The Employer's

Immigration Compliance

Desk Reference

By Gregory H. Siskind

Society for Human Resource Management
Alexandria, Virginia

The Employer's Immigration Compliance Desk Reference

By Gregory H. Siskind
Copyright © Gregory H. Siskind, 2009

Society for Human Resource Management
Alexandria, Virginia

ISBN: 978-1-586-44143-2

This publication is designed to provide accurate and authoritative information regarding the subject matter covered. It is sold with the understanding that neither the publisher nor the author is engaged in rendering legal or other professional service. If legal advice or other expert assistance is required, the services of a competent, licensed professional should be sought. The federal and state laws discussed in this book are subject to frequent revision and interpretation by amendments or judicial revisions that may significantly affect employer or employee rights and obligations. Readers are encouraged to seek legal counsel regarding specific policies and practices in their organizations.

This book is published by the Society for Human Resource Management (SHRM®). The interpretations, conclusions, and recommendations in this book are those of the author and do not necessarily represent those of the publisher.

The Society for Human Resource Management (SHRM) is the world's largest professional association devoted to human resource management. Our mission is to serve the needs of HR professionals by providing the most current and comprehensive resources, and to advance the profession by promoting HR's essential, strategic role. Founded in 1948, SHRM represents members in over 140 countries, and has a network of more than 575 affiliated chapters in the United States, as well as offices in China and India. Visit SHRM at www.shrm.org.

ILW.COM is the leading immigration law publisher. Our website has 50,000+ pages of information on immigration law. While all this information is free, our primary customers are immigration law professionals. The website was founded in 1995, our offices are located in New York City. ILW.COM's flagship publication, Immigration Daily, is the first daily newspaper on immigration law in the world. We have over 36,000 subscribers for this periodical, subscription is free. ILW.COM also publishes books for immigration law professionals and offers numerous seminars on immigration law.

Library of Congress Cataloging-in-Publication Data

Siskind, Gregory H.
The employer's immigration compliance desk reference / by Greg Siskind.
p. cm.
Includes index.
ISBN 978-1-58644-143-2
1. Alien labor--Legal status, laws, etc.--United States. 2. Alien labor certification--United States. 3. Emigration and immigration law--United States. I. Title.
KF4829.S57 2009
342.7308'2--dc22
2008046858

Cover and interior design: Shirley E.M. Raybuck

Printed in the United States of America

10 9 8 7 6 5 4 3 2 1

08-0832

Brief Table of Contents

Detailed Table of Contents

Chapter 3. Reverification

Chapter 8. Penalties and Other Risks

Chapter 9. IRCA Compliance Tips

Chapter 10. Conducting an I-9 Self-Audit

Chapter 12. Social Security No-Match Letters

Arkansas

AR.1   What does the Arkansas law bar?

AR.2   When did the Arkansas law take effect?

AR.3   Who is an "illegal immigrant" under the law?

AR.4   Who is a contractor under the Arkansas law?

AR.5   Are all contracts covered?

AR.6   Are all agencies in Arkansas covered?

AR.7   How do contractors show they have not hired unauthorized employees?

AR.8   What if it is determined that a contractor has hired "illegal immigrants"?

AR.9   Does it matter if a contractor is using the services of individuals hired by a subcontractor?

AR.10   Does the law require employers that have contracts with the state to use E-Verify?

Colorado

CO.1   What does H.B. 06-1343 bar?

CO.2   When did H.B. 06-1343 take effect?

CO.3   Who is an "illegal alien" under the law?

CO.4   Who is a "contractor" under the Colorado law?

CO.5   Are all contracts covered?

CO.6   Are all agencies in Colorado covered?

CO.7   How do contractors show they have not hired unauthorized employees?

CO.8   What if it is determined that a contractor has hired "illegal aliens"?

CO.9   Does the law require employers contracting with the state to use E-Verify?

CO.10   Does it matter if a contractor is using the services of individuals hired by a subcontractor?

CO.11   If an employer is found to have violated the law, how long will the employer remain on the list of employers barred from doing business with the state?

CO.12   What type of investigative authority does the state have under this law?

CO.13   What does H.B. 06S-1001 require?

CO.14   How does the Colorado Economic Development Commission (CEDC) determine that an employer is in compliance with IRCA?

CO.15   What happens when the CEDC determines an employer is out of compliance?

CO.16   Do employers have any right to argue against the determination of the CEDC?

CO.17   What does H.B. 06S-1017 do?

CO.18   What facts must the employer state in its affirmation?

CO.19   When did the law go into effect?

CO.20   What enforcement powers does the state have under this law?

CO.21   What penalties are faced by an employer who violates the law?

CO.22   What does H.B. 06S-1015 do?

CO.23   When does the law take effect?

CO.24   What does H.B. 06S-1020 do?

CO.25   Are there exceptions to the law?

Georgia

GA.1   What does Georgia do with respect to E-Verify?

GA.2   What is a "public employer"?

GA.3   When did this change take effect?

GA.4   What does the bill do with respect to deduction of wages paid by employers to unauthorized employees?

GA.5   What are the changes made with respect to withholding state income tax?

Missouri

MO.1   What does the new law in Missouri say generally with respect to hiring "unauthorized aliens"?

MO.2   What is a "federal work authorization program" under H.B. 1549?

MO.3   Who is a "public employer"?

MO.4   How does H.B. 1549 affect public employers?

MO.5   How does H.B. 1549 affect employers contracting with state agencies?

MO.6   Is there a safe harbor in H.B. 1549?

MO.7   Are businesses liable for the actions of contractors and subcontractors?

MO.8   How are complaints filed and handled under H.B. 1549?

MO.9   What penalties may a court impose when the attorney general brings an action under H.B. 1549?

MO.10 What happens if someone files a frivolous complaint?

MO.11 How are employer tax deductions for the wages paid to unauthorized aliens affected?

MO.12 Does the new law contain transporting provisions?

MO.13 When did H.B. 1549 become effective?

MO.14 What does the Executive Order 87-02 do?

Nevada

NV.1   How does Nevada regulate employer compliance?

New Hampshire

NH.1   How does New Hampshire regulate employer compliance?

North Carolina

NC.1   When did S.B. 1523 go into force?

NC.2   What does the law do?

NC.3   Which employers are covered?

Oklahoma

OK.1   What are OTCPA's transporting and harboring provisions?

OK.2   What are the penalties for violating the transporting and harboring provisions?

OK.3   What are OTCPA's "status verification system" provisions?

OK.4   What is OTCPA's unfair trade practices provision?

OK.5   Is there a safe harbor provision under the Oklahoma law?

Pennsylvania

PA.1   How does Pennsylvania regulate employers who fail to comply with immigration law?

Rhode Island

RI.1   What does the executive order require of state employers?

RI.2   What does the executive order state with regard to private employers doing business with state agencies?

South Carolina

SC.1   What obligation does the new law impose on government employers?

SC.2   What obligations does the new law impose on employers engaged in contracts with state agencies?

SC.3   Are there requirements applicable to all private employers?

SC.4   How are complaints against private employers investigated and violations punished?

SC.5   What is the new "employment license" created by the new law?

Chapter 18. Immigrant Visas (the "Green Card")

Chapter 19. Asylees and Refugees

Appendices

Index

List of Commonly Used Abbreviations

ALJ	administrative law judge
DHS	Department of Homeland Security
DOJ	Department of Justice
DOL	Department of Labor
DSO	Designated School Official
EAD	Employment Authorization Document
EEOC	Equal Employment Opportunity Commission
EIN	Employer Identification Number
ICE	Immigration and Customs Enforcement
IIRIRA	Illegal Immigration Reform and Immigrant Responsibility Act of 1996
IMAGE	U.S. Immigration and Customs Enforcement's Mutual Agreement between Government and Employers
INA	Immigration and Nationality Act
INS	Immigration and Naturalization Service
IRCA	Immigration Reform and Control Act of 1986
IRS	Internal Revenue Service
LCA	Labor Condition Application
LPR	lawful permanent residency
MOU	Memorandum of Understanding
OSC	Department of Justice's Office of Special Counsel for Immigration-Related Unfair Employment Practices
SSA	Social Security Administration
SSN	Social Security Number
SSNVS	Social Security Number Verification Service
Title VII	Title VII of the Civil Rights Act of 1964
TPS	Temporary Protected Status
USCIS	U.S. Citizenship and Immigration Services

Introduction

In January 2004, President George W. Bush delivered a speech from the oval office outlining a grand plan to comprehensively reform the immigration system in the United States. Most immigration legislation in the country had been on hold since the terror attacks of September 11, 2001, and the speech from the President was expected to usher in major change that would include securing the border and toughening worksite immigration compliance, introducing a large guest worker program, and legalizing millions of unauthorized employees in the country.

While the proposal was one of the few examples over the last seven years where President Bush and Democrats in Congress were largely in agreement, dissent in the President's own party as well as with a minority of conservative Democrats was enough to sink the proposal. When a final attempt to pass the bill failed in the summer of 2007, the Bush administration decided to intensify a worksite immigration enforcement strategy that has already reached unprecedented levels in the last few years. And all indications are that enforcement will remain a key priority for President Barack Obama.

The situation for today's employers is much more complex than perhaps at any time, and the situation will only get more confusing. Employers have to, of course, comply with the employer sanctions and antidiscrimination rules in the IRCA. But now employers are being targeted for a variety of additional criminal sanctions that people could not have imagined would be connected to employing unauthorized immigrants. Employers have been imprisoned on charges like harboring illegal aliens and money laundering in addition to the criminal penalties contained in IRCA.

States have been passing a patchwork of new laws aimed at employers as well. By the end of 2008, 23 states had passed employer sanctions laws. Employers are being required by states to participate in E-Verify, DHS' electronic employment eligibility verification system. And they are having their business licenses revoked and access to state contracts denied when they are found to have hired unauthorized employees.

And now employers are gearing up for new requirements like a new Social Security no-match rule that will mandate adherence to a set of protocols when the SSA sends mismatch letters (though the rule is still being challenged in the courts). And a new federal contractor regulation will require an estimated 168,000 employers begin using E-Verify in 2009.

If all of this government enforcement is not enough, employers now need to worry about matters such as losing out on contracts with companies requiring their contractors to demonstrate compliance or inheriting an immigration mess in a merger or acquisition.

The Employer's Immigration Compliance Desk Reference will help human resource managers, immigration counsel, and others charged with the task of guiding employers through these turbulent immigration waters. The array of statutes and regulations are discussed in an easy-to-understand question-and-answer format, and easy-to-understand illustrations, checklists, and sample documents are included to give you tools that will help in implementing or improving your immigration compliance program.

The book is not intended to be an overall guide to the U.S. immigration system and so you will not find in-depth information on the rules for applying for an employee's green card or transferring an employee into the U.S. from an overseas office (though I do provide an overview of the U.S. immigration system in Part II that many may find helpful). Instead, it seeks to provide in-depth information on a topic that affects every employer in the country regardless of whether the company hires foreign employees.

I welcome your feedback on this book, particularly suggestions for future editions. Please always feel free to email me at gsiskind@visalaw.com.

Greg Siskind

Writing a book is rarely a solo endeavor even if there is one name listed on the cover and that is certainly the case for this book. Many people are owed thanks for their help with this project. My law partner of 15 years Lynn Susser has been there through thick and thin and has always had faith in my crazy ideas even if the payoff won't come around for a while. I also have to thank my current and past colleagues who have given me support on this project and many others. They include Elissa Taub, Christi Hufford, Jack Richbourg, Elaine Witty, Beverly Seaton, Roz Roberts, Natasha Rhyan, Kay Miller, Ari Sauer, Ken Bragdon, Arda Beskardes, Eric Bland, Protima Daryanani, Esther Schachter, Karen Weinstock, Stacy Wagerman, Yvette Sebelist, Soky Von Dett, Gilda Bollwerk, Shmuel Susser, Mickey Torres, Monique Larocque, Melissa Lucy, and several others.

I owe a debt of gratitude to the folks at SHRM who helped with getting this work into shape, particularly Christopher Anzalone, Allen Smith and Shirley Raybuck. Many thanks also go to Sean Hanagan of Jackson Lewis LLP and Andrew Merrills of Ogletree, Deakins, Nash, Smoak & Stewart P.C. for their help in reviewing the manuscript and making very helpful suggestions. Thanks as well go to Joyce Margulies of International Paper for her helpful feedback during this project.

I owe a good deal to the great white-collar criminal lawyer Jonathan Marks of Katten Muchen Rosenman LLP for agreeing to co-write the criminal law chapter in this book and for helping to assemble an outstanding compilation of information on criminal enforcement activity in the employer compliance area. And thanks must also go to my mentor Arnold Perl of Ford & Harrison who introduced me to Jonathan and who has provided me sage advice over the years.

Finally, I owe so much to my family including my loving wife Audrey, my daughters Noa, Lily, and Eden, my mother Karen Siskind and my father Alan Siskind who is the ultimate marketing guru and who has always been there when I've needed his creative perspective.

PART I:
Complying With Immigration Laws

Form I-9 General Concepts

1.1 What is the basis for employment verification?

In 1986, Congress was debating many of the same questions as in recent years regarding illegal immigration and the best way to gain control of the border. The debate ended with passage by Congress of the IRCA, and its ratification by President Ronald Reagan.

Central to IRCA was a section that created an employer sanctions system that requires all employers in the United States to verify the identity and employment authorization of nearly all employees hired since the law was passed in 1986. Employers would basically become a central part of the immigration enforcement process by having to take over responsibility for verifying that the employers' employees are legally in the country. Shortly after the law passed, the INS created Form I-9, Employment Eligibility Verification, to document that the employer has met its IRCA obligations (see Form I-9). Employers are not permitted to knowingly hire unauthorized immigrants, and properly completing the Form I-9 is the method for employers to demonstrate they lack knowledge that an employee is not eligible to be employed.

Coupled with the provisions sanctioning employers who fail to verify the employment authorization and identity of its employees are provisions barring certain immigration-related practices by the employer, including engaging in discrimination based on citizenship or immigration status or national origin, and requiring documentation different from or in addition to what IRCA actually requires (document abuse). Employees are also protected from retaliation when they file a complaint using the antidiscrimination rules.

1.2 Which governmental agency regulates compliance with the employer sanctions rules under IRCA?

While the DOJ was responsible for enforcing compliance with IRCA's employer sanctions rules when IRCA passed, the responsibility was transferred to ICE when the DHS was created in 2002.

1.3 What is a Form I-9?

The Form I-9 is the one-page form employees complete, verifying their identity as well as proving they are allowed to work in the United States. The form itself has three parts. Section 1 includes basic biographical information of the employee and also asks the employee to certify that he or she is a citizen or permanent resident, or authorized to work under another status. The second section is completed by an employer who must verify, and attest under penalty of perjury, which documents an employee presented to prove his or her identity and right to work, and that the paperwork was completed in a timely manner. Employees may present items from List A in the I-9 instructions that prove both identity and authorization to work (such as a U.S. passport) or a combination of an identification document from List B in the instructions and a document in List C of the instructions that demonstrates employment authorization. The third section is reserved

OMB No. 1615-0047; Expires 06/30/09

Department of Homeland Security
U.S. Citizenship and Immigration Services

Form I-9, Employment Eligibility Verification

Instructions
Read all instructions carefully before completing this form.

Anti-Discrimination Notice. It is illegal to discriminate against any individual (other than an alien not authorized to work in the United States) in hiring, discharging, or recruiting or referring for a fee because of that individual's national origin or citizenship status. It is illegal to discriminate against work-authorized individuals. Employers **CANNOT** specify which document(s) they will accept from an employee. The refusal to hire an individual because the documents presented have a future expiration date may also constitute illegal discrimination. For more information, call the Office of Special Counsel for Immigration Related Unfair Employment Practices at 1-800-255-8155.

What Is the Purpose of This Form?

The purpose of this form is to document that each new employee (both citizen and noncitizen) hired after November 6, 1986, is authorized to work in the United States.

When Should Form I-9 Be Used?

All employees, citizens, and noncitizens hired after November 6, 1986, and working in the United States must complete Form I-9.

Filling Out Form I-9

Section 1, Employee

This part of the form must be completed no later than the time of hire, which is the actual beginning of employment. Providing the Social Security Number is voluntary, except for employees hired by employers participating in the USCIS Electronic Employment Eligibility Verification Program (E-Verify). **The employer is responsible for ensuring that Section 1 is timely and properly completed.**

Noncitizen Nationals of the United States

Noncitizen nationals of the United States are persons born in American Samoa, certain former citizens of the former Trust Territory of the Pacific Islands, and certain children of noncitizen nationals born abroad.

Employers should note the work authorization expiration date (if any) shown in **Section 1**. For employees who indicate an employment authorization expiration date in **Section 1**, employers are required to reverify employment authorization for employment on or before the date shown. Note that some employees may leave the expiration date blank if they are aliens whose work authorization does not expire (e.g., asylees, refugees, certain citizens of the Federated States of Micronesia or the Republic of the Marshall Islands). For such employees, reverification does not apply unless they choose to present

in Section 2 evidence of employment authorization that contains an expiration date (e.g., Employment Authorization Document (Form I-766)).

Preparer/Translator Certification

The Preparer/Translator Certification must be completed if **Section 1** is prepared by a person other than the employee. A preparer/translator may be used only when the employee is unable to complete **Section 1** on his or her own. However, the employee must still sign **Section 1** personally.

Section 2, Employer

For the purpose of completing this form, the term "employer" means all employers including those recruiters and referrers for a fee who are agricultural associations, agricultural employers, or farm labor contractors. Employers must complete **Section 2** by examining evidence of identity and employment authorization within three business days of the date employment begins. However, if an employer hires an individual for less than three business days, **Section 2** must be completed at the time employment begins. Employers cannot specify which document(s) listed on the last page of Form I-9 employees present to establish identity and employment authorization. Employees may present any List A document **OR** a combination of a List B and a List C document.

If an employee is unable to present a required document (or documents), the employee must present an acceptable receipt in lieu of a document listed on the last page of this form. Receipts showing that a person has applied for an initial grant of employment authorization, or for renewal of employment authorization, are not acceptable. Employees must present receipts within three business days of the date employment begins and must present valid replacement documents within 90 days or other specified time.

Employers must record in Section 2:

1. Document title;
2. Issuing authority;
3. Document number;
4. Expiration date, if any; and
5. The date employment begins.

Employers must sign and date the certification in **Section 2**. Employees must present original documents. Employers may, but are not required to, photocopy the document(s) presented. If photocopies are made, they must be made for all new hires. Photocopies may only be used for the verification process and must be retained with Form I-9. **Employers are still responsible for completing and retaining Form I-9.**

For more detailed information, you may refer to the *USCIS Handbook for Employers* (Form M-274). You may obtain the handbook using the contact information found under the header "USCIS Forms and Information."

Section 3, Updating and Reverification

Employers must complete **Section 3** when updating and/or reverifying Form I-9. Employers must reverify employment authorization of their employees on or before the work authorization expiration date recorded in **Section 1** (if any). Employers **CANNOT** specify which document(s) they will accept from an employee.

A. If an employee's name has changed at the time this form is being updated/reverified, complete Block A.

B. If an employee is rehired within three years of the date this form was originally completed and the employee is still authorized to be employed on the same basis as previously indicated on this form (updating), complete Block B and the signature block.

C. If an employee is rehired within three years of the date this form was originally completed and the employee's work authorization has expired **or** if a current employee's work authorization is about to expire (reverification), complete Block B; and:

    1. Examine any document that reflects the employee is authorized to work in the United States (see List A **or** C);

    2. Record the document title, document number, and expiration date (if any) in Block C; and

    3. Complete the signature block.

Note that for reverification purposes, employers have the option of completing a new Form I-9 instead of completing **Section 3.**

What Is the Filing Fee?

There is no associated filing fee for completing Form I-9. This form is not filed with USCIS or any government agency. Form I-9 must be retained by the employer and made available for inspection by U.S. Government officials as specified in the Privacy Act Notice below.

USCIS Forms and Information

To order USCIS forms, you can download them from our website at www.uscis.gov/forms or call our toll-free number at 1-800-870-3676. You can obtain information about Form I-9 from our website at www.uscis.gov or by calling 1-888-464-4218.

Information about E-Verify, a free and voluntary program that allows participating employers to electronically verify the employment eligibility of their newly hired employees, can be obtained from our website at www.uscis.gov/e-verify or by calling 1-888-464-4218.

General information on immigration laws, regulations, and procedures can be obtained by telephoning our National Customer Service Center at 1-800-375-5283 or visiting our Internet website at www.uscis.gov.

Photocopying and Retaining Form I-9

A blank Form I-9 may be reproduced, provided both sides are copied. The Instructions must be available to all employees completing this form. Employers must retain completed Form I-9s for three years after the date of hire or one year after the date employment ends, whichever is later.

Form I-9 may be signed and retained electronically, as authorized in Department of Homeland Security regulations at 8 CFR 274a.2.

Privacy Act Notice

The authority for collecting this information is the Immigration Reform and Control Act of 1986, Pub. L. 99-603 (8 USC 1324a).

This information is for employers to verify the eligibility of individuals for employment to preclude the unlawful hiring, or recruiting or referring for a fee, of aliens who are not authorized to work in the United States.

This information will be used by employers as a record of their basis for determining eligibility of an employee to work in the United States. The form will be kept by the employer and made available for inspection by authorized officials of the Department of Homeland Security, Department of Labor, and Office of Special Counsel for Immigration-Related Unfair Employment Practices.

Submission of the information required in this form is voluntary. However, an individual may not begin employment unless this form is completed, since employers are subject to civil or criminal penalties if they do not comply with the Immigration Reform and Control Act of 1986.

Paperwork Reduction Act

An agency may not conduct or sponsor an information collection and a person is not required to respond to a collection of information unless it displays a currently valid OMB control number. The public reporting burden for this collection of information is estimated at 12 minutes per response, including the time for reviewing instructions and completing and submitting the form. Send comments regarding this burden estimate or any other aspect of this collection of information, including suggestions for reducing this burden, to: U.S. Citizenship and Immigration Services, Regulatory Management Division, 111 Massachusetts Avenue, N.W., 3rd Floor, Suite 3008, Washington, DC 20529-2210. OMB No. 1615-0047. **Do not mail your completed Form I-9 to this address.**

OMB No. 1615-0047; Expires 06/30/09

Department of Homeland Security
U.S. Citizenship and Immigration Services

Form I-9, Employment Eligibility Verification

Read instructions carefully before completing this form. The instructions must be available during completion of this form.

ANTI-DISCRIMINATION NOTICE: It is illegal to discriminate against work-authorized individuals. Employers CANNOT specify which document(s) they will accept from an employee. The refusal to hire an individual because the documents have a future expiration date may also constitute illegal discrimination.

Section 1. Employee Information and Verification *(To be completed and signed by employee at the time employment begins.)*

Print Name: Last	First	Middle Initial	Maiden Name

Address *(Street Name and Number)*	Apt. #	Date of Birth *(month/day/year)*

City	State	Zip Code	Social Security #

I am aware that federal law provides for imprisonment and/or fines for false statements or use of false documents in connection with the completion of this form.

I attest, under penalty of perjury, that I am (check one of the following):

☐ A citizen of the United States

☐ A noncitizen national of the United States (see instructions)

☐ A lawful permanent resident (Alien #) _____

☐ An alien authorized to work (Alien # or Admission #) _____

until (expiration date, if applicable - *month/day/year*) _____

Employee's Signature	Date *(month/day/year)*

Preparer and/or Translator Certification *(To be completed and signed if Section 1 is prepared by a person other than the employee.) I attest, under penalty of perjury, that I have assisted in the completion of this form and that to the best of my knowledge the information is true and correct.*

Preparer's/Translator's Signature	Print Name

Address *(Street Name and Number, City, State, Zip Code)*	Date *(month/day/year)*

Section 2. Employer Review and Verification *(To be completed and signed by employer. Examine one document from List A OR examine one document from List B and one from List C, as listed on the reverse of this form, and record the title, number, and expiration date, if any, of the document(s).)*

	List A	OR	**List B**	**AND**	**List C**
Document title:	_____		_____		_____
Issuing authority:	_____		_____		_____
Document #:	_____		_____		_____
Expiration Date *(if any)*:	_____		_____		_____
Document #:	_____		_____		
Expiration Date *(if any)*:	_____		_____		

CERTIFICATION: I attest, under penalty of perjury, that I have examined the document(s) presented by the above-named employee, that the above-listed document(s) appear to be genuine and to relate to the employee named, that the employee began employment on *(month/day/year)* _____ **and that to the best of my knowledge the employee is authorized to work in the United States. (State employment agencies may omit the date the employee began employment.)**

Signature of Employer or Authorized Representative	Print Name	Title

Business or Organization Name and Address *(Street Name and Number, City, State, Zip Code)*	Date *(month/day/year)*

Section 3. Updating and Reverification *(To be completed and signed by employer.)*

A. New Name *(if applicable)*	B. Date of Rehire *(month/day/year) (if applicable)*

C. If employee's previous grant of work authorization has expired, provide the information below for the document that establishes current employment authorization.

Document Title:	Document #:	Expiration Date *(if any)*:

I attest, under penalty of perjury, that to the best of my knowledge, this employee is authorized to work in the United States, and if the employee presented document(s), the document(s) I have examined appear to be genuine and to relate to the individual.

Signature of Employer or Authorized Representative	Date *(month/day/year)*

LISTS OF ACCEPTABLE DOCUMENTS
All documents must be unexpired

LIST A	LIST B	LIST C
Documents that Establish Both Identity and Employment Authorization OR	**Documents that Establish Identity** AND	**Documents that Establish Employment Authorization**
1. U.S. Passport or U.S. Passport Card	1. Driver's license or ID card issued by a State or outlying possession of the United States provided it contains a photograph or information such as name, date of birth, gender, height, eye color, and address	1. Social Security Account Number card other than one that specifies on the face that the issuance of the card does not authorize employment in the United States
2. Permanent Resident Card or Alien Registration Receipt Card (Form I-551)		2. Certification of Birth Abroad issued by the Department of State (Form FS-545)
3. Foreign passport that contains a temporary I-551 stamp or temporary I-551 printed notation on a machine-readable immigrant visa	2. ID card issued by federal, state or local government agencies or entities, provided it contains a photograph or information such as name, date of birth, gender, height, eye color, and address	3. Certification of Report of Birth issued by the Department of State (Form DS-1350)
4. Employment Authorization Document that contains a photograph (Form I-766)	3. School ID card with a photograph	4. Original or certified copy of birth certificate issued by a State, county, municipal authority, or territory of the United States bearing an official seal
	4. Voter's registration card	
5. In the case of a nonimmigrant alien authorized to work for a specific employer incident to status, a foreign passport with Form I-94 or Form I-94A bearing the same name as the passport and containing an endorsement of the alien's nonimmigrant status, as long as the period of endorsement has not yet expired and the proposed employment is not in conflict with any restrictions or limitations identified on the form	5. U.S. Military card or draft record	
	6. Military dependent's ID card	5. Native American tribal document
	7. U.S. Coast Guard Merchant Mariner Card	
	8. Native American tribal document	6. U.S. Citizen ID Card (Form I-197)
	9. Driver's license issued by a Canadian government authority	
	For persons under age 18 who are unable to present a document listed above:	7. Identification Card for Use of Resident Citizen in the United States (Form I-179)
6. Passport from the Federated States of Micronesia (FSM) or the Republic of the Marshall Islands (RMI) with Form I-94 or Form I-94A indicating nonimmigrant admission under the Compact of Free Association Between the United States and the FSM or RMI	10. School record or report card	8. Employment authorization document issued by the Department of Homeland Security
	11. Clinic, doctor, or hospital record	
	12. Day-care or nursery school record	

Illustrations of many of these documents appear in Part 8 of the Handbook for Employers (M-274)

for employers who must periodically update the I-9 form if the employee is not authorized to permanently work in the United States.

Note that the I-9 was updated in November 2008, and all employers must be using the new form as of April 2, 2009. The form is largely unchanged except for slightly altering the list of acceptable List A, B, and C documents consistent with changes passed by section 412 of the IIRIRA and offering employees the additional choice of "non-citizen national" in identifying their status in the United States.

1.4   When must the I-9 form be completed?

The Form I-9 process must start on the day an employee starts work. The employee must complete the first section of the I-9 form on that day and must provide the supporting documents noted above within three days of the date of hire. If the documents are not presented by that point, the employee must be removed from the payroll (though it is permissible to suspend the employee rather than terminate the employee altogether). While it is possible to require people to complete the I-9 form before the *first day of employment*, many immigration lawyers caution against this. The DHS M-274 Handbook for Employer handbook (see Appendix B) tells employers that the employee must have been *offered and accepted* the job and that the form should not be used to screen job applicants lest there be a charge of nationality discrimination. To the extent an employer chooses to have I-9s completed before the date of hire, they should only be requested after a position has been offered and accepted and there should be a uniform policy for all employees receiving an offer of employment having to complete the I-9 ahead of time.

Note that the three-day requirement to produce the supporting documents also applies to recruiters and referrers for a fee, as well as state employment agencies.

1.5   What if an employee is being hired for less than a three-day period?

Employees being hired for less than a three-day period must complete Section 1 on the day of hire and the employer needs to sign the verification attestation in Section 2 as well on the day of hire. Employees for jobs that are intended to last three days or less must therefore present their documents on the day of hire.

1.6   In a nutshell, what are an employer's Form I-9 requirements?

Employers (and others required to retain the Form I-9 as described below) have six basic obligations:

- Have employees fully and properly complete Section 1 of the Form I-9 no later than the date employment commences.
- Review the documents required to provide identity and employment authorization to ensure that they are genuine and apply to the person presenting them.
- Properly complete Section 2 of the Form I-9 and sign and date the employer certification.
- Retain the Form I-9 for the required retention period.
- Reverify employment authorization for employees presenting a time-limited EAD.
- Make the Form I-9s available for inspection if requested by the DHS, OSC, or DOL.

1.7   Are employers the only entities required to verify employment eligibility using Form I-9?

Aside from employers, agricultural associations and farm labor contractors also must complete Form I-9s for individuals recruited or referred for a fee. The terms "refer for a fee" and "recruit for a fee" do not include union halls that refer union members and nonunion members.

Recruiters and referrers for a fee are permitted to designate agents to handle the I-9 process, including national associations as well as the actual employers of the employees. If the employer is designated to handle the process, the employer must provide the recruiter or referrer with a copy of the I-9 and the recruiter or referrer still is liable for IRCA violations.

Recruiters and referrers which are subject to the I-9 rules must abide by the timing and recordkeeping requirements described later in this chapter and must make the I-9 forms available to ICE, OSC, or DOL officers. Fines and penalties applicable to employers apply to these recruiters and referrers as well.

Some state employment agencies also certify people they refer to employers. State employment agencies may elect to provide employees with certification of employment authorization and, if the agency refers a job to an employer and sends a certification of employment eligibility within 21 days of the referral, the employer does not need to complete a Form I-9. Employers must still check the certification to make sure it refers to the person actually hired and must retain the certification as they would a Form I-9.

State agencies providing this service need to comply with the I-9 employment verification rules. One exception is that individuals may not present receipts for documents as they may in certain cases with I-9s completed by employers.

When a state employment agency wants to refer an individual again after he or she has previously been certified, the state agency can rely on the prior I-9 if the individual remains authorized to be employed and the employee is referred to an employer within three years of completion of the initial I-9. State agencies must retain the I-9 for a period of at least three years from the date the employee was last referred and hired.

1.8   What is the employee's responsibility in completing the Form I-9?
Employees are required to complete Section 1 of the Form I-9 stating the employee's name, address, SSN, and date of birth, and whether the employee is a U.S. citizen or national, lawful permanent resident, or an alien with authorization to be employed. If the employee is a permanent resident, he or she must provide an alien number and, if the employee is an alien with employment authorization, he or she must provide the alien or admission number and the expiration date of the employment authorization, if applicable. Employees must also sign the form attesting that the statements and documents are not false.

Employees are also required to present to the employer, recruiter or referrer for a fee, or referring state agency, documentation from the authorized lists of documents demonstrating identity and employment authorization.

1.9   Are there any employees not required to complete a Form I-9?
IRCA requires that all employers have all employees hired after 1986 complete I-9 verification paperwork. The Form I-9 requirement applies to all employees including U.S. citizens and nationals. Employees who are not hired do not need to complete I-9 forms and employers who selectively choose who will and will not complete I-9s could face penalties under the antidiscrimination rules. Volunteers are not subject to I-9 rules since they receive no remuneration for their services. Independent contractors are also not subject to the I-9 rules, but employers should note that if they contract work to companies they know use unauthorized employees, the employers could be held liable as well under IRCA. Persons transferring within a company are not required to complete an I-9 form, but the easiest practice is usually to complete a new I-9 anyway rather than having to document that the I-9 was done previously. Employees rehired by a

company need not complete a new I-9 as long as they resume work within three years of completing the initial Form I-9. Also, it is not necessary to complete a new I-9 after:
- An employee completes paid or unpaid leave (such as for illness or a vacation).
- A temporary layoff.
- A strike or labor dispute.
- Gaps between seasonal employment.

1.10   What if an employee is a volunteer or paid in ways other than with money? What if an employee receives a signing bonus prior to starting work?

For purposes of the employer sanctions rules, the DHS regulations consider a person to be hired at the time of the "actual commencement of employment" for "wages or other remuneration." "Employment" is defined to mean service or labor performed by an employee for an employer.

Based on these definitions, employees who receive a signing bonus but who have not actually begun employment would not be required to complete a Form I-9 until actual work for the employer commenced.

True volunteer positions are where no pay is received and the volunteer receives no other type of benefit in lieu of pay (such as food and lodging). While it is quite possible Congress did not intend to include positions where a charitable organization has provided meals and lodging to volunteers receiving no pay for their labor, the rules do not seem to make an exception and the charity should err on the side of completing Form I-9s for the volunteers.

1.11   Is a new I-9 required for employees who are transferred within a company?

No. Promoted and transferred employees do not require a new Form I-9.

1.12   Do independent contractors need to complete a Form I-9?

No. Employees employed by an independent contractor are to be verified by the contractor. However, ICE has targeted employers when ICE has been able to demonstrate that the employer deliberately used a contracting firm to circumvent IRCA and knew that the contractor's employees were not employment authorized.

The DHS regulations define "independent contractor" to include individuals and entities who control their own work and are subject to control only as it pertains to the results. Employers should note that just because someone is called a "contractor" and issued a 1099, or an entity is paid and then pays the employee, it does not mean that ICE will consider the arrangement to be a contractor relationship as opposed to an employer-employee relationship. The agency will examine the nature of the relationship to determine whether it should be classified as an employment relationship where employees should be completing the Form I-9.

According to ICE, the following factors are considered in determining if a relationship is a contractor or an employment arrangement:
- Who supplies the tools or materials.
- Whether the contractor makes services available to the general public.
- Whether the contractor works for a number of clients at the same time.
- Whether the contractor has an opportunity for profit or loss as a result of the services provided.
- Who invests in the facilities for work.
- Who directs the order or sequence in which the work is to be done.
- Who determines the hours during which the work is to be done.

1.13   Are domestic service employees (such as housekeepers, kitchen help, and gardeners) required to complete I-9s?

Sometimes. The term "employee" is defined by the DHS to exclude those engaged in casual domestic employment. "Casual domestic employment" includes individuals who provide "sporadic, irregular or intermittent" domestic service in a private home.

The DHS M-274, Handbook for Employers specifically notes, however, that "those who employ anyone for domestic work in their private home on a regular basis (such as every week)" are required to have the employee complete a Form I-9. (See Appendix B.)

Note that the M-274 Handbook is not controlling law in and of itself and is merely interpreting IRCA. One could argue that certain domestic employees who show up every week at a private home are independent contractors meeting the tests described in the regulations.

One way to determine whether a domestic service employee is an employee or not is if the IRS would consider an employer obligated to withhold taxes, pay Social Security, etc. If a tax specialist advises that withholding is required based on the nature of the relationship, then employment verification should occur. Even if this is not the case and even if an employee is paid in cash, it may still make sense to have the employee complete a Form I-9.

1.14   Under what circumstances would a returning employee not be required to complete a new Form I-9?

A returning employee does not need to complete a new I-9 in certain instances where he or she is considered to be continuing prior employment. These include when:

- An individual is returning from an approved paid or unpaid leave of absence (such as on account of illness, pregnancy, maternity, vacation, study, family leave, union activities, or other temporary leaves of absence approved by the employer).
- The individual is promoted or demoted or receives a significant raise.
- The individual is temporarily laid off for lack of work.
- The individual is out on strike or in a labor dispute.
- The individual is reinstated after a finding of wrongful termination.
- An individual transfers between units within the same employer (the I-9 may be transferred to the new unit).
- There is a merger, acquisition, or reorganization and the new employer assumes the Form I-9 responsibilities from the prior employer.
- The employee is engaged in seasonal employment.

The employer claiming that the employee is continuing in prior employment must show that the employee expected to resume employment at all times and that the employee's expectation was reasonable. Factors to be considered include, but are not limited to, whether the:

- Employee was employed on a "regular and substantial basis."
- Individual complied with the employer's established policies regarding absence.
- Employer's past history of recalling employees indicates the likelihood that the individual would be recalled.
- Position has not been taken over by another employee.
- Employee has not sought benefits like severance or retirement, indicating that the employee would not be resuming work.
- Financial condition of the employer indicates an ability to resume employment.
- History of communications between the employer and employee indicates the intention to resume employment.

1.15   Are employees who return to work after a labor dispute required to complete a new Form I-9?

No. The DHS regulations specifically state that employees returning after a labor dispute are considered to have been continuously employed.

1.16   Are seasonal employees required to reverify their Form I-9s?

No. The DHS regulations consider seasonal employees to be continuously employed.

1.17   Are there special rules for employer associations?

Yes. Agricultural associations that refer employees to individual employers are required to complete Form I-9s for employees referred for a fee to employers. The association can assign the task to the employer in certain cases, as well as to national associations.

1.18   Do employers of part-time employees need to complete I-9s for those employees?

Yes. There is no exemption from the verification requirements because an employee is not full-time, unless the employee is considered an independent contractor or the person is engaged in casual, nonregular, domestic work in a private home.

1.19   Can an employer require job applicants to complete Form I-9s?

No. Employers should not complete Form I-9s for individuals applying for jobs. Only those individuals who are actually offered employment and have accepted should be requested to complete the Form I-9.

1.20   What privacy protections are accorded employees when they complete Form I-9?

DHS regulations state that information contained on Form I-9 may only be used to verify an individual's identity and employment eligibility and to enforce immigration law. Presumably this bars both the government as well as employers from using I-9 information for any other purposes.

Employers with electronic I-9 systems are also required to implement a records security program which ensures that only authorized personnel have access to electronic records, that such records are backed up, that employees are trained to minimize the risk of records being altered, and that whenever a record is created, accessed, viewed, updated, or corrected, a secure and permanent trail is created establishing who accessed the record.

1.21   Which foreign nationals are always authorized to work in the United States?

In order to determine whether an employee will require sponsorship for a visa from an employer, it helps to know which types of foreign nationals are entitled to work incident to their status in the United States. The DHS lists 16 types of cases where a foreign national is entitled to work in the U.S. simply on the basis of his or her status:

- Lawful permanent residents ("green card" holders).
- Certain persons processing under IRCA, the 1986 Immigration Act (there should be very few people, if any, still in this group).
- Persons admitted as refugees.
- Persons admitted as parolees.
- Persons granted asylum status (note that the expiration date on the employment authorization card does not mean the bearer's work authorization has expired).
- K-1 fiancé or fiancée visa holders.

- N-8 parents and N-9 dependent children processing for permanent residency on the basis of a family member working in the U.S. for an international organization.
- Certain citizens of the Federated States of Micronesia or the Marshall Islands.
- K-3 spouse visa holders.
- Individuals granted withholding of deportation or removal for the period they hold that status.
- Certain persons granted voluntary departure by virtue of membership in a specific nationality group.
- Persons holding TPS for the period of time their country's nationals are granted that status.
- Individuals granted voluntary departure under the Family Unity Program of the 1990 Immigration Act.
- Persons granted Family Unity benefits under the Legal Immigration Family Equity Act (LIFE).
- Persons holding V visa status based on certain family-based "green cards" filed before 2001.
- Persons holding T visa status as victims of trafficking.

Note that with the exception of permanent residents who show their Form I-551 or "green card," the authorization to work in the other 15 categories is demonstrated by an employment card issued by the USCIS.

1.22   Which foreign nationals are sometimes authorized to work in the United States?

Certain individuals can live and work in the U.S. based on working for a specific employer and meeting certain conditions. USCIS lists 19 such categories and persons in these categories are authorized to work on the basis of possessing a valid Form I-94, Arrival-Departure Record, as opposed to an EAD:

- A-1 and A-2 foreign government officials (individuals must work only for the sponsoring foreign government entity).
- A-3 personal employees of A-1 or A-2 visa holders.
- C-2 and C-3 foreign government officials in transit (individuals must work only for the sponsoring foreign government entity).
- E-1 and E-2 treaty investors and traders employed by a qualifying company.
- F-1 students working on campus or engaged in curricular practical training (CPT) (CPT employees must have a properly annotated Form I-20 Certificate of Eligibility).
- G-1, G-2, and G-3 representatives of international organizations (individuals must work only for the sponsoring foreign government entity or international organization).
- G-5 personal employees of G-1, G-2, and G-3 visa holders.
- H-1B, H-2A, H-2B, and H-3 temporary employees and trainees.
- I representatives of foreign media organizations.
- J-1 exchange visitors (only within the guidelines set forth in the DS-2019 Certificate of Eligibility form).
- L-1 intracompany transfers.
- O-1 and O-2 aliens having extraordinary ability in the sciences, arts, education, business, or athletics, and accompanying aliens.
- P-1, P-2, and P-3 athletes, artists, or entertainers.
- Q-1 international cultural exchange visitors employed by the Q-1 petitioner.
- R-1 religious employees.
- NATO-1, NATO-2, NATO-3, NATO-4, NATO-5, and NATO-6 employees of the North Atlantic Treaty Organization (NATO).
- NATO-7 personal employees of NATO employees.
- TN professionals from Canada and Mexico working pursuant to the North American Free Trade Agreement (NAFTA).

- A-3, E-1, E-2, G-5, H-1B, H-2A, H-2B, H-3, I, J-1, L-1, O-1, O-2, P-1, P-2, P-3, R-1, and TN persons who have expired I-94s but have timely filed for an extension (employment authorization continues for 240 days or until the application is denied).

Note that the E-3 visa for Australians is not included presumably because the category is new and USCIS has not updated 8 CFR §274a.12.

There is also a group of visa categories under which an individual can apply for employment authorization, and such individuals must have an EAD to work:

- Spouses and unmarried dependent children of A-1 and A-2 visa holders.
- F-1 students seeking optional practical training in their areas of study or because of severe economic hardship (after getting support of the school's international student officer).
- Spouses and unmarried children of G-1, G-3, and G-4 international organization representatives.
- J-2 spouses and unmarried minor children of J-1 visa holders.
- M-1 students seeking practical training in an area directly related to their courses of study as recommended by a school official on Form I-20.
- Dependents of aliens classified as NATO-1 through NATO-7.
- Asylum applicants who have had their cases pending for more than 150 days.
- Individuals with an application pending to adjust their status to lawful permanent residency.
- Certain applicants with pending suspension of deportation and cancellation of removal cases.
- Parolees admitted on public interest or emergency grounds.
- B-1 visitors who are personal or domestic servants of certain nonimmigrant work visa holders.
- Domestic servants of U.S. citizens accompanying or following to join the U.S. citizen who has a permanent home or is stationed in a foreign country and who is temporarily coming to the United States.
- Employees of foreign airlines who would otherwise be entitled to E-1 visa status and who are precluded from E-1 status because they are not the same nationality as the airline.
- Individuals under final orders of removal and who are released on an order of supervision because the person's home country refuses to accept them (such cases are approved in the discretion of USCIS).
- TPS applicants.
- Certain legalization applicants under IRCA, the 1986 Immigration Act and Legal Immigration Family Equity Act (LIFE).
- Witnesses or informants in S visa status.
- Q-2 Irish peace process cultural and training program visitors.
- Immediate family members of T-1 victims of trafficking.

Completing the I-9 Form

2.1   Where can I obtain a Form I-9?

The USCIS makes the Form I-9 (see Chapter 1) available for download in a PDF format on its web site at www.uscis.gov. The form can also be ordered by telephone at the USCIS forms office at 800-870-3676 or at the USCIS National Customer Service Center at 800-375-5283.

Various case management and electronic filing systems make the I-9 available as well (see Appendix C, Electronic I-9 and E-Verify Vendors, for a list of these companies and contact information). The USCIS requires electronically generated I-9s to be legible with no change to the name, content, or sequence of information and instructions.

The USCIS permits forms to be printed on both sides (as is the actual printed form provided by the USCIS) or on single sides.

2.2   Is Form I-9 available in different languages?

The USCIS makes Form I-9 available only in English and Spanish. Note also that the Spanish form may only be used for translation purposes and the employer must retain the English language version of the form. The lone exception to this is in Puerto Rico where employers have a choice and can retain either the Spanish or English language versions of the form.

2.3   Which version of Form I-9 can an employer accept?

Employers may only accept the latest version of Form I-9 (as of publication of this edition of this book, that version was the April 2, 2009, version of the Form I-9). Furthermore, reverifications should not be made on an old version of the I-9. In cases where a new I-9 is in effect, the new I-9 should be used. To determine the latest version of Form I-9, employers should either check the USCIS web site every three or four months, subscribe to or regularly read print and online publications on immigration and employment law, or use an electronic I-9 product from a reputable vendor that regularly updates the software for its subscribers.

2.4   What documentation can an employee present that shows both identity and employment authorization?

Employees must present documentation of identity and work authorization and can present documents from a preset list included in the I-9 form's instructions. Some documents can prove both identity and work authorization. Some documents prove just identity or just work eligibility and a combination of documents must be presented in order to meet the I-9 requirements. Employers are not allowed to tell employees which documents from the preset list they must present.

Documents showing both identification and employment eligibility are provided in List A in the Form I-9's instructions. They include the following:

• A U.S. passport (unexpired or expired) or the new U.S. passport card.

- A permanent residency card (a "green card") or alien registration receipt card (Form I-551).
- An unexpired foreign passport with a temporary I-551 stamp.
- An unexpired Form I-766 EAD that contains a photograph.
- An unexpired foreign passport with an unexpired Form I-94 or Form I-94A, Arrival-Departure Record, with the same name as the passport and an endorsement showing the employee's nonimmigrant status and showing the individual is eligible to work for a particular employer.

Note that several List A items were removed from the list of acceptable documents when the USCIS released its new form in June 2007. The following items are *not* acceptable anymore:

- Certificate of U.S. Citizenship (Form N-560 or N-561).
- Certificate of Naturalization (Form N-550 or N-570).
- Alien Registration Receipt Card (I-151) (this is an old version of the "green card" that is no longer valid to prove permanent residency).
- Unexpired Reentry Permit (Form I-327).
- Unexpired Refugee Travel Document (Form I-571).

And the new April 2009 Form I-9 no longer permits employers to accept an expired U.S. passport.

Section 2 of the I-9 actually provides two spaces for listing document numbers and expiration dates. The purpose is to provide for situations where a foreign passport is used and Form I-94 is also needed to prove both identity and employment authorization. The passport number and expiration date and the I-94 number and expiration date can then be listed. Otherwise, only one document would be listed by document number and expiration date.

2.5   **What documentation can an employee present solely to provide the employee's identity?**

Form I-9's List B includes documentation acceptable to prove identity, and a List B document may be provided with a List C document. List B documents include the following:

- A driver's license or identification card issued by a state or outlying possession of the U.S., provided it contains a photograph or information such as name, date of birth, gender, height, eye color, and address.
- An identification card issued by a federal, state, or local governmental agency or entity as long as the form contains a photograph or information such as name, date of birth, gender, height, eye color, and address.
- A school identification card with a photograph.
- A voter's registration card.
- A U.S. Military Card or draft record.
- U.S. Coast Guard Merchant Mariner Card.
- Native American tribal document.
- Driver's license issued by a Canadian government authority.

Note that many states have recently enacted requirements making it significantly more difficult for nonimmigrants to obtain a driver's license. Furthermore, President George W. Bush signed the REAL ID Act in 2005 which will eventually require states to meet more stringent standards in the issuance of driver's licenses, and states not meeting the federal standards could find that their driver's licenses may no longer be acceptable documentation proving identity. If and when that happens, the USCIS would likely update the Form I-9 instructions accordingly.

For persons under the age of 18 who cannot present one of the documents listed above, the following may instead be presented:
- A school record or report card.
- A clinic, doctor, or hospital record.
- A day care or nursery school record.

2.6   What documentation can an employee present solely to provide the employee's authorization to work?

Form I-9's List C includes documentation acceptable to prove employment eligibility, and a List C document may be provided together with a List B document. List C documents include the following:
- A U.S. Social Security card issued by the SSA (other than a card stating that it is not valid for employment).
- Certification of Birth Abroad issued by the U.S. Department of State (Form FS-545 or Form DS-1350).
- Original or certified copy of a birth certificate issued by a state, county, municipal authority, or outlying possession of the U.S. bearing an official seal.
- Native American tribal document.
- U.S. citizen identification card (Form I-197).
- Identification card for use of Resident Citizen in the U.S. (Form I-179).
- Unexpired EAD issued by the DHS (other than those listed under List A).

2.7   Where can an employer find illustrations of acceptable documents in Lists A, B, and C?

Part 8 of the DHS M-274, Handbook for Employers includes a number of illustrations. (See Appendix B.)

2.8   May an employer specify which documents it will accept?

Employers may not tell employees which forms to supply. Rather, the employer must simply present the lists of acceptable documents included with the latest I-9 instructions and must allow the employee to choose what will be presented. Employers must then accept the documentation provided, as long as the documentation appears genuine. Employers who violate this requirement risk being found liable for committing an unfair immigration-related employment practice that is in violation of IRCA's antidiscrimination rules. This applies even when an employer writes down an alien number in Section 1 of the Form I-9. Employees are not required to provide documentation to prove statements in Section 1 as long as proper documentation in Section 2 is provided.

The one exception to this rule applies to employers using E-Verify, the government's electronic employment eligibility verification system. E-Verify employers may only accept List B documents with a photograph of the employee.

2.9   When will a Form I-20 presented by an F-1 student prove employment authorization?

Despite there being no reference to a Form I-20 Certificate of Eligibility on the Form I-9, F-1 nonimmigrant students may present a Form I-20 in two situations.

First, if a student works on campus at the institution sponsoring the F-1 student and the employer provides direct student services, the I-20 will serve as evidence showing employment eligibility. This also is the case for off-campus work at an employer that is educationally affiliated with the school's established curriculum or for employers contractually required to provide funded research projects at the postgraduate level where the employment is an integral part of the student's educational program.

Second, in cases where an F-1 student has been authorized by a DSO to participate in a curricular practical training program that is an integral part of an established curriculum (e.g., alternative work/study, internship, cooperative education, or other required internship offered by sponsoring employers through cooperative agreements with the school), the student must have a Form I-20 endorsed by the DSO, and the I-20 must also list the specific employer as well as the intended dates of employment.

In either case, the Form I-20 would only be used when an employee presents an unexpired foreign passport and a valid Form I-94 (essentially a third document when the other two List A documents are used).

2.10   **When will a Form DS-2019 Certificate of Eligibility presented by a J-1 exchange visitor prove employment authorization?**

J-1 nonimmigrant exchange visitors can sometimes work based on the terms of their visas. In order to document employment authorization, the J-1 visa holder can present a Form DS-2019 issued by the State Department along with an unexpired passport and a Form I-94 as acceptable List A documentation.

2.11   **Can a translator be used by an employee to assist with completing the form?**

Yes. If an employee cannot fill out Section 1 of Form I-9, he or she can receive the assistance of a translator or preparer. The preparer or translator would read the Form I-9 and instructions to the employee, help the employee fill out Section 1 of the form, and then sign the "Preparer and/or Translator Certification" block on the form. An employer can serve as translator as long as the translator block is signed, as well as the employer verification section.

2.12   **What if an employee states in Section 1 that he or she has a temporary work authorization, but presents a List C document that does not have an expiration date?**

An employer cannot specify that an employee provide documentation relating to the employee's temporary work authorization even if the employee has indicated in Section 1 that he or she has temporary work authorization. So, if an employee has a valid List B document and a valid List C document without an expiration date, the employer is not allowed to request documentation regarding the temporary status of the employee lest he or she be found guilty of immigration discrimination.

2.13   **Are there employees who may properly check the box in Section 1 indicating they are an alien without permanent residency in the United States but who do not have an expiration date for their status?**

Yes. Refugees and asylees are two fairly large groups of individuals who would fit this description. Certain nationals of Micronesia, the Marshall Islands, and Palau are authorized to work in the U.S. by virtue of their status as nationals of those countries. If an employee fits into one of these categories, they can type "N/A" in the appropriate place in Section 1.

2.14   **If an employee provides an alien number (A number) in Section 1 but presents documents without the alien number, can the employer ask to see the document with the alien number?**

No. An employer cannot ask to see a document relating to the A number or otherwise specify to an employee which documents he or she is to provide, other than presenting the employee with the lists of the acceptable documents.

2.15 **What if an employee claims to be a U.S. citizen in Section 1 but presents a "green card" as documentation of identity and work authorization?**

Employees who provide this sort of information often don't understand the question since one cannot simultaneously be a U.S. citizen and a U.S. lawful permanent resident. The matter should be brought to the attention of the employee and if a correction is needed, the employee should be able to change the I-9 form and should initial any changes. According to the DHS M-274 Handbook (question 14), an employer could be found to have reasonably known the employee was not employment eligible when it received two contradictory documents.

2.16 **What if a person claims to be a lawful permanent resident in Section 1 but provides a U.S. passport or birth certificate as documentation of status?**

As above, employees who provide this sort of information often don't understand the question since one cannot simultaneously be a U.S. citizen and a U.S. lawful permanent resident. The matter should also be brought to the attention of the employee and if a correction is needed, the employee should be able to change the I-9 form and should initial any changes. According to the DHS M-274 handbook (question 14), an employer could be found to have reasonably known the employee was not employment eligible when it received two contradictory documents.

2.17 **What types of expired documents may be accepted?**

There are a few types of expired documents which can be accepted by employers. An expired U.S. passport is an acceptable List A document as of the June 2007 version of Form I-9. That will no longer be the case on the April 2009 version. Expired identification documents may be accepted in List B. A final, very narrow instance is in the case of TPS holders who have expired EADs. Employers can accept these as well.

2.18 **What types of SSA documents may be accepted?**

Social Security cards that are marked "not valid for employment" may not be used as a List C document demonstrating employment eligibility. If an employee claims that he or she has become employment eligible, the employee will need to get a new card issued from the SSA.

Employees are also not permitted to use a printout from the SSA of the employee's particulars — name, SSN, date of birth, etc. — as a substitute for an actual Social Security card.

Employees sometimes present laminated Social Security cards. These are not per se invalid unless they say on the back "not valid if laminated."

2.19 **Are receipts for documents acceptable?**

In most cases, a receipt will not be acceptable. A common case is where an employee is waiting on an EAD and has a receipt showing the application has been filed. A receipt for an initial grant of employment authorization or a renewal of employment authorization will not suffice for Form I-9 purposes. But the USCIS is limited by law to 90 days to adjudicate EAD applications and they are required to grant an interim employment document valid for up to 240 days at that point. Still, a receipt will not be enough to begin work even after 90 days unless the interim employment authorization has actually been granted.

An exception is made in the case of a receipt for a replacement document when the document has been lost, stolen, or damaged. An employee may use the receipt to demonstrate work authorization for a 90-day period and then must present the replacement document.

A Form I-94 issued with a temporary I-551 stamp will serve as a valid receipt to replace a "green card." The individual has until the expiration date of the I-551 stamp or, if the I-551 stamp does not have an expiration date, a year from the date of the issuance of the I-94. Note that I-551 stamps are usually approved for a year anyway.

Finally, an I-94 with an unexpired refugee admission stamp may also be used as a receipt for up to 90 days after an employee is hired. The employee would then need to present a valid document demonstrating refugee status.

When an employer does receive an acceptable receipt, the employer should record the document in Section 2 of Form I-9 with the annotation "receipt" and any document number in the place for such information. Once the actual document is presented, the employer will cross out the word "receipt" and the accompanying document number, and insert the number from the new document. The employer should date and initial the amendment.

2.20   Can an employee present photocopies of documents rather than original documentation?
With the exception of a certified copy of a birth certificate, an employee is never permitted to present a photocopy of a List A, List B, or List C document.

2.21   What should a permanent resident still waiting on the actual permanent residency card to arrive present?
An applicant waiting on a permanent residency card should present the specially issued Form I-94 with an I-551 immigrant visa stamp. The I-94 form with the stamp is typically valid for a year.

2.22   What documentation should a refugee present to document authorization to work?
A refugee should present an EAD. However, if that application is being processed, the refugee can present an I-94 with a refugee admission stamp, as long as the employment card is presented within 90 days.

2.23   What if the document presented by the employee does not look valid?
This is a tricky situation for employers. On the one hand, employers are not expected to be document experts. On the other hand, if a document is obviously a phony, an employer should not be expected to be off the hook. The DHS requires employers to accept documents that "reasonably appear on their face to be genuine." Employers need to be careful, however, about being overzealous since they face the risk of being found to have committed an unfair immigration-related employment practice if they question the legitimacy of documents that appear to be genuine.

2.24   What if the name of the employee on the document is different from the name of the employee on the Form I-9?
If an employee presents a document with a different name than in Section 1, an employer would arguably have reason to believe that the documentation may not demonstrate employment eligibility. The employer should bring the discrepancy to the attention of the employee and see if there is a reasonable explanation (such as a legal name change by the employee).

2.25   What if the employee does not look like the person on the presented document or appears different from the description of the person on the document (hair color, eye color, height, race, etc.)?
An employer is required to check the presented documentation and ensure that the documents relate to the individual. If the individual presenting the docu-

mentation does not reasonably appear to be the same person in the identification document, then the employer can reject the documentation.

2.26   May an employer correct Form I-9s after they are completed?
Yes. However, the employer should be careful to make changes in a way that makes it clear to an inspecting official that the form was corrected, and how the form was corrected. Blank fields should be completed and incorrect answers should be lined through (so the original answer is visible) rather than erased. Changes in Section 1 should be initialed and dated by the employee, preparer, or translator. Changes in Section 2 should be initialed and dated by the employer.

2.27   Are employees required to supply an SSN on a Form I-9?
Employees are not required to supply an SSN unless the employer participates in the E-Verify program. Employers using E-Verify may not ask an employee to provide a specific document with an SSN.

2.28   Are there special rules for minors?
Yes. Individuals under the age of 18 who are unable to produce a List A or List B document can present the following documents to establish identity:
- A school record or report card.
- A clinic, doctor, or hospital record.
- A day care or nursery school record.

If a person under the age of 18 is not able to present a List A or List B document or one of the documents noted above, Section 1 of the Form I-9 should be completed by the parent or legal guardian and the phrase "Individual under age 18" written in the employee signature space. The parent or legal guardian should then complete the "Preparer and/or Translator Certification" block. Under List B, the phrase "Individual under age 18" should be stated.

2.29   Are there special rules for individuals with handicaps?
Yes. A special procedure can be used for individuals with handicaps who are unable to present a required identity document and who are being hired for a position in a nonprofit organization, association, or as part of a rehabilitation program.

Section 1 of the Form I-9 should be completed by the parent, legal guardian, or a representative from the nonprofit organization, association, or rehabilitation program placing the individual into a position of employment. The phrase "special placement" should be written in the employee signature space. The person completing the form would then complete the "Preparer and/or Translator Certification" block. Under List B, the phrase "special placement" should be stated.

Qualifying handicapped individuals include any person who:
- Has a physical or mental impairment, which substantially limits one or more of such person's major life activities.
- Has a record of such impairment.
- Is regarded as having such impairment.

2.30   What are the various examples of Form I-9 documents?
See Appendix B, pages 243-255.

Reverification

3.1 **What are the Form I-9 reverification requirements?**

If an employee is not a U.S. citizen or lawful permanent resident, he or she is likely working based on a status with a defined end date. For these employees, the employer must note the expiration of their documents on the Form I-9, Employment Eligibility Verification, and then must pull their I-9 form before the expiration date and reverify that the employee's status has been extended. Employers need to establish a reliable tickler system to prompt reverification. Aside from complying with the reverification rule, this system will also ensure that an employer that needs to extend a work visa for an employee will not forget to take care of this critical task (something that is, unfortunately, neglected by many employers and can result in an employee falling out of legal status). "Green cards" and passports with expiration dates do not need to be reverified.

3.2 **What if the reverification section of the form has been filled out from a prior reverification?**

In this case, an employer can complete Section 3 of a new Form I-9 (see Chapter 1). The employer should put the employee's name in Section 1 and retain the new form with the original.

3.3 **Can an employee present a Social Security card to show employment authorization at reverification when they presented an expiring EAD or I-94 form at the time of hire?**

Yes, as long as the Social Security card is not restricted with a statement such as "not valid for employment" or "valid for work only with DHS authorization" (these documents are not valid List C documents). Employers may not specify which documents an employee may present, either at the time of hire or at the time of reverification. Keep in mind that an employee may have become a permanent resident or otherwise received employment-authorized status allowing the employee to obtain a Social Security card absent the sponsorship of the employer, so the employer should not assume the employee is really unauthorized.

3.4 **What if a new Form I-9 comes out between the date the initial Form I-9 is completed and the time of reverification?**

If a new Form I-9 has been released between the date of hire and the date of reverification, the employer must complete Section 3 of the new version of the Form I-9 and only accept documentation of employment eligibility from the Lists of Acceptable Documents in the Form I-9 instructions.

3.5 **Do prior employees resuming work with a company need to complete a new Form I-9?**

Returning employees often don't need to fill out a new I-9 form, but if that is not done, the employer needs to reverify the employee's work authorization in Section 3 of the Form I-9. Remember that if a new version of the Form I-9 has come out since the last time the Form I-9 was completed, the employee will need to complete a new form. And if the form has been filled out in Section 3 from a previous reverification, the employer can complete Section 3 of a new Form I-9.

In order for an employee to be considered a "rehire," the employer must be rehiring the employee within three years of the employee's initial hiring date and the employee's previous grant of work authorization must not have expired. Reverifying employers must (a) record the rehiring date, (b) write the document title, number, and expiration date of any document presented by the employee, (c) sign and date Section 3, and (d) if the reverification is recorded on a new Form I-9, write the employee's name in Section 1.

If an employee is being updated instead of reverified, the employee must be rehired within three years of the initial date of hire and the employee must still be eligible to work on the same basis as when the original Form I-9 was completed. In other words, simply updating the Form I-9 is permitted when the employee is coming back on the same basis as with the original Form I-9 and reverification is needed when the basis for work has changed. Updating employers must (a) record the date of rehire, (b) sign and date Section 3, and (c) write the employee's name in Section 1.

Of course, it may be easier just to do new Form I-9s, and an employer can certainly opt for this.

Note that the rules on returning employees also apply to cases of recruiting or referring an individual.

3.6 What if a rehired employee is rehired after a new version of the Form I-9 is released?

If the Form I-9 has been modified since the form was filled out on the date of hire, the employer should not complete Section 3 of that form. Instead, the employer should complete Section 3 of the new form, list the employee's name in Section 1, and have the employee provide documentation of continued employment authorization from the current Lists of Acceptable Documents provided in the Form I-9 instructions.

3.7 What are examples of correctly completed I-9 forms?

See pages 53-59.

3.8 What are examples of I-9s with errors?

See pages 60-67.

OMB No. 1615-0047; Expires 06/30/08

Form I-9, Employment Eligibility Verification

Department of Homeland Security
U.S. Citizenship and Immigration Services

Please read instructions carefully before completing this form. The instructions must be available during completion of this form.

ANTI-DISCRIMINATION NOTICE: It is illegal to discriminate against work eligible individuals. Employers CANNOT specify which document(s) they will accept from an employee. The refusal to hire an individual because the documents have a future expiration date may also constitute illegal discrimination.

Section 1. Employee Information and Verification. To be completed and signed by employee at the time employment begins.

Print Name: Last	First	Middle Initial	Maiden Name
Doe	John	D.	

Address (Street Name and Number)	Apt. #	Date of Birth (month/day/year)
123 Main Street		12/20/1967

City	State	Zip Code	Social Security #
Anytown	TN	33321	987-65-4321

I am aware that federal law provides for imprisonment and/or fines for false statements or use of false documents in connection with the completion of this form.

I attest, under penalty of perjury, that I am (check one of the following):
- [✓] A citizen or national of the United States
- [ ] A lawful permanent resident (Alien #) A _____
- [ ] An alien authorized to work until _____

(Alien # or Admission #) _____

Employee's Signature	Date (month/day/year)
[employee signature]	12/30/2007

Preparer and/or Translator Certification. *(To be completed and signed if Section 1 is prepared by a person other than the employee.) I attest, under penalty of perjury, that I have assisted in the completion of this form and that to the best of my knowledge the information is true and correct.*

Preparer's/Translator's Signature	Print Name

Address (Street Name and Number, City, State, Zip Code)	Date (month/day/year)

Section 2. Employer Review and Verification. To be completed and signed by employer. Examine one document from List A OR examine one document from List B and one from List C, as listed on the reverse of this form, and record the title, number and expiration date, if any, of the document(s).

List A	OR	List B	AND	List C

Document title: US Passport

Issuing authority: Passport office

Document #: 340007237

Expiration Date (if any): 01/20/2004 ←

Document #:

Expiration Date (if any):

Note that a US passport may be expired and still serve as a valid List A document. However, this rule is expected to change as of April 2009.

CERTIFICATION - I attest, under penalty of perjury, that I have examined **the above-listed document(s) appear to be genuine and to relate to the e**mployee **that** *(month/day/year)* 12/30/2007 **and that to the best of my knowledg**e **yee began employment on** **employment agencies may omit the date the employee began employme**nt **k in the United States. (State**

Signature of Employer or Authorized Representative	Print Name	Title
[employer signature]	Emily Employer	HR Manager

Business or Organization Name and Address (Street Name and Number, City, State, Zip Code)	Date (month/day/year)
ABC Widgets, Inc.	12/30/2007

Section 3. Updating and Reverification. To be completed and signed by employer.

A. New Name *(if applicable)*	B. Date of Rehire *(month/day/year)* *(if applicable)*

C. If employee's previous grant of work authorization has expired, provide the information below for the document that establishes current employment eligibility.

Document Title:	Document #:	Expiration Date (if any):

I attest, under penalty of perjury, that to the best of my knowledge, this employee is eligible to work in the United States, and if the employee presented document(s), the document(s) I have examined appear to be genuine and to relate to the individual.

Signature of Employer or Authorized Representative	Date (month/day/year)

Form I-9 (Rev. 06/05/07) N

Department of Homeland Security U.S. Citizenship and Immigration Services	**Form I-9, Employment Eligibility Verification**

Please read instructions carefully before completing this form. The instructions must be available during completion of this form.

ANTI-DISCRIMINATION NOTICE: It is illegal to discriminate against work eligible individuals. Employers CANNOT specify which document(s) they will accept from an employee. The refusal to hire an individual because the documents have a future expiration date may also constitute illegal discrimination.

Section 1. Employee Information and Verification. To be completed and signed by employee at the time employment begins.

Print Name: Last	First	Middle Initial	Maiden Name
Doe	Jane	A.	Smith

Address (Street Name and Number)	Apt. #	Date of Birth (month/day/year)
123 Main Street		12/20/1967

City	State	Zip Code	Social Security #
Anytown	TN	33321	000-00-0000

I am aware that federal law provides for imprisonment and/or fines for false statements or use of false documents in connection with the completion of this form.

I attest, under penalty of perjury, that I am (check one of the following):

☐ A citizen or national of the United States

☐ A lawful permanent resident (Alien #) A _____

☒ An alien authorized to work until 05/01/2008

(Alien # or Admission #) I-94 #00000000000

Employee's Signature [signature]	Date (month/day/year) 06/01/2007

Preparer and/or Translator Certification. *(To be completed and signed if Section 1 is prepared by a person other than the employee.) I attest, under penalty of perjury, that I have assisted in the completion of this form and that to the best of my knowledge the information is true and correct.*

Preparer's/Translator's Signature	Print Name

Address (Street Name and Number, City, State, Zip Code)	Date (month/day/year)

Section 2. Employer Review and Verification. To be completed and signed by employer. Examine one document from List A OR examine one document from List B and one from List C, as listed on the reverse of this form, and record the title, number and expiration date, if any, of the document(s).

List A	OR	List B	AND	List C
Document title: EAD (Form I-766)				
Issuing authority: USCIS				
Document #: A00000000				
Expiration Date (if any): 05/01/2008				
Document #:				
Expiration Date (if any):				

CERTIFICATION - I attest, under penalty of perjury, that I have examined the document(s) presented by the above-named employee, that the above-listed document(s) appear to be genuine and to relate to the employee named, that the employee began employment on *(month/day/year)* 06/01/2007 **and that to the best of my knowledge the employee is eligible to work in the United States. (State employment agencies may omit the date the employee began employment.)**

Signature of Employer or Authorized Representative [signature]	Print Name Emily Employer	Title HR Manager

Business or Organization Name and Address (Street Name and Number, City, State, Zip Code) ABC Widgets, 555 Jackson Lane, Anytown, TN 33322	Date (month/day/year) 06/01/2007

Section 3. Updating and Reverification. To be completed and signed by employer.

A. New Name (if applicable)	B. Date of Rehire (month/day/year) (if applicable)

C. If employee's previous grant of work authorization has expired, provide the information below for the document that establishes current employment eligibility.

Document Title: EAD	Document #: A00000000	Expiration Date (if any): 05/01/2009

I attest, under penalty of perjury, that to the best of my knowledge, this employee is eligible to work in the United States, and if the employee presented document(s), the document(s) I have examined appear to be genuine and to relate to the individual.

Signature of Employer or Authorized Representative [signature]	Date (month/day/year) 06/01/2008

Form I-9 (Rev. 06/05/07) N

Department of Homeland Security
U.S. Citizenship and Immigration Services

Form I-9, Employment Eligibility Verification

Please read instructions carefully before completing this form. The instructions must be available during completion of this form.

ANTI-DISCRIMINATION NOTICE: It is illegal to discriminate against work eligible individuals. Employers CANNOT specify which document(s) they will accept from an employee. The refusal to hire an individual because the documents have a future expiration date may also constitute illegal discrimination.

Section 1. Employee Information and Verification. To be completed and signed by employee at the time employment begins.

Print Name: Last	First	Middle Initial	Maiden Name
Doe	Jane	A.	Smith

Address (Street Name and Number)	Apt. #	Date of Birth (month/day/year)
123 Main Street		12/20/1967

City	State	Zip Code	Social Security #
Anytown	TN	33321	000-00-0000

I am aware that federal law provides for imprisonment and/or fines for false statements or use of false documents in connection with the completion of this form.

I attest, under penalty of perjury, that I am (check one of the following):

☐ A citizen or national of the United States
☐ A lawful permanent resident (Alien #) A _____
☒ An alien authorized to work until   05/01/2008
(Alien # or Admission #) I-94 #00000000000

Employee's Signature [signature]	Date (month/day/year) 06/01/2007

Preparer and/or Translator Certification. *(To be completed and signed if Section 1 is prepared by a person other than the employee.)* I attest, under penalty of perjury, that I have assisted in the completion of this form and that to the best of my knowledge the information is true and correct.

Preparer's/Translator's Signature	Print Name

Address (Street Name and Number, City, State, Zip Code)	Date (month/day/year)

Section 2. Employer Review and Verification. To be completed and signed by employer. Examine one document from List A OR examine one document from List B and one from List C, as listed on the reverse of this form, and record the title, number and expiration date, if any, of the document(s).

List A	OR	List B	AND	List C
Document title: EAD (Form I-766)				
Issuing authority: USCIS				
Document #: A00000000				
Expiration Date (if any): 05/01/2008				
Document #:				
Expiration Date (if any):				

CERTIFICATION - I attest, under penalty of perjury, that I have examined the document(s) presented by the above-named employee, that the above-listed document(s) appear to be genuine and to relate to the employee named, that the employee began employment on *(month/day/year)* 06/01/2007 **and that to the best of my knowledge the employee is eligible to work in the United States. (State employment agencies may omit the date the employee began employment.)**

Signature of Employer or Authorized Representative [signature]	Print Name Emily Employer	Title HR Manager

Business or Organization Name and Address (Street Name and Number, City, State, Zip Code) ABC Widgets, 555 Jackson Lane, Anytown, TN 33322	Date (month/day/year) 06/01/2007

Section 3. Updating and Reverification. To be completed and signed by employer.

A. New Name (if applicable)	B. Date of Rehire (month/day/year) (if applicable)

C. If employee's previous grant of work authorization has expired, provide the information below for the document that establishes current employment eligibility.

Document Title: Social Security Card   Document #: 000-00-0000   Expiration Date (if any): _____

I attest, under penalty of perjury, that to the best of my knowledge, this employee is eligible to work in the United States, and if the employee presented document(s), the document(s) I have examined appear to be genuine and to relate to the individual.

Signature of Employer or Authorized Representative [signature]	Date (month/day/year) 02/01/2008

OMB No. 1615-0047; Expires 06/30/08

Department of Homeland Security
U.S. Citizenship and Immigration Services

Form I-9, Employment Eligibility Verification

Please read instructions carefully before completing this form. The instructions must be available during completion of this form.

ANTI-DISCRIMINATION NOTICE: It is illegal to discriminate against work eligible individuals. Employers CANNOT specify which document(s) they will accept from an employee. The refusal to hire an individual because the documents have a future expiration date may also constitute illegal discrimination.

Section 1. Employee Information and Verification. To be completed and signed by employee at the time employment begins.

Print Name: Last	First	Middle Initial	Maiden Name
Doe	Jane	A.	Smith

Address (Street Name and Number)	Apt. #	Date of Birth (month/day/year)
123 Main Street		12/20/1967

City	State	Zip Code	Social Security #
Anytown	TN	33321	000-00-0000

I am aware that federal law provides for imprisonment and/or fines for false statements or use of false documents in connection with the completion of this form.

I attest, under penalty of perjury, that I am (check one of the following):

☐ A citizen or national of the United States
☐ A lawful permanent resident (Alien #) A _____
☒ An alien authorized to work until 05/01/2009
(Alien # or Admission #) I-94 #00000000000

Employee's Signature [signature]	Date (month/day/year) 06/01/2008

Preparer and/or Translator Certification. *(To be completed and signed if Section 1 is prepared by a person other than the employee.) I attest, under penalty of perjury, that I have assisted in the completion of this form and that to the best of my knowledge the information is true and correct.*

Preparer's/Translator's Signature	Print Name

Address (Street Name and Number, City, State, Zip Code)	Date (month/day/year)

Section 2. Employer Review and Verification. To be completed and signed by employer. Examine one document from List A OR examine one document from List B and one from List C, as listed on the reverse of this form, and record the title, number and expiration date, if any, of the document(s).

List A	OR	List B	AND	List C
Document title: EAD (Form I-766)				
Issuing authority: USCIS				
Document #: 00000000				
Expiration Date (if any): 05/01/2009				
Document #:				
Expiration Date (if any):				

CERTIFICATION - I attest, under penalty of perjury, that I have examined the document(s) presented by the above-named employee, that the above-listed document(s) appear to be genuine and to relate to the employee named, that the employee began employment on (month/day/year) 06/01/2008 **and that to the best of my knowledge the employee is eligible to work in the United States. (State employment agencies may omit the date the employee began employment.)**

Signature of Employer or Authorized Representative [signature]	Print Name Emily Employer	Title HR Manager
Business or Organization Name and Address (Street Name and Number, City, State, Zip Code) ABC Widgets, 555 Jackson Lane, Anytown, TN 33322		Date (month/day/year) 06/01/2008

Section 3. Updating and Reverification. To be completed and signed by employer.

A. New Name (if applicable)	B. Date of Rehire (month/day/year) (if applicable)

C. If employee's previous grant of work authorization has expired, provide the information below for the document that establishes current employment eligibility.

Document Title:	Document #:	Expiration Date (if any):

I attest, under penalty of perjury, that to the best of my knowledge, this employee is eligible to work in the United States, and if the employee presented document(s), the document(s) I have examined appear to be genuine and to relate to the individual.

Signature of Employer or Authorized Representative	Date (month/day/year)

OMB No. 1615-0047; Expires 06/30/08

Department of Homeland Security
U.S. Citizenship and Immigration Services

Form I-9, Employment Eligibility Verification

Please read instructions carefully before completing this form. The instructions must be available during completion of this form.

ANTI-DISCRIMINATION NOTICE: It is illegal to discriminate against work eligible individuals. Employers CANNOT specify which document(s) they will accept from an employee. The refusal to hire an individual because the documents have a future expiration date may also constitute illegal discrimination.

Section 1. Employee Information and Verification. To be completed and signed by employee at the time employment begins.

Print Name: Last	First	Middle Initial	Maiden Name
Doe	John	D.	

Address (Street Name and Number)	Apt. #	Date of Birth (month/day/year)
123 Main Street		12/20/1967

City	State	Zip Code	Social Security #
Anytown	TN	33321	987-65-4321

I am aware that federal law provides for imprisonment and/or fines for false statements or use of false documents in connection with the completion of this form.

I attest, under penalty of perjury, that I am (check one of the following):

- [✓] A citizen or national of the United States
- [ ] A lawful permanent resident (Alien #) A _____
- [ ] An alien authorized to work until _____

(Alien # or Admission #)

Employee's Signature	Date (month/day/year)
[employee signature]	12/30/2007

Preparer and/or Translator Certification. *(To be completed and signed if Section 1 is prepared by a person other than the employee.) I attest, under penalty of perjury, that I have assisted in the completion of this form and that to the best of my knowledge the information is true and correct.*

Preparer's/Translator's Signature	Print Name

Address (Street Name and Number, City, State, Zip Code)	Date (month/day/year)

Section 2. Employer Review and Verification. To be completed and signed by employer. Examine one document from List A OR examine one document from List B and one from List C, as listed on the reverse of this form, and record the title, number and expiration date, if any, of the document(s).

List A	OR	List B	AND	List C
Document title: US Passport				
Issuing authority: Passport office				
Document #: 340007237				
Expiration Date (if any): 01/20/2004 ←				
Document #:				
Expiration Date (if any):				

Note that a US passport may be expired and still serve as a valid List A document. However, this rule is expected to change as of April 2009.

CERTIFICATION - I attest, under penalty of perjury, that I have exa~~min~~**[ed]** the above-listed document(s) appear to be genuine and to relate to the **[employee named,]** by the above-named employee, that **[the employ]**yee began employment on *(month/day/year)* 12/30/2007 and that to the best of my knowledg**[e]** to **[wor]**k in the United States. (State employment agencies may omit the date the employee began employme**[nt.]**

Signature of Employer or Authorized Representative	Print Name	Title
[employer signature]	Emily Employer	HR Manager

Business or Organization Name and Address (Street Name and Number, City, State, Zip Code)	Date (month/day/year)
ABC Widgets, Inc.	12/30/2007

Section 3. Updating and Reverification. To be completed and signed by employer.

A. New Name (if applicable)	B. Date of Rehire (month/day/year) (if applicable)

C. If employee's previous grant of work authorization has expired, provide the information below for the document that establishes current employment eligibility.

Document Title:	Document #:	Expiration Date (if any):

I attest, under penalty of perjury, that to the best of my knowledge, this employee is eligible to work in the United States, and if the employee presented document(s), the document(s) I have examined appear to be genuine and to relate to the individual.

Signature of Employer or Authorized Representative	Date (month/day/year)

Form I-9 (Rev. 06/05/07) N

OMB No. 1615-0047; Expires 06/30/08

Department of Homeland Security
U.S. Citizenship and Immigration Services

Form I-9, Employment Eligibility Verification

Please read instructions carefully before completing this form. The instructions must be available during completion of this form.

ANTI-DISCRIMINATION NOTICE: It is illegal to discriminate against work eligible individuals. Employers CANNOT specify which document(s) they will accept from an employee. The refusal to hire an individual because the documents have a future expiration date may also constitute illegal discrimination.

Section 1. Employee Information and Verification. To be completed and signed by employee at the time employment begins.

Print Name: Last	First	Middle Initial	Maiden Name
Doe	Jane	A.	Smith

Address (Street Name and Number)		Apt. #	Date of Birth (month/day/year)
123 Main Street			12/20/1967

City	State	Zip Code	Social Security #
Anytown	TN	33321	000-00-0000

I am aware that federal law provides for imprisonment and/or fines for false statements or use of false documents in connection with the completion of this form.

I attest, under penalty of perjury, that I am (check one of the following):

☐ A citizen or national of the United States
☒ A lawful permanent resident (Alien #) A 00 000 000
☐ An alien authorized to work until _____
(Alien # or Admission #) _____

Employee's Signature [signature]	Date (month/day/year) 06/01/2008

Preparer and/or Translator Certification. *(To be completed and signed if Section 1 is prepared by a person other than the employee.) I attest, under penalty of perjury, that I have assisted in the completion of this form and that to the best of my knowledge the information is true and correct.*

Preparer's/Translator's Signature	Print Name

Address (Street Name and Number, City, State, Zip Code)	Date (month/day/year)

Section 2. Employer Review and Verification. To be completed and signed by employer. Examine one document from List A OR examine one document from List B and one from List C, as listed on the reverse of this form, and record the title, number and expiration date, if any, of the document(s).

List A	OR	List B	AND	List C
Document title: Alien Registration ~~Card~~				
Issuing authority: USCIS				
Document #: A00 000 000				
Expiration Date (if any): 04/01/2009				
Document #:				
Expiration Date (if any):				

CERTIFICATION - I attest, under penalty of perjury, that I have examined the document(s) presented by the above-named employee, that the above-listed document(s) appear to be genuine and to relate to the employee named, that the employee began employment on *(month/day/year)* 06/01/2008 **and that to the best of my knowledge the employee is eligible to work in the United States. (State employment agencies may omit the date the employee began employment.)**

Signature of Employer or Authorized Representative [signature]	Print Name Emily Employer	Title HR Manager

Business or Organization Name and Address (Street Name and Number, City, State, Zip Code) ABC Widgets, 555 Jackson Lane, Anytown, TN 33322	Date (month/day/year) 06/01/2008

Section 3. Updating and Reverification. To be completed and signed by employer.

A. New Name (if applicable)	B. Date of Rehire (month/day/year) (if applicable)

C. If employee's previous grant of work authorization has expired, provide the information below for the document that establishes current employment eligibility.

Document Title:	Document #:	Expiration Date (if any):

I attest, under penalty of perjury, that to the best of my knowledge, this employee is eligible to work in the United States, and if the employee presented document(s), the document(s) I have examined appear to be genuine and to relate to the individual.

Signature of Employer or Authorized Representative	Date (month/day/year)

OMB No. 1615-0047; Expires 06/30/08

Department of Homeland Security
U.S. Citizenship and Immigration Services

Form I-9, Employment Eligibility Verification

Please read instructions carefully before completing this form. The instructions must be available during completion of this form.

ANTI-DISCRIMINATION NOTICE: It is illegal to discriminate against work eligible individuals. Employers CANNOT specify which document(s) they will accept from an employee. The refusal to hire an individual because the documents have a future expiration date may also constitute illegal discrimination.

Section 1. Employee Information and Verification. To be completed and signed by employee at the time employment begins.

Print Name: Last	First	Middle Initial	Maiden Name
Doe	Jane	A.	Smith

Address (Street Name and Number)	Apt. #	Date of Birth (month/day/year)
123 Main Street		12/20/1967

City	State	Zip Code	Social Security #
Anytown	TN	33321	000-00-0000

I am aware that federal law provides for imprisonment and/or fines for false statements or use of false documents in connection with the completion of this form.

I attest, under penalty of perjury, that I am (check one of the following):

- [X] A citizen or national of the United States
- [ ] A lawful permanent resident (Alien #) A _____
- [ ] An alien authorized to work until _____
(Alien # or Admission #) _____

Employee's Signature [signature]	Date (month/day/year) 06/01/2008

Preparer and/or Translator Certification. *(To be completed and signed if Section 1 is prepared by a person other than the employee.)* I attest, under penalty of perjury, that I have assisted in the completion of this form and that to the best of my knowledge the information is true and correct.

Preparer's/Translator's Signature	Print Name

Address (Street Name and Number, City, State, Zip Code)	Date (month/day/year)

Section 2. Employer Review and Verification. To be completed and signed by employer. Examine one document from List A OR examine one document from List B and one from List C, as listed on the reverse of this form, and record the title, number and expiration date, if any, of the document(s).

	List A	OR	List B	AND	List C
Document title:			Driver's License		Social Security Card
Issuing authority:			Tennessee		SSA
Document #:			000000000		000-00-0000
Expiration Date (if any):			01/01/2009		
Document #:					
Expiration Date (if any):					

CERTIFICATION - I attest, under penalty of perjury, that I have examined the document(s) presented by the above-named employee, that the above-listed document(s) appear to be genuine and to relate to the employee named, that the employee began employment on *(month/day/year)* 06/01/2008 **and that to the best of my knowledge the employee is eligible to work in the United States.** (State employment agencies may omit the date the employee began employment.)

Signature of Employer or Authorized Representative [signature]	Print Name Emily Employer	Title HR Manager

Business or Organization Name and Address (Street Name and Number, City, State, Zip Code) ABC Widgets, 555 Jackson Lane, Anytown, TN 33322	Date (month/day/year) 06/01/2008

Section 3. Updating and Reverification. To be completed and signed by employer.

A. New Name (if applicable)	B. Date of Rehire (month/day/year) (if applicable)

C. If employee's previous grant of work authorization has expired, provide the information below for the document that establishes current employment eligibility.

Document Title:	Document #:	Expiration Date (if any):

I attest, under penalty of perjury, that to the best of my knowledge, this employee is eligible to work in the United States, and if the employee presented document(s), the document(s) I have examined appear to be genuine and to relate to the individual.

Signature of Employer or Authorized Representative	Date (month/day/year)

OMB No. 1615-0047; Expires 06/30/08

Department of Homeland Security
U.S. Citizenship and Immigration Services

Form I-9, Employment Eligibility Verification

Please read instructions carefully before completing this form. The instructions must be available during completion of this form.

ANTI-DISCRIMINATION NOTICE: It is illegal to discriminate against work eligible individuals. Employers CANNOT specify which document(s) they will accept from an employee. The refusal to hire an individual because the documents have a future expiration date may also constitute illegal discrimination.

failed to check box

Section 1. Employee Information and Verification. To be completed and signed by employee at the time employment begins.

Print Name: Last	First	Middle Initial	Maiden Name
Doe	Jane	A.	Smith

Address *(Street Name and Number)*	Apt. #	Date of Birth *(month/day/year)*
123 Main Street		12/20/1967

City	State	Zip Code	Social Security #
Anytown	TN	33321	000-00-0000

I am aware that federal law provides for imprisonment and/or fines for false statements or use of false documents in connection with the completion of this form.

I attest, under penalty of perjury, that I am (check one of the following):

☐ A citizen or national of the United States
☐ A lawful permanent resident (Alien #) A _____
☐ An alien authorized to work until _____
(Alien # or Admission #) _____

Employee's Signature [signature]	Date *(month/day/year)* 06/01/2008

Preparer and/or Translator Certification. *(To be completed and signed if Section 1 is prepared by a person other than the employee.)* I attest, under penalty of perjury, that I have assisted in the completion of this form and that to the best of my knowledge the information is true and correct.

Preparer's/Translator's Signature	Print Name

Address *(Street Name and Number, City, State, Zip Code)*	Date *(month/day/year)*

Section 2. Employer Review and Verification. To be completed and signed by employer. Examine one document from List A OR examine one document from List B and one from List C, as listed on the reverse of this form, and record the title, number and expiration date, if any, of the document(s).

	List A	**OR**	**List B**	**AND**	**List C**
Document title:			Driver's License		Social Security Card
Issuing authority:			Tennessee		SSA
Document #:			000000000		000-00-0000
Expiration Date *(if any)*:			01/01/2009		
Document #:					
Expiration Date *(if any)*:					

CERTIFICATION - I attest, under penalty of perjury, that I have examined the document(s) presented by the above-named employee, that the above-listed document(s) appear to be genuine and to relate to the employee named, that the employee began employment on *(month/day/year)* 06/01/2008 **and that to the best of my knowledge the employee is eligible to work in the United States. (State employment agencies may omit the date the employee began employment.)**

Signature of Employer or Authorized Representative [signature]	Print Name Emily Employer	Title HR Manager
Business or Organization Name and Address *(Street Name and Number, City, State, Zip Code)* ABC Widgets, 555 Jackson Lane, Anytown, TN 33322		Date *(month/day/year)* 06/01/2008

Section 3. Updating and Reverification. To be completed and signed by employer.

A. New Name *(if applicable)*	B. Date of Rehire *(month/day/year) (if applicable)*

C. If employee's previous grant of work authorization has expired, provide the information below for the document that establishes current employment eligibility.

Document Title:	Document #:	Expiration Date (if any):

I attest, under penalty of perjury, that to the best of my knowledge, this employee is eligible to work in the United States, and if the employee presented document(s), the document(s) I have examined appear to be genuine and to relate to the individual.

Signature of Employer or Authorized Representative	Date *(month/day/year)*

OMB No. 1615-0047; Expires 06/30/08

Department of Homeland Security
U.S. Citizenship and Immigration Services

Form I-9, Employment Eligibility Verification

Please read instructions carefully before completing this form. The instructions must be available during completion of this form.

ANTI-DISCRIMINATION NOTICE: It is illegal to discriminate against work eligible individuals. Employers **CANNOT** specify which document(s) they will accept from an employee. The refusal to hire an individual because the documents have a future expiration date may also constitute illegal discrimination.

Section 1. Employee Information and Verification. To be completed and signed by employee at the time employment begins.

Print Name: Last	First	Middle Initial	Maiden Name
Doe	Jane	A.	Smith

Address (Street Name and Number)		Apt. #	Date of Birth (month/day/year)
123 Main Street			12/20/1967

City	State	Zip Code	Social Security #
Anytown	TN	33321	000-00-0000

I am aware that federal law provides for imprisonment and/or fines for false statements or use of false documents in connection with the completion of this form.

I attest, under penalty of perjury, that I am (check one of the following):

[X] A citizen or national of the United States

[ ] A lawful permanent resident (Alien #) A _____

[ ] An alien authorized to work until _____

(Alien # or Admission #) _____

Employee's Signature [signature]	Date (month/day/year) 06/01/2008

Preparer and/or Translator Certification. *(To be completed and signed if Section 1 is prepared by a person other than the employee.) I attest, under penalty of perjury, that I have assisted in the completion of this form and that to the best of my knowledge the information is true and correct.*

Preparer's/Translator's Signature	Print Name

Address (Street Name and Number, City, State, Zip Code)

Section 2. Employer Review and Verification. To be completed and signed by employer. ~~one document from List A OR~~ examine one document from List B and one from List C, as listed on the reverse of this ~~~~ ~~number and~~ expiration date, if any, of the document(s).

> List A document is inconsistent with status indicated by employee in Section 1

List A	OR	List B	AND	List C
Document title: Alien Registration ~~Card~~				
Issuing authority: USCIS				
Document #: A00 000 000				
Expiration Date (if any): 04/01/2009				
Document #:				
Expiration Date (if any):				

CERTIFICATION - I attest, under penalty of perjury, that I have examined the document(s) presented by the above-named employee, that the above-listed document(s) appear to be genuine and to relate to the employee named, that the employee began employment on *(month/day/year)* 06/01/2008 **and that to the best of my knowledge the employee is eligible to work in the United States. (State employment agencies may omit the date the employee began employment.)**

Signature of Employer or Authorized Representative [signature]	Print Name Emily Employer	Title HR Manager

Business or Organization Name and Address (Street Name and Number, City, State, Zip Code) ABC Widgets, 555 Jackson Lane, Anytown, TN 33322	Date (month/day/year) 06/01/2008

Section 3. Updating and Reverification. To be completed and signed by employer.

A. New Name (if applicable)	B. Date of Rehire (month/day/year) (if applicable)

C. If employee's previous grant of work authorization has expired, provide the information below for the document that establishes current employment eligibility.

Document Title:	Document #:	Expiration Date (if any):

I attest, under penalty of perjury, that to the best of my knowledge, this employee is eligible to work in the United States, and if the employee presented document(s), the document(s) I have examined appear to be genuine and to relate to the individual.

Signature of Employer or Authorized Representative	Date (month/day/year)

OMB No. 1615-0047; Expires 06/30/08

Department of Homeland Security
U.S. Citizenship and Immigration Services

Form I-9, Employment Eligibility Verification

Please read instructions carefully before completing this form. The instructions must be available during completion of this form.

ANTI-DISCRIMINATION NOTICE: It is illegal to discriminate against work eligible individuals. Employers CANNOT specify which document(s) they will accept from an employee. The refu~~signature missing~~ecause the documents have a future expiration date may also constitute illegal discrimination.

Section 1. Employee Information and Verification. To be completed and signed by employee at the time employment begins.

Print Name: Last	First	Middle Initial	Maiden Name
Doe	Jane	A.	Smith

Address (Street Name and Number)	Apt. #	Date of Birth (month/day/year)
123 Main Street		12/20/1967

City	State	Zip Code	Social Security #
Anytown	TN	33321	000-00-0000

I am aware that federal law provides for imprisonment and/or fines for false statements or use of false documents in connection with the completion of this form.

I attest, under penalty of perjury, that I am (check one of the following):

[X] A citizen or national of the United States
[ ] A lawful permanent resident (Alien #) A _____
[ ] An alien authorized to work until _____
(Alien # or Admission #) _____

Employee's Signature	Date (month/day/year)
	06/01/2008

Preparer and/or Translator Certification. *(To be completed and signed if Section 1 is prepared by a person other than the employee.) I attest, under penalty of perjury, that I have assisted in the completion of this form and that to the best of my knowledge the information is true and correct.*

Preparer's/Translator's Signature	Print Name

Address (Street Name and Number, City, State, Zip Code)	Date (month/day/year)

Section 2. Employer Review and Verification. To be completed and signed by employer. Examine one document from List A OR examine one document from List B and one from List C, as listed on the reverse of this form, and record the title, number and expiration date, if any, of the document(s).

List A	OR	List B	AND	List C
Document title:		Driver's License		Social Security Card
Issuing authority:		Tennessee		SSA
Document #:		000000000		000-00-0000
Expiration Date (if any):		01/01/2009		
Document #:				
Expiration Date (if any):				

CERTIFICATION - I attest, under penalty of perjury, that I have examined the document(s) presented by the above-named employee, that the above-listed document(s) appear to be genuine and to relate to the employee named, that the employee began employment on *(month/day/year)* 06/01/2008 **and that to the best of my knowledge the employee is eligible to work in the United States. (State employment agencies may omit the date the employee began employment.)**

Signature of Employer or Authorized Representative	Print Name	Title
[signature]	Emily Employer	HR Manager

Business or Organization Name and Address (Street Name and Number, City, State, Zip Code)	Date (month/day/year)
ABC Widgets, 555 Jackson Lane, Anytown, TN 33322	06/01/2008

Section 3. Updating and Reverification. To be completed and signed by employer.

A. New Name (if applicable)	B. Date of Rehire (month/day/year) (if applicable)

C. If employee's previous grant of work authorization has expired, provide the information below for the document that establishes current employment eligibility.

Document Title:	Document #:	Expiration Date (if any):

I attest, under penalty of perjury, that to the best of my knowledge, this employee is eligible to work in the United States, and if the employee presented document(s), the document(s) I have examined appear to be genuine and to relate to the individual.

Signature of Employer or Authorized Representative	Date (month/day/year)

Form I-9 (Rev. 06/05/07) N

OMB No. 1615-0047; Expires 06/30/08

Form I-9, Employment Eligibility Verification

Department of Homeland Security
U.S. Citizenship and Immigration Services

Please read instructions carefully before completing this form. The instructions must be available during completion of this form.

ANTI-DISCRIMINATION NOTICE: It is date missing **inst work eligible individuals. Employers CANNOT** specify which document(s) they will accept from an employee. The refusal to hire an individual because the documents have a future expiration date may also constitute illegal discrimination.

Section 1. Employee Information and Verification. To be completed and signed by employee at the time employment begins.

Print Name: Last	First	Middle Initial	Maiden Name
Doe	Jane	A.	Smith

Address *(Street Name and Number)*	Apt. #	Date of Birth *(month/day/year)*
123 Main Street		12/20/1967

City	State	Zip Code	Social Security #
Anytown	TN	33321	000-00-0000

I am aware that federal law provides for imprisonment and/or fines for false statements or use of false documents in connection with the completion of this form.

I attest, under penalty of perjury, that I am (check one of the following):
- ☐ A citizen or national of the United States
- ☒ A lawful permanent resident (Alien #) A   00 000 000
- ☐ An alien authorized to work until _____
(Alien # or Admission #) _____

Employee's Signature [signature]	Date *(month/day/year)*

Preparer and/or Translator Certification. *(To be completed and signed if Section 1 is prepared by a person other than the employee.)* I attest, under penalty of perjury, that I have assisted in the completion of this form and that to the best of my knowledge the information is true and correct.

Preparer's/Translator's Signature	Print Name

Address *(Street Name and Number, City, State, Zip Code)*	Date *(month/day/year)*

Section 2. Employer Review and Verification. To be completed and signed by employer. Examine one document from List A OR examine one document from List B and one from List C, as listed on the reverse of this form, and record the title, number and expiration date, if any, of the document(s).

List A	OR	List B	AND	List C
Document title: Alien Registration Card				
Issuing authority: USCIS				
Document #: A00 000 000				
Expiration Date *(if any):* 04/01/2009				
Document #:				
Expiration Date *(if any):*				

CERTIFICATION - I attest, under penalty of perjury, that I have examined the document(s) presented by the above-named employee, that the above-listed document(s) appear to be genuine and to relate to the employee named, that the employee began employment on *(month/day/year)* 06/01/2008 **and that to the best of my knowledge the employee is eligible to work in the United States.   (State employment agencies may omit the date the employee began employment.)**

Signature of Employer or Authorized Representative [signature]	Print Name Emily Employer	Title HR Manager
Business or Organization Name and Address *(Street Name and Number, City, State, Zip Code)* ABC Widgets, 555 Jackson Lane, Anytown, TN 33322		Date *(month/day/year)* 06/01/2008

Section 3. Updating and Reverification. To be completed and signed by employer.

A. New Name *(if applicable)*	B. Date of Rehire *(month/day/year) (if applicable)*

C. If employee's previous grant of work authorization has expired, provide the information below for the document that establishes current employment eligibility.

Document Title:	Document #:	Expiration Date (if any):

I attest, under penalty of perjury, that to the best of my knowledge, this employee is eligible to work in the United States, and if the employee presented document(s), the document(s) I have examined appear to be genuine and to relate to the individual.

Signature of Employer or Authorized Representative	Date *(month/day/year)*

OMB No. 1615-0047; Expires 06/30/08

Department of Homeland Security
U.S. Citizenship and Immigration Services

Form I-9, Employment Eligibility Verification

Please read instructions carefully before completing this form. The instructions must be available during completion of this form.

ANTI-DISCRIMINATION NOTICE: It is illegal to discriminate against work eligible individuals. Employers CANNOT specify which document(s) they will accept from an employee. The refusal to hire an individual because the documents have a future expiration date may also constitute illegal discrimination.

Section 1. Employee Information and Verification. To be completed and signed by employee at the time employment begins.

Print Name: Last	First	Middle Initial	Maiden Name
Doe	Jane	A.	Smith

Address (Street Name and Number)	Apt. #	Date of Birth (month/day/year)
123 Main Street		12/20/1967

City	State	Zip Code	Social Security #
Anytown	TN	33321	000-00-0000

I am aware that federal law provides for imprisonment and/or fines for false statements or use of false documents in connection with the completion of this form.

I attest, under penalty of perjury, that I am (check one of the following):

☐ A citizen or national of the United States
☒ A lawful permanent resident (Alien #) A   00 000 000
☐ An alien authorized to work until _____
(Alien # or Admission #) _____

Employee's Signature [signature]	Date (month/day/year) 06/01/2008

Preparer and/or Translator Certification. *(To be completed and signed if Section 1 is prepared by a person other than the employee.) I attest, under penalty of perjury, that I have assisted in the completion of this form and that to the best of my knowledge the information is true and correct.*

Preparer's/Translator's Signature	Print Name

Address (Street Name and Number, City, State, Zip Code)	Date (month/day)

Section 2. Employer Review and Verification. To be completed and signed by employer. Examine one document from List B and one from List C, as listed on the reverse of this form, and record the expiration date, if any, of the document(s).

> Overdocumentation (Complete either List A only or provide a combination of a List B and List C document)

List A	OR	List B	AND	
Document title: ~~Alien Registration Card~~		Drivers License		Social Security Card
Issuing authority: USCIS		State of Tennessee		SSA
Document #: A00 000 000		00000000		000-00-0000
Expiration Date (if any): 04/01/2009		05/20/2009		
Document #:				
Expiration Date (if any):				

CERTIFICATION - I attest, under penalty of perjury, that I have examined the document(s) presented by the above-named employee, that the above-listed document(s) appear to be genuine and to relate to the employee named, that the employee began employment on *(month/day/year)* 06/01/2008 **and that to the best of my knowledge the employee is eligible to work in the United States. (State employment agencies may omit the date the employee began employment.)**

Signature of Employer or Authorized Representative [signature]	Print Name Emily Employer	Title HR Manager

Business or Organization Name and Address (Street Name and Number, City, State, Zip Code) ABC Widgets, 555 Jackson Lane, Anytown, TN 33322	Date (month/day/year) 06/01/2008

Section 3. Updating and Reverification. To be completed and signed by employer.

A. New Name (if applicable)	B. Date of Rehire (month/day/year) (if applicable)

C. If employee's previous grant of work authorization has expired, provide the information below for the document that establishes current employment eligibility.

Document Title:	Document #:	Expiration Date (if any):

I attest, under penalty of perjury, that to the best of my knowledge, this employee is eligible to work in the United States, and if the employee presented document(s), the document(s) I have examined appear to be genuine and to relate to the individual.

Signature of Employer or Authorized Representative	Date (month/day/year)

OMB No. 1615-0047; Expires 06/30/08

Department of Homeland Security
U.S. Citizenship and Immigration Services

Form I-9, Employment Eligibility Verification

Please read instructions carefully before completing this form. The instructions must be available during completion of this form.

ANTI-DISCRIMINATION NOTICE: It is illegal to discriminate against work eligible individuals. Employers CANNOT specify which document(s) they will accept from an employee. The refusal to hire an individual because the documents have a future expiration date may also constitute illegal discrimination.

Section 1. Employee Information and Verification. To be completed and signed by employee at the time employment begins.

Print Name: Last	First	Middle Initial	Maiden Name
Doe	Jane	A.	Smith

Address (*Street Name and Number*)		Apt. #	Date of Birth (*month/day/year*)
123 Main Street			12/20/1967

City	State	Zip Code	Social Security #
Anytown	TN	33321	000-00-0000

I am aware that federal law provides for imprisonment and/or fines for false statements or use of false documents in connection with the completion of this form.

I attest, under penalty of perjury, that I am (check one of the following):

☐ A citizen or national of the United States
☐ A lawful permanent resident (Alien #) A _____
☒ An alien authorized to work until 05/01/2009
(Alien # or Admission #) I-94 #00000000000

Employee's Signature [signature]	Date (*month/day/year*) 06/01/2008

Preparer and/or Translator Certification. (*To be completed and signed if Section 1 is prepared by a person other than the employee.*) I attest, under penalty of perjury, that I have assisted in the completion of this form and that to the best of my knowledge the information is true and correct.

Preparer's/Translator's Signature	Print Name

Address (*Street Name and Number, City, State, Zip Code*)	Date (*month/day/year*)

Section 2. Employer Review and Verification. To be completed and signed by employer. Examine one document from List A OR examine one document from List B and one from List C, as listed on the reverse of this form, and record the title, number and expiration date, if any, of the document(s).

List A	OR	List B	List C
Document title: EAD (Form I-766)		blank document number and no expiration date	
Issuing authority: USCIS			
Document #:			
Expiration Date (*if any*):			
Document #:			
Expiration Date (*if any*):			

CERTIFICATION - I attest, under penalty of perjury, that I have examined the document(s) presented by the above-named employee, that the above-listed document(s) appear to be genuine and to relate to the employee named, that the employee began employment on (*month/day/year*) 06/01/2008 **and that to the best of my knowledge the employee is eligible to work in the United States.** (State employment agencies may omit the date the employee began employment.)

Signature of Employer or Authorized Representative [signature]	Print Name Emily Employer	Title HR Manager
Business or Organization Name and Address (*Street Name and Number, City, State, Zip Code*) ABC Widgets, 555 Jackson Lane, Anytown, TN 33322		Date (*month/day/year*) 06/01/2008

Section 3. Updating and Reverification. To be completed and signed by employer.

A. New Name (*if applicable*)	B. Date of Rehire (*month/day/year*) (*if applicable*)

C. If employee's previous grant of work authorization has expired, provide the information below for the document that establishes current employment eligibility.

Document Title:	Document #:	Expiration Date (if any):

I attest, under penalty of perjury, that to the best of my knowledge, this employee is eligible to work in the United States, and if the employee presented document(s), the document(s) I have examined appear to be genuine and to relate to the individual.

Signature of Employer or Authorized Representative	Date (*month/day/year*)

OMB No. 1615-0047; Expires 06/30/08

Department of Homeland Security
U.S. Citizenship and Immigration Services

Form I-9, Employment Eligibility Verification

Please read instructions carefully before completing this form. The instructions must be available during completion of this form.

ANTI-DISCRIMINATION NOTICE: It is illegal to discriminate against work eligible individuals. Employers CANNOT specify which document(s) they will accept from an employee. The refusal to hire an individual because the documents have a future expiration date may also constitute illegal discrimination.

Section 1. Employee Information and Verification. To be completed and signed by employee at the time employment begins.

Print Name: Last	First	Middle Initial	Maiden Name
Doe	Jane	A.	Smith

Address *(Street Name and Number)*	Apt. #	Date of Birth *(month/day/year)*
123 Main Street		12/20/1967

City	State	Zip Code	Social Security #
Anytown	TN	33321	000-00-0000

I attest, under penalty of perjury, that I am (check one of the following):

- [ ] A citizen or national of the United States
- [ ] A lawful permanent resident (Alien #) A _____
- [x] An alien authorized to work until 05/01/2009
  (Alien # or Admission #) I-94 #00000000000

I am aware that federal law provides for ~~imprisonment and/or~~ **fines for false statements or** ~~use of false document~~**s in connection with the** ~~completion of this fo~~**rm.**

> documents should have been included in List A

Employee's Signature   [signature]

Date *(month/day/year)*
06/01/2008

Preparer and/or Translator Certification. *(To be completed and signed if Section 1 is prepared by a person other than the employee.)* I attest, under penalty of perjury, that I have assisted in the completion of this form and that to the best of my knowledge the information is true and correct.

Preparer's/Translator's Signature	Print Name

Address *(Street Name and Number, City, State, Zip Code)*	Date *(month/day/year)*

Section 2. Employer Review and Verification. To be completed and signed by employer. Examine one document from List A OR examine one document from List B and one from List C, as listed on the reverse of this form, and record the title, number and expiration date, if any, of the document(s).

	List A	OR	List B	AND	List C
Document title:			Passport		Form I-94
Issuing authority:			Government of Germany		USCIS
Document #:			0000000000000		00000000000
Expiration Date *(if any):*			05/10/2010		05/01/2009
Document #:					
Expiration Date *(if any):*					

CERTIFICATION - I attest, under penalty of perjury, that I have examined the document(s) presented by the above-named employee, that the above-listed document(s) appear to be genuine and to relate to the employee named, that the employee began employment on *(month/day/year)* 06/01/2008 **and that to the best of my knowledge the employee is eligible to work in the United States. (State employment agencies may omit the date the employee began employment.)**

Signature of Employer or Authorized Representative	Print Name	Title
[signature]	Emily Employer	HR Manager

Business or Organization Name and Address *(Street Name and Number, City, State, Zip Code)*	Date *(month/day/year)*
ABC Widgets, 555 Jackson Lane, Anytown, TN 33322	06/01/2008

Section 3. Updating and Reverification. To be completed and signed by employer.

A. New Name *(if applicable)*	B. Date of Rehire *(month/day/year) (if applicable)*

C. If employee's previous grant of work authorization has expired, provide the information below for the document that establishes current employment eligibility.

Document Title:	Document #:	Expiration Date (if any):

I attest, under penalty of perjury, that to the best of my knowledge, this employee is eligible to work in the United States, and if the employee presented document(s), the document(s) I have examined appear to be genuine and to relate to the individual.

Signature of Employer or Authorized Representative	Date *(month/day/year)*

OMB No. 1615-0047; Expires 06/30/08

Department of Homeland Security
U.S. Citizenship and Immigration Services

Form I-9, Employment Eligibility Verification

Please read instructions carefully before completing this form. The instructions must be available during completion of this form.

ANTI-DISCRIMINATION NOTICE: It is illegal to discriminate against work eligible individuals. Employers CANNOT specify which document(s) they will accept from an employee. The refusal to hire an individual because the documents have a future expiration date may also constitute illegal discrimination.

Section 1. Employee Information and Verification. To be completed and signed by employee at the time employment begins.

Print Name: Last	First	Middle Initial	Maiden Name
Doe	Jane	A.	Smith

Address (*Street Name and Number*)	Apt. #	Date of Birth (*month/day/year*)
123 Main Street		12/20/1967

City	State	Zip Code	Social Security #
Anytown	TN	33321	000-00-0000

I am aware that federal law provides for imprisonment and/or fines for false statements or use of false documents in connection with the completion of this form.

I attest, under penalty of perjury, that I am (check one of the following):

☐ A citizen or national of the United States
☒ A lawful permanent resident (Alien #) A   00 000 000
☐ An alien authorized to work until _____

(Alien # or Admission #) _____

Employee's Signature [signature]	Date (*month/day/year*) 06/01/2008

Preparer and/or Translator Certification. (*To be completed and signed if Section 1 is prepared by a person other than the employee.*) I attest, under penalty of perjury, that I have assisted in the completion of this form and that to the best of my knowledge the information is true and correct.

Preparer's/Translator's Signature	Print Name

Address (*Street Name and Number, City, State, Zip Code*)	Date (*month/day/year*)

Section 2. Employer Review and Verification. To be completed and signed by employer. Examine one document from List A OR examine one document from List B and one from List C, as listed on the reverse of this form, and record the title, number and expiration date, if any, of the document(s).

List A	OR	**List B**	AND	**List C**
Document title: Alien Registration Card				
Issuing authority: USCIS			blank	
Document #: A00 000 000				
Expiration Date (*if any*): 04/01/2009				blank
Document #:				
Expiration Date (*if any*):				

CERTIFICATION - I attest, under penalty of perjury blank document(s) presented by the above-named employee, that the above-listed document(s) appear to be genuine and to relate to the employee named, that the employee began employment on (*month/day/year*) _____ and that to the best of my knowledge the employee is eligible to work in the United States. (State employment agencies may omit the date the employee began employment.)

Signature of Employer or Authorized Representative [signature]	Print Name Emily Employer	Title
Business or Organization Name and Address (*Street Name and Number, City, State, Zip Code*) ABC Widgets, 555 Jackson Lane, Anytown, TN 33322		Date (*month/day/year*)

Section 3. Updating and Reverification. To be completed and signed by employer.

A. New Name (*if applicable*)	B. Date of Rehire (*month/day/year*) (*if applicable*)

C. If employee's previous grant of work authorization has expired, provide the information below for the document that establishes current employment eligibility.

Document Title:	Document #:	Expiration Date (if any):

I attest, under penalty of perjury, that to the best of my knowledge, this employee is eligible to work in the United States, and if the employee presented document(s), the document(s) I have examined appear to be genuine and to relate to the individual.

Signature of Employer or Authorized Representative	Date (*month/day/year*)

Form I-9 (Rev. 06/05/07) N

Recordkeeping

4.1 **What are the Form I-9 recordkeeping requirements?**

Employers must keep I-9 forms for all current employees, though the forms of certain terminated employees can be destroyed. In the case of an audit from a governmental agency, the forms must be produced for inspection. The forms may be retained in either paper or electronic formats as well as in microfilm or microfiche formats (see discussion below for more information on this subject).

4.2 **When can Form I-9 be destroyed?**

For terminated employees (the date employment in the U.S. ceased for employees transferred abroad), the form must be retained for at least three years from the date of hire or for at least one year after the termination date, whichever comes later.

Employers should figure out two dates when an employee is terminated. The first is the date three years from the employee's date of hire. The second is the date one year from the termination date. The later date is the date until which the Form I-9 must be retained.

Note that there is a different rule for recruiters or referrers for a fee. Those entities are only required to maintain the Form I-9s for a three-year period from the date of hire, regardless of whether the employee has been terminated.

In addition to establishing a reminder system to reverify Form I-9s, employers should also establish a tickler system to destroy forms no longer required to be retained.

4.3 **Should recordkeeping be centralized at a company?**

Keeping records in one location is generally advisable because it makes it easier to conduct internal audits to ensure the employer is complying with IRCA's rules and also easier to prepare for a government inspection, since having the forms at one location will allow more time for review.

The forms themselves can be kept on-site or at an off-site storage facility, as long as the employer is able to produce the documentation within three days of an audit request from a federal agency.

4.4 **Does an employer need to keep copies of the documents presented by the employee?**

No. Retaining copies of the supporting documents is voluntary. Employers can retain copies of documents and must keep the copies with the specific Form I-9. While some would argue that maintaining copies of documents leaves an unnecessary paper trail for government inspectors, it is also true that maintaining documentation could provide a good-faith defense for an employer in showing that it had reason to believe an employee was authorized even if the paperwork was not properly completed. IRCA compliance officers may also be suspicious of employers that don't keep copies of documents. It is also easier for an employer to conduct internal audits to ensure compliance when they can see what documents were actually provided to the human resource representative responsible for completion of the Form I-9. Finally, whatever a company decides, however, it is important that the policy be consistently applied. Keep all the documents or keep none of them, since keeping copies only for certain employees could expose the employer to charges of discrimination. Also, it is important to remember that simply having copies of the documents does not relieve the employer of its responsibility for fully completing Section 2 of Form I-9.

4.5   Can a Form I-9 completed on paper be stored in another format?

Yes. In addition to paper, Form I-9s may be retained in electronic, microfilm, or microfiche formats.

The DHS suggests the following with respect to microfilm or microfiche:
- Use film stock that will last the entire retention period (which could exceed 20 years for some businesses).
- Use equipment that allows for a high degree of readability and for copying onto paper.
- For microfilm, place the index at the beginning or end of the series, and for microfiche, place the index on the last microfiche.

Form I-9s can also be retained in an electronic format. (See Chapter 5 for further information on the requirements for electronic I-9 systems.)

4.6   Should Form I-9 records be kept with the personnel records?

This is generally a bad idea. First, it could compromise the privacy of employees by allowing government inspectors to review items that are completely unrelated to the Form I-9. Employers that want to prevent this would have to manually go through the personnel records and pull the Form I-9 paperwork, something that could cost valuable time as the employer prepares for the government inspection. Keeping the Form I-9s separately will also make it easier to conduct internal audits to ensure compliance with IRCA and to reverify forms as needed.

Electronic I-9 Systems

For the past few years, employers have been eligible to file and store Form I-9s electronically. As the national crackdown on employers of illegal immigrants grows more intense and as a number of vendors now offer electronic I-9 products, employers are starting to weigh the benefits of ditching paper I-9s and going digital. This chapter first discusses the laws surrounding filing and then reviews why companies would want to switch.

5.1 Can a Form I-9 be completed electronically?

In October 2004, President George W. Bush signed a law, which for the first time authorized employers to retain employment eligibility verification forms (Form I-9s) in an electronic format. In April 2005, the law took effect and employers began to manage their Form I-9s electronically. ICE issued rules setting standards for using electronic I-9s in June 2006 (8 CFR §274a.2), and the agency is actively encouraging employers to store their Form I-9s electronically.

5.2 Why would companies want to switch to electronic I-9 systems?

There are numerous reasons why companies would prefer electronic I-9s over paper-based systems.

- Most of the major vendors use web-based systems, which means employers do not have to install software and only need Internet access and a web browser.
- Employees are not able to complete Form I-9 unless the data is properly entered. Many vendors offer systems that guide workers and human resource officials through proper completion of the forms.
- Some of the systems are "intelligent" and ensure that, based on answers provided in Section 1 of the Form I-9, only appropriate documents show up in Section 2.
- Some systems allow for certain sections of the form that are the same from applicant-to-applicant to be prefilled to save time.
- The better electronic I-9 systems include "help" features that make it easier for human resource officials and employees to answer questions on the Form I-9.
- Employers with employees at multiple sites can more easily monitor I-9 compliance at remote locations.
- Reverification is automated and employers are less likely to incur liability due to an inadvertent failure to update an employee's I-9. Many systems send e-mail Employers can integrate the system with E-Verify or other electronic employment verification systems in order to minimize the chances that unauthorized workers end up employed.
- Using an electronic I-9 system reduces the risk of identity theft from the robbery of paper I-9 records (a problem that has been occurring with more frequency of late). By law, electronic I-9s must have built-in security systems to protect the privacy of employees and the integrity of the data.
- Using an electronic I-9 system can make it easier to respond to ICE audits. In addition to creating the audit trails required by regulation, some of the systems archive communications relating to the I-9.
- Electronic I-9 systems can be integrated with payroll and employee database systems.

- Data from the electronic Form I-9 can be automatically uploaded into E-Verify, the government's electronic employment verification system. Several electronic I-9 vendors are federally approved E-Verify designated agents, thus allowing them to automate the entry of an employer's data in E-Verify.
- An electronic I-9 system allows for the automation of purging Form I-9s for employees who are no longer with the employer and whose Form I-9s no longer need to be retained.
- Some of the systems contain instructions in multiple languages for employees who have difficulty understanding English.
- Employers can potentially achieve cost savings by storing Form I-9s electronically rather than using conventional filing and storage of paper copies or converting paper forms to microfilm or microfiche.
- Electronically retained I-9s are more easily searchable and, hence, often a time-saver for HR personnel. The better systems produce a variety of reports that make it easier to monitor I-9 compliance.
- Some of the systems also track visa and I-94 expiration dates.

5.3   Are there downsides to using an electronic I-9 system?
There are some potential problems with using a digital system. They include the following:

- There are no 100 percent secure electronic systems (though the law requires that electronic I-9 vendors and their employer-customers implement security measures).
- The electronic systems do not totally stop identity theft, since a person can present doctored identification and employment authorization paperwork making it appear that the employee is another person (though employers can undertake additional background-checking to reduce the likelihood of problems).
- A paper I-9 form is free (aside from indirect costs like storage, training, etc.). Electronic systems typically charge a flat monthly fee or a per-employee fee (though the per-employee costs are usually no more than a few dollars with any of the major vendors).
- Most I-9s are Internet dependent. When the Internet is not available, the I-9 form cannot be completed (though an employer may use a paper I-9 in such a case).
- If an electronic I-9 vendor goes out of business, the employer could be in a bind if precautions are not in place to make it easy to retrieve the employee's data (such as having backups on the employer's own computer system).

5.4   What requirements must electronic I-9 systems meet?
The June 2006 rules issued by ICE set standards for completing forms electronically and also for the scanning and storage of existing I-9 forms. Since the change in the law, a number of software products have come onto the market allowing for the electronic filing of I-9s. There are advantages to using such a system, including improving accuracy in completing forms and setting up automated systems to prompt employers to reverify I-9s for employees with temporary work authorizations.

The DHS regulations require that electronically generated I-9s meet the following standards:

- The forms must be legible when seen on a computer screen, microfiche, or microfilm, or when printed on paper.
- The name, content, and order of data must not be altered from the paper version of the form.
- There are reasonable controls to ensure the accuracy and reliability of the electronic generation or storage system.
- There are reasonable controls designed to prevent and detect the unauthorized or accidental creation, deletion, or deterioration of stored Form I-9s.

- The software must have an indexing system allowing for searches by any field.
- There must be the ability to reproduce legible hard copies.
- The software must not be subject to any agreement that would limit or restrict access to and use of the electronic generation system by a governmental agency on the premises of the employer, recruiter, or referrer for a fee (including personnel, hardware, software, files, indexes, and software documentation).
- Compression or formatting technologies may be used as long as the standards defined above are met.
- There is a system to identify anyone who has created, accessed, viewed, updated, or corrected an electronic Form I-9, and also to see what action was taken.

Employers that know or should reasonably have known that an action or lack of action would result in the loss of electronic Form I-9 records can be held liable under IRCA.

Employers may use more than one kind of electronic I-9 system as long as each system meets the standards noted above.

Employers using an electronic I-9 system must also make available, upon request, descriptions of the electronic generation and storage system, the indexing system, and the business process that create, modify, and maintain the retained Form I-9s and establish the authenticity and integrity of the forms, such as audit trails. The I-9 software vendor should, of course, provide such documentation to the employer, though this is not a requirement in the regulations.

There are special audit requirements for electronically stored I-9s and a discussion of those requirements is set out below in the section of this chapter discussing the regulation of government inspections.

5.5   How is an electronic Form I-9 "signed" by an employee and employer?
The DHS regulations require that electronic I-9s can be "signed" electronically through a system where the person providing the information will acknowledge that he or she has read the attestation.

The signature must be affixed to the document at the time the attestation is provided. The form must also be printed and provided to the person providing the signature at the time the document is signed. This applies to the employee as well as to the employer, recruiter, or referrer for a fee.

5.6   What are the Form I-9 recordkeeping requirements for electronic I-9s?
Employers must keep I-9 forms for all current employees, though the forms of certain terminated employees can be destroyed. In the case of an audit by a governmental agency, the forms must be produced for inspection. The forms may be retained in either paper or electronic formats, as well as in microfilm or microfiche formats.

5.7   What privacy protections are accorded employees when they complete Form I-9 electronically?
Employers with electronic I-9 systems are required to implement a records security program that ensures that only authorized personnel have access to electronic records, that such records are backed up, that employees are trained to minimize the risk of records being altered, and that whenever a record is created, accessed, viewed, updated, or corrected, a secure and permanent trail is created establishing who accessed the record.

5.8   **How does an employer who uses an electronic I-9 system respond to an ICE audit?**

Original I-9 forms must normally be provided for inspection to ICE examiners. If an employer retains Form I-9s in an electronic format, the employer must retrieve and reproduce the specific forms requested by the inspecting officer as well as the associated audit trails showing who accessed the computer system and the actions performed on the system in a specified period of time. The inspecting officer must also be provided with the necessary hardware and software, as well as access to personnel and documentation in order to locate, retrieve, read, and reproduce the requested Form I-9 documentation and associated audit trails, reports, and other related data.

Finally, an inspecting officer is permitted to request an electronic summary of all the immigration fields on an electronically stored Form I-9.

5.9   **Can a company using an electronic I-9 system batch load data to E-Verify?**

Yes. The DHS has a real-time batch method that requires a company to develop an interface between its personal system or electronic Form I-9 system and the E-Verify database. Employers interested in more information, including design specifications, should call ICE at 800-741-5023.

5.10   **Can employers convert existing I-9s to an electronic format?**

Yes. Many employers are scanning and indexing their current I-9 forms and storing them electronically using electronic I-9 software.

5.11   **Where can I find out which companies offer electronic Form I-9 products and services?**

A list of electronic I-9 vendors can be found in Appendix C. Links to vendors can also be found at the author's employer immigration compliance blog at www.visalaw.com/blog_i9/blog_i9.htm..

Knowledge of Unlawful Immigration Status

6.1   **What if an employer knows an employee is not authorized to be employed even though the Form I-9 was properly completed?**

An employer who knows the employee is not authorized to work — even though everything on the Form I-9 appears valid — is violating IRCA because the employer is considered to have actual knowledge that an employee is not employment eligible. But note that an employer who simply suspects an employee is ineligible to work should be extremely careful before terminating an employee or even asking for additional documentation until the employer has a very solid foundation for the belief. Taking an action after merely hearing from another employee that a particular employee is unauthorized to be in the U.S. is a recipe for a discrimination lawsuit, since IRCA does not require employers to make inquiries under these circumstances. On the other hand, if an employee actually provides information to the employer regarding their immigration status, the employer would be considered to have knowledge.

6.2   **When will an employer be considered to have "constructive knowledge"?**

The DHS regulations not only hold employers liable when they have actual knowledge that an employee is not authorized to work, but also when knowledge may be inferred through notice of certain facts which would "lead a person, through the exercise of reasonable care, to know about a certain condition." This is called "constructive knowledge" and the DHS lists several examples in its rules:

- The employer fails to complete or improperly completes the Form I-9.
- The employer has information which would indicate the alien is not authorized to work, such as a labor certification (but note that this would generally only apply when an employee was already claiming to be a U.S. citizen or permanent resident on the Form I-9).
- The employer acts with reckless and wanton disregard for the legal consequences of permitting another individual to introduce an unauthorized employee into its workforce.

This is not an exhaustive list and employers also need to be cognizant of the anti-discrimination rules. Also, failing to reverify a Form I-9 that requires reverification could be considered constructive knowledge.

A more difficult situation arises in cases where an employer receives a "no-match" letter from the SSA regarding an employee whose name does not properly match the SSN he or she has provided. At the time of this book's publication, an August 2007 regulation that would outline when an employer is deemed to have knowledge that an employee is unauthorized based on a no-match letter was tied up in litigation. The chief purpose of the regulation was to clarify for employers what to do when letters from the SSA are received. Until a no-match rule become effective, there are no clear rules on how much follow-up is required on the part of the employer. While some lawyers advise their clients not to fire employees in no-match cases since the mismatch may be attributable to computer errors, typographical mistakes, or other issues, others have taken the position that an employee's failure to resolve the problem after a reasonable period of time could be construed to provide constructive knowledge. A clearer situation is found when an employer receives a notice from ICE that an employee has submitted fraudulent documentation. The courts have generally held that such a notification provides an employer with constructive knowledge of a problem and the employer needs to reverify. ICE notifications are also covered in the August 2007 rule, though the litigation enjoining the enforcement of the rule does not create as much confusion in these cases.

6.3   What if an employee later presents an SSN different from the SSN provided when the I-9 was completed?

Because a person is only assigned one SSN in his or her lifetime, an employee who comes to an employer with a number different from the one provided at the time of hire should be viewed with suspicion. The odds are that the employee used a false number to begin work and has somehow been able to obtain a valid SSN later (such as through a "green card" application filed independently of the employer).

Employers will, of course, want to speak to labor and employment counsel regarding a violation of an employer's policies concerning making false statements during the hiring process. With respect to IRCA, the employer will want to inquire regarding the circumstances surrounding obtaining the new SSN. However, the employer is not required to terminate the employee even if the employee admits to making a false statement, and the employer could continue employing the employee if the employer had no knowledge of the employee's lack of work authorization. In this case, the employer should have the employee update the Form I-9 to correct the problem, and the employer would also want to correct the SSN with the IRS so taxes are properly withheld.

6.4   Is an employer on notice that an employee is not authorized to work if the employee requests that the employer petition for the employee's permanent residency?

The DHS regulations list an employer being requested to file a "green card" application as an example of a situation where there may be constructive knowledge that an employee is not eligible to work. This would be the case, for example, when the employer is requested to file a "green card" application for an employee who stated on the I-9 that he or she was a U.S. citizen or lawful permanent resident. There are situations, however, where an employee may request an employer to file for permanent residence that would not indicate a problem. The obvious example is where an employee is on a nonimmigrant work visa sponsored by the employer. But it may also happen when an employee is in a status which allows for employment, but is not actual permanent residency. This may be the case if, for example, an employee is in TPS or asylum status, or has a "green card" application pending through another petition, and the employee wants to have a backup strategy to get permanent residency.

6.5   What if the employee states in Section 1 that he or she is a permanent resident or U.S. citizen, but then presents an employment document with an expiration date?

The employer in this situation should ask the employee if he or she properly understood the question in Section 1 regarding status, since the document presented is facially inconsistent with the status claimed. Perhaps the employee has a pending permanent residency petition and has an EAD associated with that application. If the employee erred, then he or she should either correct and initial the attestation or present documents that are not inconsistent with the claim of being a permanent resident (including documents that do not show permanent residency, but do show identity and work authorization, such as a driver's license and a Social Security card without annotations). The employee may also complete a new Form I-9. If the employee states that he or she is, in fact, a U.S. citizen or permanent resident, then the employer should not accept an EAD since the document directly contradicts the employee's stated status.

6.6 **Should an employer reverify a Form I-9 for an employee who is subject to a Social Security no-match letter?**

The rules regarding SSA letters telling an employer that an employee's name and SSN do not match are completely unsettled as of the publication of this book. In August 2007, the DHS released a rule that would require an employer to reverify a Form I-9 after going through a series of set procedures in a specified time frame. The rule was to take effect on September 14, 2007. However, a coalition of business and labor groups sued to overturn the regulation and succeeded in convincing a court to issue an injunction blocking the regulation from taking effect. That injunction continues and, though the DHS has released a new rule, the injunction remains in place.

In the interim, lawyers' opinions differ over the meaning of receiving a no-match letter. Does the letter itself mean an employer has knowledge that an employee's SSN is suspect? Because there are many reasons why a letter from the SSA may have nothing to do with an employee's immigration status, an employer cannot assume that the employee is improperly documented.

The employer should initially check to make sure that an error has not been made on the employer's part. After it is clear that the problem is not the employer's fault, the employer should notify the employee. Beyond that, it is not clear under current law what an employer should do. The no-match letters in the past have stated that they are not to be construed by the employer as being a statement about an employee's immigration status. And a recent case out of the Ninth Circuit Court of Appeals held that the mere receipt of a no-match letter by an employer does not equate to the employer having constructive knowledge that an employee is unauthorized to work.

Likewise, a December 23, 1997, legacy INS opinion letter indicated that receiving a no-match letter does not alone constitute notice that an employee is not eligible to work. The 1997 letter did indicate that an SSN with the following characteristics might lead to a duty to reverify:
- The number has more than nine digits.
- The number has less than nine digits.
- The number's first three digits are "000."
- The number's first digit is "8" or "9."
- The middle two digits are "00."
- The last four digits of the number are "0000."

A no-match letter regarding an SSN with these characteristics would be a reasonable indication that the employee's SSN is falsified.

A later April 12, 1999, opinion letter from the general counsel of the legacy INS stated that receiving a no-match letter in and of itself does not put an employer on notice that an employee is not authorized to work. The 1999 letter, however, warned employers, "We emphasize that although it is incorrect to assume that an SSA discrepancy necessarily indicates unauthorized status, it would be equally incorrect for an employer to assume that in all cases it may safely ignore any possible INA relevance or consequence of SSA discrepancies."

The letter then noted that an SSA no-match letter in combination with other information the employer receives regarding the employee may be enough to put the employer on notice that an employee's status is not valid for work authorization. The letter specifically warned employers that the INS would be likely to consider the employer to have violated IRCA if the employer had given an employee the opportunity to explain and reconcile a reported discrepancy with SSA records and the employee failed to do so satisfactorily. In other words, if an employer starts to make inquiries into SSN discrepancies and then ignores the findings, that is worse than not making the inquiry at all.

6.7   What if an employer receives a DHS notice that there is a problem with a document presented in connection with a Form I-9?

Like receipt of an SSA no-match letter, there is currently uncertainty regarding the appropriate actions for an employer to take when it receives a notification from ICE. The DHS issued a regulation in August 2007 that would require an employer to take specific steps in a prescribed time frame when it receives notification from the DHS that a document presented by an alien for employment verification purposes is invalid or fraudulent. However, unlike the case of Social Security mismatches described above, employers always need to follow up. The main uncertainty surrounds how quickly an employer needs to respond and to what extent.

An employer who receives this type of notice will not violate IRCA's antidiscrimination rules if it requests an employee to provide additional documentation. The courts have held that ICE need not provide irrefutable proof that the employee is ineligible to work. It is enough that ICE provides information that arouses suspicion. As for timing, there is no firm amount of time an employer has to act, but the courts have used a standard of what is "reasonable." In one case, waiting two weeks was held to be reasonable. The courts will look at how long it took an employer to reverify the employee's work authorization and how long it took an employer to discharge an employee after that.

When an employer follows up with an employee, the question also arises regarding what action must be taken. What if the employee provides valid documentation that does not include the suspect document? In this case, the employer still must abide by IRCA's antidiscrimination rules and would have a defense against a later charge of knowingly employing an unauthorized employee.

The timing and nature of reverification will be clarified if the August 2007 regulation is allowed to take effect, and employers should monitor developments in the case.

6.8   What if an employer is told that an employee is unauthorized by another employee?

The employer should not consider a mere tip from another employee to constitute knowledge that an employee is out of status. An employer acting on such a tip alone could very well be vulnerable to being found to have violated antidiscrimination rules. On the other hand, an April 12, 1999, opinion letter from the INS general counsel noted that if an employer receives a tip from another employee indicating that an employee is not authorized to be employed and the employer later receives a Social Security no-match letter, the employer would likely have constructive knowledge based on a "totality of the circumstances."

6.9   Are employers liable if they use a contractor and know the contractor's employees are not authorized to work?

Yes. The DHS regulations state that any person who uses a contract, subcontract, or exchange to obtain the labor or services of a foreign employee in the U.S., knowing that the employee is unauthorized to work, shall be considered to have hired the employee, for purposes of determining if a person has violated IRCA. Indeed, ICE has recently been aggressively pursuing companies under this provision.

6.10   May an employer be deemed to have constructive knowledge when it failed to complete a Form I-9 for an employee or the form is completed improperly?

Yes. This has been found in various court cases, and employers have been held to have had constructive knowledge that an employee was unauthorized to work even if the employer had no direct knowledge of the employee's employment status. Courts have also held that employers are not off the hook simply because there is a Form I-9, if the form itself was not properly completed. A court would look to the circumstances surrounding the particular form and use a standard of what is reasonable to determine if an employer should have known that an employee is likely not authorized.

6.11   May an employer be deemed to have constructive knowledge when it fails to reverify a Form I-9?

Yes. Courts have found that an employer that fails to reverify a Form I-9 where such reverification is required could have constructive knowledge that an employee is unauthorized to work. The more complicated question is what to do when the employee presents documentation that does not relate to the expired document presented at the time of hire. ICE and the courts have held that an employer had an obligation to make an inquiry regarding the continuing employment authorization. This would seem to violate the antidiscrimination rules in IRCA that bar employers from specifying which documents an employee may submit. However, Congress addressed this issue in §421 of the IIRIRA, which only prohibits employers from making inquiries regarding continuing work authorization when such inquiries are made for the purpose or with the intent of discriminating against an individual.

Unfair Immigration Practices

7.1 **What are the IRCA antidiscrimination and document abuse rules?**
While employers need to be diligent about complying with IRCA's employment verification rules, they should not be so overzealous that they penalize qualified employees. IRCA also has antidiscrimination rules that can result in an employer facing stiff sanctions. Employers of more than three employees are covered by the IRCA antidiscrimination rules (as opposed to the 15 or more employees required by Title VII). IRCA protects most U.S. citizens, permanent residents, temporary residents or asylees, and refugees from discrimination on the basis of national origin or citizenship status, if the person is authorized to work. Aliens illegally in the United States are not protected.

Under IRCA, employers may not refuse to hire someone because of their national origin or citizenship status, and they may not discharge employees on those grounds either. The employer is also barred from requesting specific documents in completing an I-9 form and cannot refuse to accept documents that appear genuine on their face. But note that an employer must be shown to have had the intent to discriminate.

Employers can be sanctioned separately based on legislation passed in 1990 if they request more or different documents than required by the I-9 rules. Employers originally were held strictly liable for violations under this category, but in 1996 legislation was passed requiring a showing that employers intended to discriminate.

7.2 **How is enforcement responsibility split between the OSC and the EEOC?**
The OSC and the EEOC split jurisdiction over national origin discrimination charges.

The EEOC handles matters involving employers with 15 or more employees, while the OSC has responsibility for smaller employers with between four and 14 employees. The OSC covers national origin claims involving intentional acts of discrimination with respect to hiring, firing, and recruitment. The EEOC has broader jurisdiction under Title VII.

The OSC has exclusive jurisdiction to rule on citizenship and immigration status discrimination claims against employers with four or more employees. The OSC also has jurisdiction over document abuse claims for employers with four or more employees.

7.3 **How is a complaint made for an IRCA antidiscrimination violation?**
The OSC accepts charges filed by individuals or their representatives who believe they have been the victims of employment discrimination. DHS officers may also file charges.

Discrimination charges must be filed with six months of the alleged discriminatory acts. After the claim is filed, the OSC has 10 days to notify the employer and then either file a complaint with an ALJ within 120 days or notify the charging party that it will not file a complaint. The charging party may independently file a complaint with an ALJ within 90 days of receiving this notice from the OSC. The OSC may also reverse its decision and file a complaint within the 90-day period. The ALJ then will have a hearing and issue a decision, or the parties may independently reach a settlement agreement.

7.4   What is "document abuse"?

"Document abuse" refers to discriminatory practices related to the verification of employment eligibility in the Form I-9 process. Employers who treat individuals differently based on national origin or citizenship commit document abuse when they engage in one of four types of activity:

- Improperly requesting employees to produce more documentation than is required to show identity and employment authorization.
- Improperly asking employees to produce a particular document to show identity or employment eligibility.
- Improperly rejecting documents that appear to be genuine and belonging to the employee.
- Improperly treating groups of applicants differently (e.g., based on looking or sounding foreign) when they complete the Form I-9.

All individuals authorized to be employed can file a claim under the document abuse rules if an employer has four or more employees.

7.5   What is "citizenship or immigration status discrimination"?

"Citizenship or immigration status discrimination" refers to when a person or entity discriminates against any individual (other than an unauthorized immigrant) with respect to the hiring, recruitment, or referral for a fee of the individual for employment, or the firing of the individual from employment because of the individual's citizenship or immigration status.

7.6   What is "national origin discrimination"?

"National origin discrimination" refers to when a person or entity discriminates against any individual (other than an unauthorized immigrant) with respect to the hiring, recruitment, or referral for a fee of the individual for employment, or the firing of the individual from employment because of the individual's national origin.

7.7   What are examples of prohibited practices?

The DHS lists various examples of prohibited practices in its M-174, Handbook for Employers (see Appendix B):

- Setting different employment eligibility verification standards or requiring different documents based on national origin or citizenship status. (One example would be requiring non-U.S. citizens to present DHS-issued documents like "green cards.")
- Requesting to see employment eligibility verification documents before hire and completion of the Form I-9 because an employee appears foreign or the employee indicates that he or she is not a U.S. citizen.
- Refusing to accept a document or to hire an individual because an acceptable document has a future expiration date.

- Requiring an employee during reverification to present a new unexpired EAD if the employee presented an employment document during the initial verification. (Note that this appears to contradict earlier legacy INS statements and at least one court case holding that an employer may have a responsibility to ask an employee whether employment authorization has been extended. An employer should consult with counsel in such a situation.)
- Limiting jobs to U.S. citizens, unless a job is limited to citizens by law.
- Asking to see a document with an employee's alien or admission number when completing Section 1 of Form I-9.
- Asking a lawful permanent resident to reverify employment eligibility because the person's "green card" has expired.

7.8   Are employees protected from retaliation if they complain about discrimination?

Yes. Employers cannot retaliate against an employee who files a charge with the OSC or the EEOC. The employee is also protected if he or she is a witness or participant in an investigation or prosecution of a discrimination complaint or if the employee asserts rights under IRCA's antidiscrimination provisions or under Title VII.

7.9   How does the Civil Rights Act of 1964 provide employees additional protections?

Title VII bars employment discrimination based on national origin, race, color, religion, and sex. Only employers with 15 or more employees for 20 or more weeks in the preceding or current calendar year are covered. Title VII covers discrimination in any aspect of employment.

7.10   What is the basis for regulating immigration-related unfair employment practices?

Section 274B of the INA specifically prohibits discrimination based on national origin or citizenship status.

7.11   Can employers discriminate against employees requiring visa sponsorship?

Nonimmigrant aliens (whether work authorized or not), aliens not in legal status in the U.S., and others requiring visa sponsorship are not protected by the anti-discrimination provisions in IRCA. However, Title VII offers some protections to these individuals insofar as employers who appear to be inconsistent in whom they consider for sponsorship and whom they don't may be found to have engaged in national origin discrimination under that law.

7.12   Can employers discriminate against employees with an expiring EAD?

No. Generally the existence of a future expiration date should not be considered in determining whether a person is qualified for a position, and considering a future employment authorization expiration date may be deemed employment discrimination. In other words, you may not refuse to hire a person because he or she only has temporary employment authorization. This does not, of course, preclude reverification upon the expiration of employment authorization.

7.13   What information can be requested of an individual prior to the commencement of employment?

Employers who require applicants to complete Form I-9 prior to beginning employment need to be very careful because of the possibility of national origin discrimination. At a minimum, the employer should wait until an offer is extended and accepted before requesting completion of the I-9. After that, the employer can start the Form I-9 process. It is a smart practice to have a uniform policy regarding completion of the Form I-9 or, if an exception is made, to have a sound reason.

7.14   Who is a "protected individual" under IRCA and can an employer discriminate against those not included?

A "protected individual" under IRCA's antidiscrimination rules includes anyone who is a U.S. citizen, as well as an individual who fits into the following categories:

- Lawful permanent residents ("green card" holders).
- Refugees.
- Certain beneficiaries of the 1986 legalization program (very few of these people have not become "green card" holders at this point).
- Asylees.

Employers are not required to consider applicants who are outside of this list under IRCA's antidiscrimination rules. Employers should be careful, however, to be consistent in applying the policy so as to avoid a finding that a particular group has been disparately treated. Such inconsistency could lead to a finding of national origin discrimination under the Civil Rights Act of 1964.

7.15   Can an employer maintain a policy of only employing U.S. citizens?

No. Employers must consider all protected individuals under IRCA. Discriminating against protected individuals under IRCA would be considered discrimination.

7.16   Can an employer require employees to post indemnity bonds against potential liability under IRCA?

No. Such a practice is specifically prohibited under the DHS regulations, including any other type of indemnification required by an employer against potential liability arising under IRCA. However, the regulations do say that an employer may still require an employee to agree to a "performance clause" where an employee unable to perform the job duties may be held accountable to the employer. Whether or not such a clause is enforceable is a question of contract and labor law, of course, and counsel should be consulted.

7.17   Can an employer request DHS' verification of the status of the employee when it is not sure whether documents for a new hire are valid?

Only employers participating in E-Verify can validate the status of an employee through the DHS. (See Chapter 11 for more information.) Employers are permitted, however, to contact the DHS if the employer has a reason to believe that the employee's documentation is suspicious. If the DHS believes the matter to be worth pursuing, ICE could follow up to investigate the matter. Employers who contact the DHS about documents they suspect are invalid would not be liable for discrimination if they genuinely believe the documents to be potentially invalid and were not singling out an employee on the basis of appearing or sounding foreign.

Note that an employer can contact the SSA to verify the validity of an SSN. Information on this online service can be found at www.ssa.gov/bso/services. htm.

7.18   Who may file a complaint under IRCA against an employer for violations of the employer sanctions rules?

Any person having knowledge of a violation or potential violation of IRCA may submit a signed, written complaint in person or by mail to the local DHS office having jurisdiction over the employer.

7.19 **What is the procedure to file a complaint under IRCA against an employer for violation of the antidiscrimination rules? What about a complaint under Title VII?**

The complaint must detail the allegations, identify the parties, and list the relevant dates of the alleged violations. The complaint must be filed within 180 days of the alleged discriminatory act.

Individuals who believe they have been the victim of discrimination prohibited by IRCA can also call the OSC employee hotline at 800-255-7688 or visit their web site at www.usdoj.gov/crt/osc/ for more information and to download a charge form. The OSC also has a telephone intervention program where employers and employees can speak with an OSC representative and attempt to resolve a matter without resorting to the formal complaint process. The employer telephone number for this service is 800-255-8155 and the employee number is 800-255-7688.

Individuals seeking to file a complaint under Title VII can call the EEOC at 800-USA-EEOC or go to www.eeoc.gov.

7.20 **How does the OSC investigate complaints?**

First, the OSC must determine if the claim has merit. If the OSC decides to investigate a complaint, it will notify the employer in writing about the opening of an investigation and it will request in writing information and documentation relating to the complaint. The documents may be subpoenaed if an employer refuses to cooperate.

The OSC has 120 days to determine if the charge is true and whether to bring a complaint. If it makes this determination, it will issue a notice of intent to fine or, instead, a warning notice. It can also send a letter to the complaining party during that 120-day period indicating it will not file a complaint.

The charging party may file a complaint directly with the chief administrative hearing officer within 90 days of getting the notification from the OSC that it is not pursuing the case.

Employers who wish to contest the fine must file a written request for a hearing before a hearing officer or judge.

7.21 **How many complaints does the OSC receive each year?**

In 2007, the OSC received 277 charges that it reviewed. The OSC also handled 21,000 hotline calls. One-half of all charges were voluntarily resolved.

Penalties and Other Risks

8.1   What penalties does an employer face for Form I-9 violations?

Employers can face stiff penalties for IRCA violations, which include substantial fines and debarment from government contracts. Penalties can be imposed for hiring unauthorized employees as well as for simply committing paperwork violations even if all employees are authorized to work. Fines for hiring unauthorized employees will amount to anywhere from $250 to $16,000 per employee, depending on the prior history of violations. Employers can also be barred from competing for government contracts for a year if they knowingly hire or continue to employ unauthorized aliens. Paperwork violations can also result in significant fines. Each mistake or missing item on a form can result in a $110 penalty, up to $1,100 for each form. A missing form would automatically be assessed at $1,000. An employer, for example, that had 100 employees and did not complete I-9 forms might face a $100,000 fine. IRCA investigators have considerable discretion in assessing fines and will look at factors like the size of the company, the seriousness of the violations, whether the employer was trying to comply in good faith, and the pattern of past violations.

Employers should also be cautioned that knowingly accepting fraudulent documents from employees is a different kind of violation that can be criminally prosecuted under other immigration laws.

Aside from federal violations, several states have passed, or are considering passing, laws that would penalize employers violating IRCA, including barring such employers from state contracts and revoking their business licenses.

Civil and criminal penalties are as follows for IRCA violations:
Civil Penalties (effective March 27, 2008)

Hiring or continuing to employ unauthorized aliens
Fines will vary depending on past violations:
- First offense: $375 to $3,200 for each unauthorized employee.
- Second offense: $3,200 to $6,500 for each unauthorized employee.
- Subsequent offenses: $4,300 to $16,000 for each unauthorized employee.

Failing to comply with the Form I-9 requirements
The fine is $110 to $1,100 per individual employee for failing to properly complete, retain, and/or make available for inspection Form I-9s. The DHS will consider the following factors in setting the fine:
- Business size.
- Employer's good faith.
- Seriousness of the violation.
- Whether the individual was, in fact, unauthorized to work.
- History of violations by the employer.

Injunctions

If the attorney general has reasonable cause to believe that an employer is engaged in a pattern of unlawful employment, recruitment, or referral activities, the attorney general may bring a civil action in the appropriate U.S. District Court requesting relief, such as a temporary or permanent injunction, restraining order, or other order against an IRCA violator.

Indemnification

If an employer unlawfully requires an employee to put up a bond or indemnify the employer against an IRCA violation, the employer is liable for paying a civil penalty of $1,000 for each violation and making restitution to the person who was required to pay the indemnity or to the U.S. Treasury.

Criminal Penalties

Employers can also be criminally sanctioned for IRCA violations. Employers who engage in a practice or pattern of hiring or continuing to employ unauthorized employees face fines up to $3,000 per employee and imprisonment for up to six months.

Injunctions

The DHS may seek a temporary or permanent injunction or other order against a person or entity believed to be engaged in a pattern or practice of employment, recruitment, or referral in violation of IRCA's employer sanctions rules.

Indemnity Bonds

Employers who require employees to post a bond or indemnify the employer against IRCA violations can be fined up to $1,000 per violation and subjected to an order to return the money to the employee.

Document Fraud

Employers who assist in the production and use of false documents for employees to demonstrate employment eligibility are, not surprisingly, subject to penalties. Fines range from $275 to $6,500 per document depending on whether it is an employer's first offense or not. Criminal penalties may be imposed on persons who fail to disclose that they have prepared or assisted in the preparation of false documents. Fines and imprisonment up to five years may be imposed for a first offense, and subsequent offenses may result in 15 years of imprisonment.

Other Criminal Sanctions

For an extensive discussion of other criminal sanctions an employer may face, see Chapter 14.

8.2   What are the penalties for unlawful discrimination?

The OSC can seek several remedies when an employer has been found to have engaged in prohibited discriminatory practices under IRCA. It has the power to seek an order requiring an employer to:

- Hire adversely affected individuals, with or without back pay (if back pay is ordered, there is a limit of two years).
- Post notices to employees about their rights and the employer's obligations.
- Educate all personnel involved in IRCA compliance about IRCA's antidiscrimination rules.
- Remove (in applicable cases) a false performance review or false warning from a personnel file.
- Lift (in applicable cases) restrictions on an employee's assignments, work shifts, or movements.

Significant financial penalties may also be ordered. As of March 27, 2008, they are as follows:
- First offense: $375 to $3,200 for each individual subjected to discrimination.
- Second offense: $3,200 to $6,500 for each individual subjected to discrimination.

- Subsequent offenses: $4,300 to $16,000 for each individual subjected to discrimination.

Document abuse comes with a separate penalty of $110 to $1,100 for each individual subjected to discrimination. The size of the penalty will depend on:
- The size of the business.
- The seriousness of the violations.
- Whether the employee covered in the particular Form I-9 was an unauthorized immigrant.
- The history of previous violations of the employer.

Employers found to have violated Title VII may be ordered to do one or more of the following:
- Hire, reinstate, or promote with back pay and retroactive seniority the individual subjected to discrimination.
- Post notices for employees regarding their rights and the employer's obligations.
- Remove false information from an employee's personnel file.

Financial penalties may also be imposed under Title VII for financial losses and mental anguish, as well as for punitive damages against employers who act with malice or reckless indifference.

Finally, under either IRCA or the Civil Rights Act, the prevailing party may be ordered to pay attorney's fees. Under IRCA, reasonable attorney's fees may be awarded if the losing party's argument is without reasonable foundation in law and fact. IRCA states that the U.S. government cannot be held liable for attorney's fees, so this effectively means only the employer would pay this cost. Under Title VII, a judge may award reasonable attorney's fees (including expert fees) to either prevailing party and the U.S. government may be held liable for costs the same as the employer.

8.3   Can employers who tried in good faith to comply avoid penalties?

Yes. If an employer has actually complied with the Form I-9 requirements in good faith and then has been found to have hired an unauthorized employee, the employer would have a good-faith defense. The government would need to show the employer actually knew the employee was unlawfully present. For paperwork violations that are technical or procedural, employers who have made a good-faith attempt to comply may be excused. This good-faith provision won't apply if the DHS notified the employer of problems and the employer did not correct the problems within 10 days. This good-faith provision also does not apply to employers who have been engaged in a pattern or practice of violations.

8.4   Which cases must be investigated by ICE?

ICE may investigate cases on its own initiative and need not have received a complaint. When ICE does receive a complaint, it has the discretion to decide whether the complaint has a reasonable probability of validity and whether to investigate (8 CFR 274a.9(b)).

8.5   What is the process for imposing penalties?

If ICE investigates and determines that a violation of the employer sanctions rules has occurred, it may issue a notice of intent to fine or, in the alternative, a warning notice. A warning notice must contain a statement of the basis for the violations and which sections of the law have been violated.

If a notice of intent to fine is issued, the notice must contain the basis for the charge, the sections of the law violated, and the penalty being imposed. It must also advise the employer of the right to counsel, that any statement given by the employer may be used against the employer, and that the employer is entitled to a hearing before an ALJ.

If an employer wants to fight the fine, it must file for a hearing in front of an ALJ within 30 days from being served with the notice. If a written request for a hearing is not filed, ICE will issue a final order 45 days from the issuance of the notice of intent to fine.

8.6   Are entities at a company liable in addition to the one division targeted for penalties?

When an order is issued against a specific entity in a family of distinct corporations, separate entities in the corporate family that do their own hiring are not considered subject to the order.

8.7   Does ICE have to provide advance notice of a Form I-9 audit?

The DHS, OSC, and DOL are each required to provide three days' notice before they can inspect Form I-9s. The forms must be made available by the employer at the location requested by the agency inspecting the forms.

8.8   In what format must Form I-9s be provided to ICE auditors?

The original forms must be provided for inspection, except that recruiters or referrers for a fee who designate an employer to handle Form I-9 completion may present a copy of the Form I-9s.

If an employer retains Form I-9s in an electronic format, the employer must retrieve and reproduce the specific forms requested by the inspecting officer, as well as the associated audit trails showing who accessed the computer system and the actions performed on the system in a specified period of time. The inspecting officer must also be provided with the necessary hardware and software as well as access to personnel and documentation in order to locate, retrieve, read, and reproduce the requested Form I-9 documentation and associated audit trails, reports, and other related data.

Finally, an inspecting officer is permitted to request an electronic summary of all the immigration fields on an electronically stored Form I-9.

8.9   What if records are kept at a location different from where the ICE agents will be visiting?

If forms are stored at a location other than the worksite, the employer must inform the inspecting officer where they are kept and cooperate with the inspector in making the forms available either at the location where they are kept or at the office of the governmental agency conducting the inspection.

8.10   Can an employer be penalized if they properly completed an I-9, but the employee turns out to be unauthorized?

No. Employers who follow IRCA's rules will have a good-faith defense against any penalties that might be imposed for knowingly hiring an unauthorized employee. This assumes, of course, that the employer did not otherwise have knowledge, actual or constructive, that the employee was not authorized to work.

8.11   Aside from penalties under IRCA, are there other risks associated with not properly completing I-9s?

Yes. There are a number of other reasons why an employer needs to be diligent in complying with IRCA's Form I-9 requirements. They include:

- Qualifying to do business with large employers that now require contractors to be in compliance.
- Qualifying for government contracts with local, state, and federal agencies that require compliance.
- Avoiding problems in a merger or acquisition where an employer's I-9 records are requested as part of a due diligence review. (See Chapter 13 for more information on immigration issues in mergers and acquisitions.)
- Avoiding liability under new state laws which penalize employers for Form I-9 violations (including revoking business licenses and barring access to state contracts).
- Avoiding lawsuits filed by employees who have faced immigration problems as a result of an employer's errors (particularly when such errors might have been identified if an employer reverified an employee's Form I-9 and such reverification failed to take place).

Immigration Reform and Control Act (IRCA) Compliance Tips

9.1 What are the best ways to prevent being prosecuted for I-9 employer sanctions violations?

Employers can minimize the chances for being found to have violated IRCA's employment verification rules by undertaking several steps:

- Appoint an IRCA compliance officer and establish an IRCA compliance policy.
- Conduct a preventative internal audit of the I-9 files to see if there is a pattern of violations requiring remediation. Such an audit should be conducted by, or under the close supervision of, an immigration lawyer familiar with IRCA.
- Establish a regular training program for human resource professionals regarding I-9 compliance rules. The training should be conducted by an attorney familiar with IRCA rules.
- Establish uniform company policies regarding I-9s. Should copies of documents be retained or not? What kinds of questions can be asked about national origin and citizenship status before the date of hire? Is their uniformity in terms of when the employment verification is commenced? Are employees all treated the same when there is a Social Security mismatch letter?
- Establish a re-verification tickler system to ensure I-9s are checked in a timely manner.
- Centralize the I-9 Form recordkeeping process.
- Establish a process for human resource professionals to check quickly with counsel when there are any problems in the verification process.
- Establish a backup system to ensure timely compliance with I-9 rules when a human resource professional is out of the office.
- Segregate Forms I-9 from personnel records.
- Consider using an electronic I-9 product in order to automate the collection of information, speed up the production of information in the case of a government audit and ensure timely re-verification of I-9 forms.

9.2 What are the best ways to avoid immigration-related employment discrimination?

The OSC suggests the following 10 steps be taken to avoid liability under IRCA's anti-discrimination rules:

- Treat all people the same when announcing a job, taking applications, interviewing, offering a job, verifying eligibility to work, and in hiring and firing.
- Accept documentation presented by an employee if it establishes identity and employment eligibility; is included in the list of acceptable documents; and reasonably appears to be genuine and to relate to the person.
- Accept documents that appear to be genuine. You are not expected to be a document expert, and establishing the authenticity of a document is not your responsibility.
- Avoid "citizen-only" or "permanent resident-only" hiring policies unless required by law, regulation or government contract. In most cases, it is illegal to require job applicants to be U.S. citizens or have a particular immigration status.
- Give out the same job information over the telephone to all callers, and use the same application form for all applicants.

- Base all decisions about firing on job performance and/or behavior, not on the appearance, accent, name, or citizenship status of your employees.
- Complete the I-9 Form and keep it on file for at least three years from the date of employment or for one year after the employee leaves the job, whichever is later. This means that you must keep I-9s on file for all current employees. You must also make the forms available to government inspectors upon request.
- On the I-9 Form, verify that you have seen documents establishing identity and work authorization for all employees hired after November 6, 1986, including U.S. citizens.
- Remember that many work authorization documents (I-9 Form lists A and C) must be renewed. On the expiration date, you must re-verify employment authorization and record the new evidence of continued work authorization on the I-9 Form. You must accept any valid document your employee chooses to present, whether or not it is the same document provided initially. Individuals may present an unrestricted Social Security card to establish continuing employment eligibility.
  » Permanent resident cards should not be re-verified.
  » Identity documents should not be re-verified.
- Be aware that U.S. citizenship, or nationality, belongs not only to persons born in the U.S. but also to all individuals born to a U.S. citizen, and those born in Puerto Rico, Guam, the Virgin Islands, the Commonwealth of Northern Mariana Islands, American Samoa, and Swains Island. Citizenship is granted to legal immigrants after they complete the naturalization process.

9.3   Should a company have an IRCA compliance officer?

Yes. Employers should ensure that an official at the company is thoroughly trained in IRCA's employer sanctions and anti-discrimination rules and is able to supervise all persons charged with handling Forms I-9. The officer should be responsible for the following additional functions:

- ensuring that Form I-9 records are properly retained.
- ensuring that a reliable system is in place to re-verify Forms I-9.
- acting in concert with employees, managers, subcontractors, customers, recruiters, and others to ensure that the company's IRCA compliance policy is followed.
- working with outside counsel to ensure that regular Forms I-9 preventative audits are conducted.
- working with outside counsel to conduct regular training programs for human resource professionals and others at a company charged with hiring employees.
- consulting with counsel to properly respond to Social Security Mismatch letters.
- working with outside counsel to establish an action plan should the company be the subject of an audit or investigation by DHS, DOL, or OSC.
- ensuring that contractors supplying labor are properly screened to ensure IRCA compliance.
- overseeing the company's IRCA compliance policy to ensure it is readily available and periodically updated by counsel.

9.4   Should a company have an IRCA compliance policy?

Yes. Employers should establish a standard IRCA compliance policy that is included with the company's other personnel policies and materials. The IRCA compliance policy should:

- Name the company's IRCA compliance officer.
- Advise on complying with IRCA's employer sanctions and anti-discrimination rules.
- Contain rules for working with outside contractors.
- Set training requirements for those completing the Forms I-9.
- Have a zero tolerance policy for the employment of individuals who cannot comply with IRCA's employment verification rules.

- Establish the timing and procedures for regular internal Form I-9 audits.
- Contain rules on who has access to Form I-9 records.
- List procedures for using E-Verify.
- Set protocols for interacting with government officials in connection with IRCA compliance.
- Outline re-verification procedures.

9.5   Should companies have special Form I-9 policies for dealing with outside contractors?

Over the last few years, ICE has increasingly targeted companies that use contractors employing unauthorized employees. IRCA specifically states that a person or entity who uses a contract to obtain the labor of an alien knowing that the alien is unauthorized to work shall be considered to have hired the alien for employment in the United States.

This was the basis of the government's targeting of Wal-Mart in 2005. Sixty Wal-Mart stores were raided by ICE, and 245 unauthorized employees were discovered working as night janitors and cleaners. The employees were actually the employees of a contracting firm and the government argued that Wal-Mart was responsible for the contractor's actions. The retail giant eventually paid an $11 million fine to resolve the dispute. In response, Wal-Mart has now established a compliance program that is considered one of the most rigorous in the country.

Employers are also, as noted above, sometimes held to be the actual employer of unauthorized employees as opposed to the contractor that ostensibly employs them. The lesson is that employers may very well need to focus on IRCA compliance by its contractors.

Given the risks associated with using contract labor, many companies are beginning to demand that their contractors adhere to IRCA and provide documentation of their compliance. Consult with your attorney regarding developing appropriate protective measures.

9.6   How do mergers, acquisitions, and other major changes affect Form I-9 requirements?

While a closing may be a cause for celebration at a company, it can also be the cause of a nightmare for a company since it can instantly render all completed I-9s for an acquired company invalid. An employer who continues to employ some or all of a previous employer's workforce in cases involving a corporate reorganization, merger, or sale of stock or assets may accept the I-9s previously prepared by the predecessor company. However, the Forms I-9 should be checked in the due diligence process to ensure that the acquired forms are in compliance, as any errors or omissions on the adopted forms become the responsibility of the acquiring employer. Employers should consider adding Forms I-9 to a merger checklist and have all employees of the combined company complete new forms on the day of closing or beforehand. In any case, an immigration lawyer should be consulted in any merger, acquisition, or divestiture to ensure that the transaction does not result in immigration problems. (For an in depth discussion of the immigration consequences of mergers and acquisitions, see Chapter 13.)

9.7   Can an employer who does not wish to assume an acquired company's liability for Form I-9 violations re-verify the entire work force?

Yes. In such a case, the succeeding employer may have all employees complete new Forms I-9. The benefit of this is that employers will have the opportunity to correct past problems and ensure compliance. Also, if any employees requiring a visa transfer as a result of the merger or acquisition, the employer will have an additional chance to discover the issue.

9.8   Are there ICE best hiring practices?

Yes. They are:

- Use E-Verify for all hiring.
- Establish an internal training program, with annual updates, on how to manage completion of Form I-9 (Employee Eligibility Verification Form), how to detect fraudulent use of documents in the I-9 process, and how to use E-Verify.
- Permit the I-9 and E-Verify process to be conducted only by individuals who have received this training — and include a secondary review as part of each employee's verification to minimize the potential for a single individual to subvert the process.
- Arrange for annual I-9 audits by an external auditing firm or a trained employee not otherwise involved in the I-9 and electronic verification process.
- Establish a self-reporting procedure for reporting to ICE any violations or discovered deficiencies.
- Establish a protocol for responding to no-match letters received from the SSA.
- Establish a Tip Line for employees to report activity relating to the employment of unauthorized aliens, and a protocol for responding to employee tips.
- Establish and maintain safeguards against use of the verification process for unlawful discrimination.
- Establish a protocol for assessing the adherence to the "best practices" guidelines by the company's contractors/subcontractors.
- Submit an annual report to ICE to track results and assess the effect of participation in the IMAGE program.

Source: www.ice.gov/partners/opaimage/.

9.9   Is there useful contract language for contractors?

Yes, consider the following:

CONTRACTOR represents and warrants that all necessary visa or work authorization petitions have been timely and properly filed on behalf of any employees requiring a visa stamp, I-94 status document, EAD, or any other immigration document necessary for such employees to legally work in the U.S. CONTRACTOR has complied in all respects with the provisions of the Immigration Reform and Control Act of 1986 including properly completing, retaining and re-verifying Forms I-9. CONTRACTOR has complied in all respects with any state or local laws relating to employers that knowingly or intentionally hire unauthorized immigrants. There are no claims, lawsuits, actions, arbitrations, administrative or other proceedings, governmental investigations or inquiries pending or threatened against the CONTRACTOR relating to the CONTRACTOR's compliance with local, state or federal immigration laws and regulations.

There have been no letters received from the Social Security Administration (SSA) regarding the failure of CONTRACTOR's employees' SSNs to match their name in the SSA database. There have been no letters or other correspondence received from the Department of Homeland Security or other agencies regarding the employment authorization of any employees of CONTRACTOR. If the CONTRACTOR operates in a state or has contracts with a state or federal agency that requires or provides a safe harbor if an employer participates in the Department of Homeland Security's e-Verify electronic employment verification system, the CONTRACTOR has been participating in e-Verify for the entire period such participation has been required or available as a safe harbor or as long as the company has been operating in such state or contracting with such agency.

CONTRACTOR agrees to conduct a self-audit on an [annual] basis of its personnel records to ensure compliance with IRCA's I-9 requirements. CONTRACTOR agrees to certify [annually] to ABC Corporation that it is in compliance with all immigration laws and requirements and is not being investigated by any government agency with respect to compliance with immigration law. CONTRACTOR agrees to provide ABC Corporation with copies of Forms I-9 for all employees working at ABC Corporation. CONTRACTOR shall only provide employees to ABC Corporation that have consented in writing to the disclosure of their Form I-9 to ABC Corporation. CONTRACTOR shall provide ABC Corporation with a copy of its IRCA compliance policy and procedures.

CONTRACTOR agrees to indemnify and hold harmless ABC Corporation from any liability for CONTRACTOR's failure to comply with any U.S. immigration law or regulation.

[NOTE: Language should be included reciting that the relationship is an independent contractor relationship and listing factors showing this is the case.]

Conducting an I-9 Self-Audit

10.1   What should be asked when preparing for an I-9 audit?
To assess IRCA compliance practices, the auditor should interview the employer to determine the following:

- Are I-9s completed by a single office in the organization? If not, how is the responsibility divided (by department, branch, etc.)?
- If the responsibility for the forms is centralized, how many people are responsible? Identify all individuals with this responsibility.
- Has each person who is responsible for I-9s received training in immigration compliance and immigration-related antidiscrimination rules?
- Does the employer have a manual or electronic I-9 system? If the latter, which system is used and when was it implemented?
- Where are the files kept and are they in good physical order?
- Are I-9s completed on the date of hire consistently? If they are ever completed earlier than the date of hire, is the form ever completed before the employee has been offered the position and has actually accepted an offer of employment? If I-9s are completed earlier than the first day of employment, is the employer consistent in having employees complete the form early and, if not, is there a sound basis for varying from this?
- Does the employer ever instruct employees which documents to present?
- Has the employer ever revoked a job offer or terminated an employee because he or she put an expiration date in Section 1 of the I-9 form?
- Prior to signing Section 2 of the I-9, do employees responsible for I-9s actually review the original List A, B, and C documents in order to determine if the documents reasonably appear to be genuine and to relate to the employee in question?
- Does the employer have a system to identify and destroy I-9s that no longer are required to be maintained for terminated employees?
- Does the company keep copies of Section 2 documents in all cases? In none? If the answer is only sometimes, why the inconsistency?
- Does the employer have a tickler system to reverify work authorization and complete Section 3 of forms requiring such reverification? Describe the system.
- When was the last time an audit was conducted? What was its scope (full or partial)? What were the findings?
- Has the employer had previous immigration violations or previously been audited regarding any immigration matters?
- Has the employer ever received a Social Security no-match letter?
- Does the employee use the E-Verify electronic verification system?
- Does the employer verify employment authorization or identification independently such as through the use of a background-checking service?
- Does the employer have contracts with government agencies? If so, which government agencies?

10.2   Should employers prepare a spreadsheet for an I-9 audit?

Yes. It should include the following information:

- The names of all employees hired since the company opened or since November 8, 1986, whichever is later.
- The date of hire of each employee.
- The date of termination for each employee no longer employed.
- Dates of rehire and termination, if the employee's employment has been periodic.
- Whether an I-9 form has been located for the employee identified by payroll records as having been employed by the company since the company opened or since November 8, 1986, whichever is later.
- If the employee has been terminated, whether the I-9 form has been destroyed.
- Whether the employee fits into any of the following categories: the employee is under 18, is handicapped, is returning from a layoff or labor dispute, or has had employment authorization verified by a state employment service, or the employer is not required to receive an I-9 because the employer is part of a qualifying employer association.

Depending on the size, budget, immigration history, and overall vulnerability of an employer, either all I-9 records should be pulled for review or a random selection. If a random selection is chosen, the selection should be varied in terms of departments, types of employee, dates of hire, whether the employee is still with the company, and whether the employee's form must be reverified. The number in a sample should be large enough to be a statistically close representation of the actual situation at the company in order to meaningfully estimate the liability exposure.

10.3   I-9 Should employers use an audit checklist?

Yes, consider using the following

Section 1. Employee Information and Verification.

☐ Yes   ☐ No   Is the employee's name correct and does it exactly match the employer's records and the supporting documents?

☐ Yes   ☐ No   Is the employee's SSN properly stated?

☐ Yes   ☐ No   Is the date of birth properly stated?

☐ Yes   ☐ No   Is the employee's address properly stated?

☐ Yes   ☐ No   Is one of the boxes checked stating that the employee is a U.S. citizen/national, a lawful permanent resident or employment authorized alien?

☐ Yes   ☐ No   In the box above, if the employee has indicated that he or she is a lawful permanent resident or a work authorized alien, has the applicable alien or admission number been included and has an expiration?

☐ Yes   ☐ No   In the box above, if the employee has indicated that he or she is a work authorized alien, has the expiration date of the employment authorization been stated?

☐ Yes   ☐ No   Has the employee signed his or her name?

☐ Yes   ☐ No   Has the employee dated the signature on the first
                     date of employment?

☐ Yes   ☐ No   If a translator or preparer has been used, has that
                     person signed and dated the attestation, printed his
                     or her name, and provided his or her address?

Section 2. Employer Review and Verification

List A (only complete if applicable)

☐ Yes   ☐ No   If a List A document is used, has a proper docu-
                     ment been referenced?

☐ Yes   ☐ No   If a List A document is used, has the issuing author-
                     ity been listed?

☐ Yes   ☐ No   If a List A document is used, has the document has
                     been used, is a document number been provided?

☐ Yes   ☐ No   If a List A document is used, has the document
                     expiration date been provided?

☐ Yes   ☐ No   ☐ N/A   If a receipt for a List A document is provided in lieu
                     of showing the actual document, has the original
                     document been presented within 90 days of pre-
                     senting the receipt?

☐ Yes   ☐ No   If a List A document is provided, has the employee
                     left blank all information in List B and/or List C?

List B (only complete if applicable)

☐ Yes   ☐ No   If a List B document is used, has a proper docu-
                     ment been referenced?

☐ Yes   ☐ No   If a List B document is used, has the issuing au-
                     thority been listed?

☐ Yes   ☐ No   If a List B document is used, has the document has
                     been used, is a document number been provided?

☐ Yes   ☐ No   If a List B document is used, has the document
                     expiration date been provided?

☐ Yes   ☐ No   ☐ N/A   If a receipt for a List B document is provided
                     in lieu of showing the actual document, has the
                     original document been presented within 90 days
                     of presenting the receipt?

☐ Yes   ☐ No   If a List B document is provided, has the employee
                     left blank all information in List A and provided
                     information in List C?

List C (only complete if applicable)

☐ Yes ☐ No — If a List C document is used, has a proper document been referenced?

☐ Yes ☐ No — If a List C document is used, has the issuing authority been listed?

☐ Yes ☐ No — If a List C document is used, has the document has been used, is a document number been provided?

☐ Yes ☐ No — If a List C document is used, has the document expiration date been provided?

☐ Yes ☐ No ☐ N/A — If a receipt for a List B document is provided in lieu of showing the actual document, has the original document been presented within 90 days of presenting the receipt?

☐ Yes ☐ No — If a List C document is provided, has the employee left blank all information in List A and provided information in List B?

Documentation

☐ Yes ☐ No — Copies of the List A or List B/List C documents are included in the I-9 file and appear valid.

☐ Yes ☐ No — If documents were not provided on the date of hire, was Section 2 completed and the documents shown no later than the third business day after hiring?

☐ Yes ☐ No — Do the documents presented appear consistent with the status described in Section 1 (e.g., a lawful permanent resident card is shown, but the applicant claims to be a U.S. citizen)?

Employer Certification

☐ Yes ☐ No — Has an authorized representative of the company filled out this portion of the form?

☐ Yes ☐ No — Has the authorized representative properly listed the date he or she examined the form?

☐ Yes ☐ No — Has the authorized representative signed the form?

☐ Yes ☐ No — Has the authorized representative printed his or her name?

☐ Yes ☐ No — Has the authorized representative listed his or her title?

☐ Yes ☐ No — Has the employer's name and address been properly stated?

☐ Yes   ☐ No   Has the authorized representative dated the form?

Section 3. Employer Review and Verification (only complete if applicable)

☐ Yes   ☐ No   If the employee provided an expiration date for work authorization in Section 1, has Section 3 been completed before the expiration date listed in Section 1?

☐ Yes   ☐ No   ☐ N/A   If the employee's name has changed, has the new name been provided?

☐ Yes   ☐ No   ☐ N/A   If the employee is a re-hire, has the re-hire date been provided?

☐ Yes   ☐ No   Has a proper document been presented demonstrating continuing employment authorization?

☐ Yes   ☐ No   Has a document title been properly stated?

☐ Yes   ☐ No   Has the document number been properly stated?

☐ Yes   ☐ No   Has the new expiration date been properly stated?

☐ Yes   ☐ No   Has the authorized representative of the company properly signed Section 3?

☐ Yes   ☐ No   Has the authorized representative dated Section 3?

Additional Notes: _____

_____

_____

_____

_____

_____

_____

_____

E-Verify, IMAGE, and SSNVS

11.1   What is E-Verify?

E-Verify, formerly known as the Basic Pilot Program, is a free Internet-based system that employers use to confirm the legal status of newly hired employees. The system was authorized and created under the IIRIRA. The system compares SSN data and information in the DHS' immigration databases to the employee's name and other Form I-9 information to confirm the employee matches. The SSA has 425 million numbers in its database and the DHS has 60 million records in its system. If an employee's information does not match up, the USCIS will notify the employer of the nonconfirmation. The average response time in E-Verify is three-to-five seconds.

11.2   How many employees are typically run through E-Verify in a year?

As of January 2009, there were over 100,000 employers using E-Verify. During the most recent fiscal year, nearly two million queries were made in the E-Verify system. That number is expected to increase dramatically as several states are requiring that E-Verify be used by the states' employees. Ninety-two percent of verification queries are instantly verified. According to the DHS, the top industries using E-Verify are food services, drinking establishments, administrative and support personnel, professional and technical services, other information services, and clothing and accessories stores.

11.3   Who administers E-Verify?

E-Verify is a partnership of the DHS and the SSA that is administered by the USCIS.

11.4   How does E-Verify work?

Employers submit information provided on an employee's Form I-9 into the E-Verify web site. The E-Verify system will return one of three results:

- "Employment authorized" — The employee is employment authorized.
- "SSA Tentative NonConfirmation" — The SSA database is showing the employee's name and SSN are not matching.
- "DHS Verification in Process" — The DHS will respond within 24 hours with either an "Employment Authorized" or "DHS Tentative NonConfirmation."

If an employee shows up as "employment authorized," the employer will record the system-generated verification number on the Form I-9.

If an employer gets a "tentative nonconfirmation," the employer must promptly provide the employee with information about how to challenge the information mismatch, and the employee can then contest the determination and resolve the mismatch with the SSA or the DHS. The employee will have eight days to resolve the issue. The employee may continue to work while the case is being resolved.

If the employee does not contest the finding, the determination is considered final and the employer may terminate the employee and resolve the case.

Employers are also required to post a notice in an area visible to prospective employees that the company is an E-Verify participant. And the employer must post an antidiscrimination notice issued by the OSC in an area visible to prospective employees.

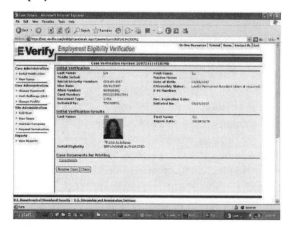

11.5   How does E-Verify handle H-1B portability cases?

According to an advisory e-mail provided to the author, E-Verify does not check who the employer-sponsor is and the new employer can use the employee's I-94 information from the previous employer in an H-1B portability situation.

11.6   What computer requirements are necessary to use E-Verify?

Users need an Internet-capable, Windows-based personal computer and a web browser of Internet Explorer 5.5 or Netscape 4.7 or higher (with the exception of Netscape 7.0).

The USCIS warns employers to "white list" this e-mail address in their spam filters: Employer.Pilots@dhs.gov.

11.7   Can a company batch load data to E-Verify?

Yes. The DHS has a real-time batch method that requires a company to develop an interface between its personal system or electronic Form I-9 system and the E-Verify database. Employers interested in more information, including design specifications, should call 800-741-5023.

11.8   What is the required timetable for using E-Verify?

An employer can complete E-Verify anytime after an offer of employment is accepted and after the Form I-9 is completed. This can be before the start date (as long as an employer is not prescreening applicants), but in no case later than three business days after the new employee's actual start date. Note that this doesn't apply in cases where there is no SSN and when the employer should wait until the number is available (see Question 11.12 below regarding employees without SSNs). A query may be submitted before the actual start date, but the employer needs to be careful not to prescreen applicants and may not delay training or an actual start date based on a tentative nonconfirmation, and the employee may not face adverse consequences as a result of the use of E-Verify unless a query results in a nonconfirmation. And an employer cannot accelerate a start date for an employee because employment authorization is confirmed. Employers also must always be consistent in the timing of a query so as to avoid discrimination.

11.9   Does E-Verify tell an employer anything about the immigration status of a new hire?
No. The system only verifies an employee's authorization to work and not immigration status.

11.10   What is E-Verify's photo screening tool?
The E-Verify photo tool was incorporated into E-Verify in September 2007 and enables employers to match the photo on an employee's EAD or a permanent residence card ("green card") to the photo that the USCIS has on file for that employee. The tool enables employers to detect instances of document fraud.

11.11   What information does an employer need to supply for each employee?
After an employee completes an I-9, the employer must submit a query that includes:
- The employee's name and date of birth.
- The employee's SSN.
- The citizenship status he or she attests to.
- An A number or I-94 number, if applicable.
- The type of document provided on the Form I-9 to establish work authorization status.
- Proof of identity and its expiration date, if applicable.

11.12   What about employees who don't have SSNs yet?
E-Verify cannot be used for employees who do not yet have an SSN. The I-9 form still needs to be completed and after the SSN is received, the query needs to be filed with E-Verify. If an employee otherwise meets the requirements to begin work without the SSN, the employee should be permitted to work until the SSN is received and the employee has gotten a negative response from the DHS on the name check.

11.13   What happens if E-Verify issues a nonconfirmation finding?

11.13.1 For SSA nonconfirmations:
If the employer receives a tentative nonconfirmation from the SSA, the employer must print the notice and provide it to the employee so the employee can decide whether or not to contest the finding. If the employer erred in the data input, the employer should attempt to refile with E-Verify.

The employer must then record the case verification number, review the data input in the system to make sure there was no error, and find out if the employee will contest the tentative nonconfirmation.

If the employee will contest the finding, E-Verify will provide the employer with instructions on referring the employee to the SSA field offices. The employer will print instructions on how to seek correction with the SSA and provide the letter to the employee with instructions that the matter must be resolved within eight federal government workdays.

After 10 federal government workdays, the employer will requery E-Verify in order to get a confirmation or a final nonconfirmation, unless the SSA instructs otherwise.

11.13.2 For DHS nonconfirmations:

If the employer receives a tentative nonconfirmation from the DHS, the employer must print the notice and provide it to the employee so the employee can decide whether or not to contest the finding. If the employer erred in the data input, the employer should attempt to re-file with E-Verify.

If the employer finds a photographic nonmatch for an employee who provides a document for which E-Verify has transmitted a photograph, the employer must print the photographic nonconfirmation notice and present it to the employee so the employee can decide on contesting the finding.

If the employee will contest a regular nonconfirmation case, the employer will print instructions and the employee must phone the DHS within eight business days to attempt to resolve the matter. In the case of a photographic nonconfirmation, the employer will provide the employee with a referral letter to the DHS. The DHS will provide the results within 10 days of the referral unless it determines it needs more time.

In photographic nonconfirmation cases, the employer will send a copy of the employee's Form I-551 permanent residency card or I-766 EAD by scanning and uploading the document or mailing a photocopy via express mail (to be paid by the DHS). Where an employer cannot decide if the photograph matches or not, the employer should forward the photographic document to the DHS for the DHS to decide.

11.14 Can employers selectively choose which employees are verified in the electronic system?

No. Employers must verify *all* newly hired employees including both citizens and noncitizens. Employers may not pick and choose which employees are put through the verification system.

11.15 Can an employer prescreen job applicants through E-Verify?

No. The employer needs to be careful not to prescreen applicants and may not delay training or an actual start date based on a tentative nonconfirmation, and the employee may not face adverse consequences as a result of the use of E-Verify unless a query results in a nonconfirmation. And an employer cannot accelerate a start date for an employee because employment authorization is confirmed. Employers also must always be consistent in the timing of a query so as to avoid discrimination.

11.16 Is E-Verify voluntary?

For most employers, E-Verify is voluntary. However, a few states require E-Verify for all employers. Others limit the requirement to state agencies and employers with government contracts. (A full discussion of state laws is included in Chapter 16.)

Also, on June 6, 2008, President George W. Bush signed an executive order calling on the DHS to issue regulations requiring federal contractors to participate in the E-Verify program. DHS issued a final regulation set to take effect in May 2009, but at the time of writing this book, litigants were seeking to block the rule.

11.17 What if a company does not have a computer or Internet access? Can a third-party agent be used to manage E-Verify filings?

Employers can outsource to a third-party agent the ability to submit employment eligibility verification queries. E-Verify designated agents must register online and sign a MOU, and an agent can represent multiple clients. The employer would still need to separately register and complete an MOU, and will have a unique client number. Designated agents can track their client's reporting, billing, and compliance.

11.18 What is an E-Verify corporate administrator?

An employer can designate an employee as a corporate administrator who has management authority over an employer's hiring sites participating in E-Verify. This person generally would not conduct the actual inquiries, but, after registering, would be able to register company sites, add and delete users at company sites, and view reports generated by company sites.

11.19 How does an employer sign up for E-Verify?

To participate in E-Verify, an employer must register online at the DHS E-Verify web page and accept the electronic MOU that details the responsibilities of the SSA, the DHS, and the employer.

The registration page for E-Verify is at www.vis-dhs.com/EmployerRegistration.

11.20 What are the government's obligations with regard to privacy and data security?

In the MOU, the SSA agrees to safeguard the information provided by an employer and limit access to individuals responsible for the verification of SSNs and for the evaluation of E-Verify. The DHS agrees to safeguard the information provided by the employer and to limit access to individuals responsible for the verification of alien employment eligibility and for the evaluation of E-Verify. Information can only be used to verify the accuracy of SSNs and employment eligibility, to enforce the INA and federal criminal laws, and to ensure accurate wage reports to the SSA.

11.21 What are the employer's obligations under the MOU?

The employer agrees to:

- Display the notices supplied by the DHS.
- Provide the DHS with the names and contact information of the employer representatives responsible for E-Verify.
- Comply with the E-Verify manual supplied by the DHS.
- Ensure that the employer representative takes the E-Verify tutorial before attempting to file an E-Verify case.
- Comply with I-9 rules except that List B documents proving identity must have a photograph. Also, if an employee presents an I-551 permanent residency card or an I-766 EAD, the employer must keep a copy of the document.
- Notify the DHS of any employee the employer continues to employ after a final nonconfirmation and be liable for fines of between $500 and $1,000 for each failure.

- Not use E-Verify to engage in pre-employment screening or to support any unlawful employment practice.
- Not use E-Verify to selectively check only some employees as opposed to all new hires.
- Not use E-Verify to reverify employees with I-9s requiring reverification or run existing employees through E-Verify.
- To follow the rules with respect to dealing with tentative nonconfirmations.
- Not to terminate an employee until a final nonconfirmation is received from the DHS, unless an employer gains actual knowledge beforehand that an employee is not work eligible.
- Comply with the INA §274B antidiscrimination rules.
- Safeguard the information provided to and received from E-Verify, subject to criminal penalties.
- Permit the DHS and the SSA to make periodic visits to the employer for the purpose of reviewing E-Verify records.

11.22   Can a large employer have a controlled rollout of E-Verify instead of including every location? Can a large employer change the sites participating?

Yes. An employer with multiple sites has flexibility. The employer can have one of its sites verify new hires at all of its sites or it can have each site perform its own verification inquiries. Whether one site is handling queries or multiple sites, each site must sign a separate MOU (though the DHS has recently informed the American Immigration Lawyers Association that a single MOU may be used by employers with more than 1,000 employees and multiple sites). Employers with multiple sites should select "multiple site registration" and give the number of sites per state it will be verifying. An employer can also choose to only include some of its sites and can control the rollout of E-Verify across its organization. However, at each worksite, all new hires for that site must be verified.

11.23   What are the benefits of participating?

Employers are presumed not to have violated the employer sanctions rules in §274A of the INA with respect to the hiring of any individual, if it obtains confirmation of the identity and employment eligibility in compliance with the terms and conditions of E-Verify. Note that the DHS does not consider using E-Verify to provide a safe harbor from worksite enforcement. Some states, such as Tennessee, do, however, consider using E-Verify a safe harbor from violation of the state's new law which can lead to the revocation of a business license for an employer's knowingly hiring unauthorized immigrants.

Using E-Verify will likely result in the elimination of no-match letters being received by a company. However, there are private companies that provide similar services, albeit at a cost. The DHS also touts E-Verify as a way to improve the accuracy of wage and tax reporting, protecting jobs for authorized U.S. employees, and helping U.S. employers maintain a legal workforce.

11.24   Are there risks associated with participating?

An employer will have a rebuttable presumption that it knowingly employs someone ineligible to work if it continues to employ someone after receiving a final nonconfirmation. If an employer believes E-Verify is incorrect, the employer will have a strong incentive to terminate an employee anyway in order to minimize the risk, since an employer acting in good faith on information received from E-Verify is immunized from civil and criminal liability.

Employers must agree to permit the DHS and SSA officials to visit their worksites to review E-Verify records and other employment records related to E-Verify. And the DHS and the SSA may interview an employer's authorized agents or designees regarding the employer's experience with E-Verify for the purpose of evaluating E-Verify.

Employers who have buyer's remorse and choose to stop using E-Verify must continue using the program for 30 days after giving written notice to the USCIS that it wants to stop using the system.

11.25   Can an employer verify existing employees as well as new hires?
No. E-Verify may not be used to go back to check employees hired before the company signed the MOU or to reverify employees who have temporary work cards. The planned federal contractor E-Verify rule modifies this requirement to include employees specifically.

11.26   Can an employer quit using E-Verify?
Yes, assuming state law does not require it. The federal government is considering legislation to require beneficiaries of certain government agencies' contracts to use E-Verify, but no such law has passed yet.

For employers to stop using the system, they must, per the signed MOU, provide 30 days' written notice to the government before they discontinue using the system.

11.27   Is an employer protected from an investigation if they use E-Verify?
No. Worksite enforcement is still permitted, but an employer using E-Verify is presumed not to knowingly have hired unauthorized aliens.

11.28   What can employees do if they feel they have been subject to discrimination?
Employers may not take any adverse action against an employee because the employee contests the information mismatch. This would include firing, suspending, withholding pay or training, or otherwise infringing on the employee's employment. Employees who think they have been subject to discrimination because of their national origin, citizenship, or immigration status with respect to hiring, firing, recruitment, or referral for a fee, through an employer's use of E-Verify or when completing Form I-9, should call the OSC at 1-800-225-7688 for assistance.

11.29   What states require E-Verify?
A complete list of states that require E-Verify for all or some of a state's employers can be found in Table 16.1 in Chapter 16.

11.30   What special E-Verify rules apply to student visa holders?
In April 2008, the USCIS released a new rule allowing for certain F-1 students to get an additional 17 months of optional practical training (OPT) on top of the currently available 12 months, if an employer participates in E-Verify. This is seen as highly useful given the extreme demand for H-1B visas. Eligible students now will have an additional one or two opportunities to try for success in the annual H-1B lottery.

F-1 students who have degrees in science, technology, engineering, or mathematics and who are already in a period of approved post-completion OPT can apply to extend that period by up to 17 months (for a total of 29 months of OPT) if the student has accepted employment with an employer registered and in good standing with E-Verify, USCIS' electronic employment eligibility verification system.

"STEM" stands for science, technology, engineering, and math. The USCIS refers to a "STEM Designated Degree Program List" that is based on the U.S.

Department of Education's Classification of Instructional Programs (CIP) 2000 report, which can be found online at http://nces.ed.gov/pubsearch/pubsinfo.asp?pubid=2002165.

According to the USCIS, the list of degrees currently includes those degrees in the following fields:
- Actuarial Science. NCES CIP Code 52.1304.
- Computer Science: NCES CIP Codes 11.xxxx (except Data Entry/Microcomputer Applications, NCES CIP Codes 11.06xx).
- Engineering: NCES CIP Codes 14.xxxx.
- Engineering Technologies: NCES CIP Codes 15.xxxx.
- Biological and Biomedical Sciences: NCES CIP Codes 26.xxxx.
- Mathematics and Statistics: NCES CIP Codes 27.xxxx.
- Military Technologies: NCES CIP Codes 29.xxxx.
- Physical Sciences: NCES CIP Codes 40.xxxx.
- Science Technologies: NCES CIP Codes 41.xxxx.
- Medical Scientist (MS, PhD): NCES CIP Code 51.1401.

For more detailed information on this rule, you can go to blogs.ilw.com/gregsiskind/files/ead_extension_faq.pdf.

Note that students already working for an employer need not be run through E-Verify since the system is only for new employees. Also, the USCIS currently takes the position that the location where the student is working must be using E-Verify.

The USCIS also takes the position that all employers employing students under the Curricular Practical Training (CPT) program must use E-Verify for CPT students. According to the USCIS, since E-Verify cannot automatically check a student's I-20 to produce an automatic confirmation of employment eligibility, students under CPT will always be sent to secondary verification. But employment eligibility should still be confirmed within 24 hours, provided the student's record can be located within the Student Exchange Visitor Information System.

11.31   How reliable is E-Verify in accurately identifying unauthorized employees? What other problems are showing up in the system?
On November 21, 2007, the USCIS released a report it commissioned from Westat, Inc., which it retained to evaluate E-Verify. While the report found that the number of false positives had decreased (the number of approved queries had increased from 79 percent to 92 percent), there were still numerous problems.

E-Verify does not detect identity theft. In fact, Swift and Company, the meat processing company that was raided early in 2007 and had more than 1,500 employees arrested, used the E-Verify system. The employees subject to the raid were accused of identity theft. The new photo tool in E-Verify is designed to address this problem.

One of the more disturbing findings in the Westat report indicated that foreign-born, work-authorized employees are much more likely to receive a tentative nonconfirmation than U.S.-born employees. In fact, a foreign-born employee was 30 times more likely to receive a false-positive nonconfirmation than a U.S.-born employee.

The Westat report also found employer compliance problems with E-Verify, including employers failing to properly train employees using E-Verify, employers terminating employees improperly, and other employers not promptly firing employees who receive final nonconfirmation notices. Employers were also found to be restricting work assignments, delaying training, reducing pay, or requiring employees to work longer hours during the period when a nonconfirmation was being tested.

The Westat report can be found online at www.uscis.gov/files/article/ WebBasicPilotRprtSept2007.pdf. DHS claims that it has further reduced errors and cites a new report showing a 99 percent accuracy rate.

11.32   Is there an alternative available to employers that want to check the authenticity of SSNs of new hires without using E-Verify?

Yes. The SSA has a new Social Security Number Verification Service (SSNVS). The SSNVS is found online at www.ssa.gov/employer/ssnv.htm. Employers and authorized third parties can verify that names and SSNs match, and employers can upload an entire payroll database to determine if a company's workforce has matching numbers.

11.33   What is the E-Verify rule for federal contractors?

On June 6, 2008, President George W. Bush issued Executive Order 13465 "Economy and Efficiency in Government Procurement through Compliance with Certain Immigration and Nationality Act Provisions and the Use of an Electronic Employment Eligibility Verification System." The order mandated that all federal agencies that enter in to contracts shall require, as a condition of each contract, that the contractor agrees to use an electronic employment eligibility verification system designated by the DHS to verify all new employees and all persons assigned by the contractor to perform work within the U.S. on the federal contract. The order also mandated that the Department of Defense, NASA, and the General Services Administration (GSA) amend the Federal Acquisition Regulation (FAR) to carry out the order. On June 9, 2008, DHS designated E-Verify as the system to be used in carrying out the order.

On November 14, 2008, the Department of Defense, the GSA, and NASA jointly released a final regulation amending the FAR requiring an estimated 168,000 employers contracting and subcontracting with the federal government to begin using E-Verify. The rule was to have taken effect on January 15, 2009, and as of that date, federal agencies were to be required to include a section in their agreements with covered employers that specifically calls on the employer to use the E-Verify program in order to comply with the contract. However, the rule has been the subject of litigation and as of the writing of this book, the rule has been delayed until May 21, 2009.

11.34   How does the federal contractor rule affect contracts signed before the rule took effect?

While contracts executed after May 21, 2009, are covered under the federal contractor regulations (assuming the agreement is not exempt under various categories outlined below), only certain existing contracts would be covered. Government agency contracting officers are required to modify existing "indefinite-delivery/indefinite quantity" (ID-IQ) contracts if the remaining period of performance under the contract extends at least six months after May 21, 2009, and if the remaining work under the contract is expected to be "substantial."

11.35   Can the requirement to include the E-Verify clause in federal contracts be waived?

Yes. In exceptional circumstances, the head of the contracting activity at an agency may waive the requirement. This authority may not be delegated.

11.36 **Are any contracts exempt from the new federal contractor rule?**

Yes. The following types of contracts do not require inclusion of the E-Verify clause:

- Contracts for commercially available off-the-shelf (COTS) items as well as items that would be classified as COTS items but for minor modifications.
- Prime contracts that have a value less than $100,000 and subcontracts under those contracts that have a value of less than $3,000.
- Contracts waived based on exceptional circumstances by the head of contracting authority at the agency.
- Contracts that are less than 120 days in duration.
- Contracts for work that will be performed outside the United States (the 50 states, the District of Columbia, Guam, Puerto Rico, and the U.S. Virgin Islands).

11.37 **How much time does a federal contractor employer have to start running employees' names through the E-Verify system?**

There are a few key timelines to watch in complying with the regulation. For employers not yet enrolled as a federal contractor in E-Verify:

- Employers have 30 calendar days to enroll as a federal contractor in E-Verify after a contract is awarded.
- Within 90 calendar days of enrollment in E-Verify, the employer must begin verifying employment eligibility for all new hires working in the United States.
- For all employees assigned to the contract, the employer must begin verification within 90 calendar days of enrollment in E-Verify or within 30 calendar days of the employee's assignment to the contract, whichever date is later.

For employers already enrolled as a federal contractor in E-Verify when the contract is awarded, the following timelines apply:

- For employers already enrolled for 90 calendar days or more, the employer must initiate verification of all new hires within three business days after date of hire (except certain universities, state and local government employers and federally recognized Indian tribes).
- For employers enrolled less than 90 calendar days, within 90 calendar days after enrollment as a federal contractor, the employer shall initiate verification of all new hires.
- For each employee assigned to the contract, the employer shall begin verification within 90 calendar days after the date of the contract award or within 30 days after assignment to the contract, whichever date is later. Note that the 90-day clock starts on the date the contract is awarded instead of 90 days from the date of enrollment as would be the case for employers enrolled less than 90 days when the contract is awarded.

11.38 **Which types of employers only need to verify employees assigned to work on the federal contract?**

- Institutions of higher education.
- State and local governments.
- Federally recognized Indian tribes.
- Sureties performing under a takeover agreement entered into with a federal agency pursuant to a performance bond.

11.39 **Can an employer verify all existing employees under the federal contractor rule as opposed to just employees working on the contract?**

Yes. Contractors can choose to verify all employees of the contractor. If this option is exercised, the employer must notify DHS and must initiate verifications for the contractor's entire workforce within 180 day of notice being given to DHS. To notify DHS that the entire workforce will be verified, the employer should update its company profile through the "Maintain Company" page on E-Verify.

11.40 Does a company already enrolled in E-Verify need to re-enroll in order to comply with the federal contractor rule?

No. However, an employer does need to update its profile on E-Verify's "Maintain Company" page. There is an option for federal contractors where employees and employers will need to take a brief federal contractor tutorial that explains the new policies and features that are unique to contractors. Once the federal contractor option is selected, an employer will not be able to verify new employees until it takes the refresher tutorial.

11.41 What are a company's obligations under the federal contractor rule once the contract is over?

After the contract is over, the company should update its Maintain Company page to reflect the revised status. After that, existing employees may not be run through E-Verify. If the company chooses to terminate participation in E-Verify, it can select "request termination" in the E-Verify system.

11.42 How does the federal contractor rule treat commercially available off-the-shelf contracts?

The new rule does not apply to contracts to supply "commercially available off-the-shelf" (COTS) items. This applies to items of supply that are commercial items sold in substantial quantities in the commercial marketplace and offered to the government, without modification, in the same form in which they are sold in the commercial marketplace. The new rule also does not apply to contracts to supply bulk cargo such as agricultural products and petroleum products. Contracts for items that would be COTS items but for minor modifications are also not covered. The preamble to the rule specifically notes that food is an item of supply and most agricultural suppliers will not be affected by the new rule.

Services related to supplying the COTS items that are procured at the same time the COTS items are procured and supplied by the same employer providing the COTS items are also not subject to the rule. The services also must be typical or normal for the COTS provider.

11.43 Which employees associated with work on a contract must be verified under the new federal contractor rule?

The rule covers employees hired after November 6, 1986, who are directly performing work in the U.S. under the contract. An employee is not considered to be directly performing work under the contract if the employee
- normally performs support work, such as indirect or overhead functions, and
- does not perform any substantial duties applicable to the contract.

The rule exempts employees who hold an active security clearance of confidential, secret, or top secret. Employees for which background investigations have been completed and credentials issued pursuant to the Homeland Security Presidential Directive (HSPD) – 12, "Policy for a Common Identification Standard for Employees and Contractors," issued on August 27, 2004.

11.44 Under the federal contractor rule, how should an employer treat a Form I-9 for an existing employee that is not a current Form I-9?

Employers may use a previously completed Form I-9 as the basis for initiating E-Verify verification of an assigned employee as long as that Form I-9 complies with the E-Verify documentation requirements and the employee's work authorization has not expired, and as long as the employer has reviewed the Form I-9 with the employee to ensure that the employee's stated basis for work authorization has not changed. If the Form I-9 does not comply with the current E-Verify requirements, or the employee's basis for work authorization has expired or changed, the employer should complete a new Form I-9. If the Form I-9 is up to date, but reflects documentation (such as a U.S. passport or green card) that expired after completing the Form I-9, the employer shouldn't use E-Verify's photo screening tool unless USCIS issues further instructions on the subject at some later point.

11.45   Are subcontractors also responsible for participating in E-Verify under the federal contractor rule?

Yes. Any subcontractor furnishing commercial or noncommercial services or construction under a prime contract or a subcontract covered by the rule must participate in E-Verify. The value of the contract must be more than $3,000 and the work to be performed must be in the United States.

11.46   What is the contractor language that must be included in contracts of employers covered by the federal contractor rule?

EMPLOYMENT ELIGIBILITY VERIFICATION (JAN 2009)

(a) Definitions. As used in this clause—

Commercially available off-the-shelf (COTS) item—

(1) Means any item of supply that is—

(i) A commercial item (as defined in paragraph (1)

of the definition at 2.101);

(ii) Sold in substantial quantities in the commercial marketplace; and

(iii) Offered to the Government, without modification, in the same form in which it is sold in the commercial marketplace; and

(2) Does not include bulk cargo, as defined in section 3 of the Shipping Act of 1984 (46 U.S.C. App. 1702), such as agricultural products and petroleum products. Per 46 CFR 525.1 (c)(2), "bulk cargo" means cargo that is loaded and carried in bulk onboard ship without mark or count, in a loose unpackaged form, having homogenous characteristics. Bulk cargo loaded into intermodal equipment, except LASH or Seabee barges, is subject to mark and count and, therefore, ceases to be bulk cargo.

Employee assigned to the contract means an employee who was hired after November 6, 1986, who is directly performing work, in the United States, under a contract that is required to include the clause prescribed at 22.1803. An employee is not considered to be directly performing work under a contract if the employee—

(1) Normally performs support work, such as indirect or overhead functions; and

(2) Does not perform any substantial duties applicable to the contract.

Subcontract means any contract, as defined in 2.101, entered into by a subcontractor to furnish supplies or services for performance of a prime contract or a subcontract. It includes but is not limited to purchase orders, and changes and modifications to purchase orders.

Subcontractor means any supplier, distributor, vendor, or firm that furnishes supplies or services to or for a prime Contractor or another subcontractor.

United States, as defined in 8 U.S.C. 1101(a)(38), means the 50 states, the District of Columbia, Puerto Rico, Guam, and the U.S. Virgin Islands.

(b) Enrollment and verification requirements. (1) If the Contractor is not enrolled as a Federal Contractor in E-Verify at time of contract award, the Contractor shall—

(i) Enroll. Enroll as a Federal Contractor in the E-Verify program within 30 calendar days of contract award;

(ii) Verify all new employees. Within 90 calendar days of enrollment in the E-Verify program, begin to use E-Verify to initiate verification of employment eligibility of all new hires of the Contractor, who are working in the United States, whether or not assigned to the contract, within 3 business days after the date of hire (but see paragraph (b)(3) of this section); and

(iii) Verify employees assigned to the contract.

For each employee assigned to the contract, initiate verification within 90 calendar days after date of enrollment or within 30 calendar days of the employee's assignment to the contract, whichever date is later (but see paragraph (b)(4) of this section).

(2) If the Contractor is enrolled as a Federal Contractor in E-Verify at time of contract award, the Contractor shall use E-Verify to initiate verification of employment eligibility of—

(i) All new employees. (A) Enrolled 90 calendar days or more. The Contractor shall initiate verification of all new hires of the Contractor, who are working in the United States, whether or not assigned to the contract, within 3 business days after the date of hire (but see paragraph (b)(3) of this section); or

(B) Enrolled less than 90 calendar days. Within 90 calendar days after enrollment as a Federal Contractor in E-Verify, the Contractor shall initiate verification of all new hires of the Contractor, who are working in the United States, whether or not assigned to the contract, within 3 business days after the date of hire (but see paragraph(b)(3) of this section); or

(ii) Employees assigned to the contract. For each employee assigned to the contract, the Contractor shall initiate verification within 90 calendar days after date of contract award or within 30 days after assignment to the contract, whichever date is later (but see paragraph (b)(4) of this section).

(3) If the Contractor is an institution of higher education (as defined at 20 U.S.C. 1001(a)); a State or local government or the government of a Federally recognized Indian tribe; or a surety performing under a takeover agreement entered into with a Federal agency pursuant to a performance bond, the Contractor may choose to verify only employees assigned to the contract, whether existing employees or new hires. The Contractor shall follow the applicable verification requirements at (b)(1) or (b)(2) respectively, except that any requirement for verification of new employees applies only to new employees assigned to the contract.

(4) Option to verify employment eligibility of all employees. The Contractor may elect to verify all existing employees hired after November 6, 1986, rather than just those employees assigned to the contract. The Contractor shall initiate verification for each existing employee working in the United States who was hired after November 6, 1986, within 180 calendar days of—

(i) Enrollment in the E-Verify program; or

(ii) Notification to E-Verify Operations of the Contractor's decision to exercise this option, using the contact information provided in the E-Verify program Memorandum of Understanding (MOU).

(5) The Contractor shall comply, for the period of performance of this contract, with the requirements of the E-Verify program MOU.

(i) The Department of Homeland Security (DHS) or the Social Security Administration (SSA) may terminate the Contractor's MOU and deny access to the E-Verify system in accordance with the terms of the MOU. In such case, the Contractor will be referred to a suspension or debarment official.

(ii) During the period between termination of the MOU and a decision by the suspension or debarment official whether to suspend or debar, the Contractor is excused from its obligations under paragraph (b) of this clause. If the suspension or debarment official determines not to suspend or debar the Contractor, then the Contractor must re-enroll in E-Verify.

(c) Web site. Information on registration for and use of the E-Verify program can be obtained via the Internet at the Department of Homeland Security Web site: http://www.dhs.gov/E-Verify.

(d) Individuals previously verified. The Contractor is not required by this clause to perform additional employment verification using E-Verify for any employee:

(1) Whose employment eligibility was previously verified by the Contractor through the E-Verify program;

(2) Who has been granted and holds an active U.S. Government security clearance for access to confidential, secret, or top secret information in accordance with the National Industrial Security Program Operating Manual; or

(3) Who has undergone a completed background investigation and been issued credentials pursuant to Homeland Security Presidential Directive (HSPD) - 12, Policy for a Common Identification Standard for Federal Employees and Contractors.

(e) Subcontracts. The Contractor shall include the requirements of this clause, including this paragraph (e) (appropriately modified for identification of the parties), in each subcontract that—

(1) Is for— (i) Commercial or noncommercial services (except for commercial services that are part of the purchase of a COTS item (or an item that would be a COTS item, but for minor modifications), performed by the COTS provider, and are normally provided for that COTS item); or
(ii) Construction;
(2) Has a value of more than $3,000; and
(3) Includes work performed in the United States.

11.47   What is IMAGE?

IMAGE is a joint government and private sector initiative designed to "combat unlawful employment and reduce vulnerabilities that help illegal aliens gain such employment." The initiative is basically designed to improve employer self-compliance.

Under the IMAGE program, employers receive education and training from ICE on proper hiring procedures, fraudulent document detection, use of E-Verify, and antidiscrimination procedures. To participate in IMAGE, employers must submit to a Form I-9 audit by ICE and verify all of their employees' SSNs through the SSNVS.

After completing the program, an employer will be deemed "IMAGE Certified." ICE believes that this will become an industry standard.

11.48 Will participating in IMAGE guarantee that an employer will not be found liable in an enforcement action?

No. But participation in IMAGE will be considered a mitigating factor in the determination of fines, should they be levied.

11.49 What obligations do IMAGE participants face?

All IMAGE participants must meet the following requirements:

- Participate in E-Verify.
- Establish an internal training program covering Form I-9 compliance, detecting fraudulent identity documents, and using E-Verify.
- Ensure that only trained employees complete the Form I-9 and use E-Verify.
- Establish a secondary review process to ensure that one person cannot subvert the process.
- Conduct I-9 audits semiannually using a neutral party.
- Establish self-reporting procedures to inform ICE of violations or deficiencies.
- Set protocols for responding to no-match letters.
- Establish a tip line for employees to report violations or deficiencies.
- For companies with 50 employees or more, designate a compliance officer to ensure employment practices are in accordance with IMAGE guidelines.
- Report annually to ICE the number of employees removed and denied employment as a result of IMAGE participation, any major organizational changes, and any changes in the contact information of the company's IMAGE liaison to ICE.
- Report immediately to ICE the discovery or allegations of any criminal violations.

11.50 What is the SSNVS?

The SSNVS was created in 2006 by the SSA to allow employers to verify SSNs via a web site. It is a free service available to any employer.

The SSNVS can only be used by employers and payroll services to verify that a SSN matches a particular name and only for the purpose of completing a W-2 form. The SSNVS will not indicate whether an employee is authorized to work in the United States.

Employers can verify up to 10 names at a time and receive results instantly. They can also upload files with up to 250,000 names and get a response in one business day.

The SSA has posted a detailed tutorial on using SSNVS online at www.ssa.gov/employer/SSNVS.pdf.

11.51 What restrictions are placed on employers seeking to use the SSNVS?

- Employers cannot use the system to prescreen applicants.
- Employers cannot use the system by itself to take punitive actions against an employee whose name does not match.
- Employers must establish policies that are applied consistently to all employees (including, for example, using the system on all newly hired employees or verifying all employees at an employer).

- Privacy must be protected by ensuring that third-party use of the SSNVS is limited to organizations that handle annual wage reporting responsibilities under contract to the employer.
- The SSNVS should not be used by third-party companies that conduct identity verification or background checks, or for nonwage-reporting purposes.

11.52 What is the DHS/Employer E-Verify MOU?

ARTICLE I
PURPOSE AND AUTHORITY

This Memorandum of Understanding (MOU) sets forth the points of agreement between the Social Security Administration (SSA), the Department of Homeland Security (DHS) and _____ (Employer) regarding the Employer's participation in E-Verify. E-Verify is a pilot program in which the employment eligibility of all newly hired employees will be confirmed after the Employment Eligibility Verification Form (Form I-9) has been completed.

Authority for the E-Verify is found in Title IV, Subtitle A, of the Illegal Immigration Reform and Immigrant Responsibility Act of 1996 (IIRIRA), Pub. L. 104-208, 110 Stat. 3009, as amended (8 U.S.C. § 1324a note).

ARTICLE II
FUNCTIONS TO BE PERFORMED

A. RESPONSIBILITIES OF THE SSA

1. Upon completion of the Form I-9 by the employee and the Employer, and provided the Employer complies with the requirements of this MOU, SSA agrees to provide the Employer with available information that allows the Employer to confirm the accuracy of Social Security Numbers provided by all newly hired employees and the employment authorization of U.S. citizens.

2. The SSA agrees to provide to the Employer appropriate assistance with operational problems that may arise during the Employer's participation in E-Verify. The SSA agrees to provide the Employer with names, titles, addresses, and telephone numbers of SSA representatives to be contacted during E-Verify.

3. The SSA agrees to safeguard the information provided by the Employer through the E-Verify procedures, and to limit access to such information, as is appropriate by law, to individuals responsible for the verification of Social Security Numbers and for evaluation of the E-Verify or such other persons or entities who may be authorized by the SSA as governed by the Privacy Act (5 U.S.C. § 552a), the Social Security Act (42 U.S.C. 1306(a)), and SSA regulations (20 CFR Part 401).

4. SSA agrees to establish a means of automated verification that is designed (in conjunction with the Department of Homeland Security's automated system if necessary) to provide confirmation or tentative nonconfirmation of U.S. citizens' employment eligibility and accuracy of SSA records for both citizens and aliens within 3 Federal Government work days of the initial inquiry.

5. SSA agrees to establish a means of secondary verification (including updating SSA records as may be necessary) for employees who contest SSA tentative nonconfirmations that is designed to provide final confirmation or nonconfirmation U.S. citizens' employment eligibility and accuracy of SSA records for both citizens and aliens within 10 Federal Government work days of the date of referral to SSA,

unless SSA determines that more than 10 days may be necessary. In such cases, SSA will provide additional verification instructions.

B. RESPONSIBILITIES OF THE DEPARTMENT OF HOMELAND SECURITY

1. Upon completion of the Form I-9 by the employee and the Employer and completion of SSA verification procedures required prior to initiation of Department of Homeland Security verification procedures by the Employer, the Department of Homeland Security agrees to provide the Employer access to selected data from the Department of Homeland Security's database to enable the Employer to conduct:

- Automated verification checks on newly hired alien employees by electronic means, and
- Photographic verification checks (when available) on newly hired alien employees.

2. The Department of Homeland Security agrees to provide to the Employer appropriate assistance with operational problems that may arise during the Employer's participation in E-Verify. The Department of Homeland Security agrees to provide the Employer names, titles, addresses, and telephone numbers of Department of Homeland Security representatives to be contacted during E-Verify.

3. The Department of Homeland Security agrees to provide to the Employer a manual containing instructions on E-Verify policies, procedures and requirements for both SSA and Department of Homeland Security, including restrictions on use of E-Verify procedures (the E-Verify Manual). The Department of Homeland Security agrees to provide training materials on E-Verify.

4. The Department of Homeland Security agrees to provide to the Employer a notice, which indicates the Employer's participation in E-Verify. The Department of Homeland Security also agrees to provide to the Employer anti-discrimination notices issued by the Office of Special Counsel for Immigration-Related Unfair Employment Practices (OSC), Civil Rights Division, and U.S. Department of Justice.

5. The Department of Homeland Security agrees to issue the Employer a user identification number and password that permits the Employer to verify information provided by alien employees with the Department of Homeland Security's database.

6. The Department of Homeland Security agrees to safeguard the information provided to the Department of Homeland Security by the Employer, and to limit access to such information to individuals responsible for the verification of alien employment eligibility and for evaluation of the E-Verify, or to such other persons or entities as may be authorized by applicable law. Information will be used only to verify the accuracy of Social Security Numbers and employment eligibility, to enforce the INA and federal criminal laws, and to ensure accurate wage reports to the SSA.

7. The Department of Homeland Security agrees to establish a means of automated verification that is designed (in conjunction with SSA verification procedures) to provide confirmation or tentative nonconfirmation of employees' employment eligibility within 3 Federal Government work days of the initial inquiry.

8. The Department of Homeland Security agrees to establish a means of secondary verification (including updating Department of Homeland Security records as

may be necessary) for employees who contest Department of Homeland Security tentative nonconfirmations and photographic non-match tentative nonconfirmations that is designed to provide final confirmation or nonconfirmation of the employees' employment eligibility within 10 Federal Government work days of the date of referral to the Department of Homeland Security, unless DHS determines that more than 10 days may be necessary. In such cases, the Department of Homeland Security will provide additional verification instructions.

C. RESPONSIBILITIES OF THE EMPLOYER

1. The Employer agrees to display the notices supplied by the Department of Homeland Security in a prominent place that is clearly visible to prospective employees.

2. The Employer agrees to provide to the SSA and the Department of Homeland Security the names, titles, addresses, and telephone numbers of the Employer representatives to be contacted regarding E-Verify.

3. The Employer agrees to become familiar with and comply with the E-Verify Manual.

4. The Employer agrees that any Employer Representative who will perform employment verification queries will complete the E-Verify Tutorial before that individual initiates any queries.

5. The Employer agrees to comply with established Form I-9 procedures, with two exceptions:
- If an employee presents a "List B" identity document, the Employer agrees to only accept "List B" documents that contain a photograph. (List B documents identified in 8 C.F.R. § 274a.2(b)(1)(B)) can be presented during the Form I-9 process to establish identity).
- If an employee presents a DHS Form I-551 (Permanent Resident Card) or Form I-766 (EAD) to complete the Form I-9, the Employer agrees to make a photocopy of the document and to retain the photocopy with the employee's Form I-9. The employer will use the photocopy to verify the photograph and to assist the Department with its review of photographic non-matches that are contested by employees. Note that employees retain the right to present any List A, or List B and List C, documentation to complete the Form I-9. DHS may in future designate other documents for the photographic screening tool.

6. The Employer understands that participation in E-Verify does not exempt the Employer from the responsibility to complete, retain, and make available for inspection Forms I-9 that relate to its employees, or from other requirements of applicable regulations or laws, except for the following modified requirements applicable by reason of the Employer's participation in E-Verify: (1) identity documents must have photographs, as described in paragraph 5 above; (2) a rebuttable presumption is established that the Employer has not violated section 274A(a)(1)(A) of the Immigration and Nationality Act (INA) with respect to the hiring of any individual if it obtains confirmation of the identity and employment eligibility of the individual in compliance with the terms and conditions of E-Verify ; (3) the Employer must notify the Department of Homeland Security if it continues to employ any employee after receiving a final nonconfirmation, and is subject to a civil money penalty between $500 and $1,000 for each failure to notify the Department of Homeland Security of continued employment following a final nonconfirmation; (4) the Employer is subject to a rebuttable presumption that it has knowingly employed an unauthorized alien in violation of section 274A(a)(1)(A) if the Employer continues to employ any employee after receiving a final nonconfirmation; and (5) no person or entity participating in E-Verify is civilly

or criminally liable under any law for any action taken in good faith on information provided through the confirmation system. The Department of Homeland Security reserves the right to conduct Form I-9 compliance inspections during the course of E-Verify, as well as to conduct any other enforcement activity authorized by law.

7. The Employer agrees to initiate E-Verify verification procedures within 3 Employer business days after each employee has been hired (but after both sections 1 and 2 of the Form I-9 have been completed), and to complete as many (but only as many) steps of the E-Verify process as are necessary according to the E-Verify Manual. The Employer is prohibited from initiating verification procedures before the employee has been hired and the Form I-9 completed. If the automated system to be queried is temporarily unavailable, the 3-day time period is extended until it is again operational in order to accommodate the Employer's attempting, in good faith, to make inquiries during the period of unavailability. In all cases, the Employer must use the SSA verification procedures first, and use the Department of Homeland Security verification procedures and photo screening tool only as directed by the SSA verification response.

8. The Employer agrees not to use E-Verify procedures for pre-employment screening of job applicants, support for any unlawful employment practice, or any other use not authorized by this MOU. The Employer will not verify selectively; it agrees to use the E-Verify procedures for all new hires as long as this MOU is in effect. The Employer agrees not to use E-Verify procedures for re-verification, or for employees hired before the date this MOU is in effect. The Employer understands that if the Employer uses E-Verify procedures for any purpose other than as authorized by this MOU, the Employer may be subject to appropriate legal action and the immediate termination of its access to SSA and Department of Homeland Security information pursuant to this MOU.

9. The Employer agrees to follow appropriate procedures (see Article IIIB below) regarding tentative non-confirmations, including notifying employees of the finding, providing written instructions to employees, allowing employees to contest the finding, and not taking adverse action against employees if they choose to contest the finding. Further, when employees contest a tentative non-confirmation based upon a photographic non-match, the Employer is required to take affirmative steps (see Article IIIB below) to contact the Department of Homeland Security with information necessary to resolve the challenge.

10. The Employer agrees not to take any adverse action against an employee based upon the employee's employment eligibility status while SSA or the Department of Homeland Security is processing the verification request unless the Employer obtains knowledge (as defined in 8 C.F.R. § 274a.1(l)) that the employee is not work authorized. The Employer understands that an initial inability of the SSA or Department of Homeland Security automated verification to verify work authorization, a tentative nonconfirmation, or the finding of a photo non-match, does not mean, and should not be interpreted as, an indication that the employee is not work authorized. In any of the cases listed above, the employee must be provided the opportunity to contest the finding, and if he or she does so, may not be terminated until secondary verification by SSA or the Department of Homeland Security has been completed to determine the final confirmation or non-confirmation. If the employee does not choose to contest the Employer's initial finding, then the Employer can find the employee is not work authorized and take the appropriate action.

11. The Employer agrees to comply with section 274B of the INA by not discriminating unlawfully against any individual in hiring, firing, or recruitment practices

because of his or her national origin or, in the case of a protected individual as defined in section 274B(a)(3) of the INA, because of his or her citizenship status. The Employer understands that such illegal practices can include discharging or refusing to hire eligible employees because of their foreign appearance or language, and that any violation of the unfair immigration-related employment practices provisions of the INA could subject the Employer to civil penalties pursuant to section 274B of the INA and the termination of its participation in the E-Verify. If the Employer has any questions relating to the anti-discrimination provision, it should contact OSC at 1-800-255-7688 or 1-800-237-2515 (TDD).

12. The Employer agrees to record the case verification number on the employee's Form I-9 or to print the screen containing the case verification number and attach it to the employee's Form I-9.

13. The Employer agrees that it will use the information it receives from the SSA or the Department of Homeland Security pursuant to E-Verify and this MOU only to confirm the employment eligibility of newly-hired employees after completion of the Form I-9. The Employer agrees that it will safeguard this information, and means of access to it (such as PINS and passwords) to ensure that it is not used for any other purpose and as necessary to protect its confidentiality, including ensuring that it is not disseminated to any person other than employees of the Employer who need it to perform the Employer's responsibilities under this MOU.

14. The Employer acknowledges that the information which it receives from SSA is governed by the Privacy Act (5 U.S.C. § 552a(i)(1) and (3)) and the Social Security Act (42 U.S.C. 1306(a)), and that any person who obtains this information under false pretenses or uses it for any purpose other than as provided for in this MOU may be subject to criminal penalties.

15. The Employer agrees to allow the Department of Homeland Security and SSA, or their authorized agents or designees, to make periodic visits to the Employer for the purpose of reviewing E-Verify -related records, i.e., Forms I-9, SSA Transaction Records, and Department of Homeland Security verification records, which were created during the Employer's participation in the E-Verify Program. In addition, for the purpose of evaluating the E-Verify, the Employer agrees to allow the Department of Homeland Security and SSA or their authorized agents or designees, to interview it regarding its experience with E-Verify, to interview employees hired during E-Verify concerning their experience with the pilot, and to make employment and E-Verify related records available to the Department of Homeland Security and the SSA, or their designated agents or designees.

ARTICLE III
REFERRAL OF INDIVIDUALS TO THE SSA AND THE DEPARTMENT OF HOMELAND SECURITY

A. REFERRAL TO THE SSA

1. If the Employer receives a tentative nonconfirmation issued by SSA, the Employer must print the tentative nonconfirmation notice as directed by the automated system and provide it to the employee so that the employee may determine whether he or she will contest the tentative nonconfirmation.

2. The Employer will refer employees to SSA field offices only as directed by the automated system based on a tentative nonconfirmation, and only after the Employer records the case verification number, reviews the input to detect any transaction errors, and determines that the employee contests the tentative

nonconfirmation. The Employer will transmit the Social Security Number to SSA for verification again if this review indicates a need to do so. The Employer will determine whether the employee contests the tentative nonconfirmation as soon as possible after the Employer receives it.

3. If the employee contests an SSA tentative nonconfirmation, the Employer will provide the employee with a referral letter and instruct the employee to visit an SSA office to resolve the discrepancy within 8 Federal Government work days. The Employer will make a second inquiry to the SSA database using E-Verify procedures on the date that is 10 Federal Government work days after the date of the referral in order to obtain confirmation, or final nonconfirmation, unless otherwise instructed by SSA.

4. The Employer agrees not to ask the employee to obtain a printout from the Social Security Number database (the Numident) or other written verification of the Social Security Number from the SSA (other than the Social Security Number Card).

B. REFERRAL TO THE DEPARTMENT OF HOMELAND SECURITY

1. If the Employer receives a tentative nonconfirmation issued by the Department of Homeland Security, the Employer must print the tentative nonconfirmation notice as directed by the automated system and provide it to the employee so that the employee may determine whether he or she will contest the tentative nonconfirmation.

2. If the Employer finds a photographic non-match for an alien who provides a document for which the automated system has transmitted a photograph, the employer must print the photographic non-match tentative non-confirmation notice as directed by the automated system and provide it to the employee so that the employee may determine whether he or she will contest the finding.

3. The Employer agrees to refer individuals to the Department of Homeland Security only when the employee chooses to contest a tentative nonconfirmation received from the Department of Homeland Security automated verification process or when the Employer issues a tentative non-confirmation based upon a photo non-match. The Employer will determine whether the employee contests the tentative nonconfirmation as soon as possible after the Employer receives it.

4. If the employee contests a tentative nonconfirmation issued by the Department of Homeland Security, the Employer will provide the employee with a referral letter and instruct the employee to contact the Department through its toll-free hotline within 8 Federal Government work days.

5. If the employee contests a tentative nonconfirmation based upon a photographic non-match, the Employer will provide the employee with a referral letter to the Department of Homeland Security. The Department of Homeland Security will electronically transmit the result of the referral to the Employer within 10 Federal Government work days of the referral unless it determines that more than 10 days may be necessary.

6. The Employer agrees that if an employee contests a tentative non-confirmation based upon a photograph non-match, the Employer will send a copy of the employee's Form I-551 or Form I-766 to DHS for review by:
- Scanning and uploading the document, or
- Sending a photocopy of the document by an express mail account (furnished and paid for by DHS).

7. The Employer understands that if it cannot determine whether there is a photo match/non-match, the Employer is required to forward the employee's documentation to DHS by scanning and uploading, or by sending the document as described in the preceding paragraph, and resolving the case as specified by the Immigration Services Verifier at DHS who will determine the photo match or non-match.

ARTICLE IV
SERVICE PROVISIONS

The SSA and the Department of Homeland Security will not charge the Employer for verification services performed under this MOU. The Employer is responsible for providing equipment needed to make inquiries. To access E-Verify, an Employer will need a personal computer with Internet access.

ARTICLE V
PARTIES

This MOU is effective upon the signature of all parties, and shall continue in effect for as long as the SSA and the Department of Homeland Security conduct E-Verify unless modified in writing by the mutual consent of all parties, or terminated by any party upon 30 days prior written notice to the others. Termination by any party shall terminate the MOU as to all parties. The SSA or the Department of Homeland Security may terminate this MOU without prior notice if deemed necessary because of the requirements of law or policy, or upon a determination by SSA or the Department of Homeland Security that there has been a breach of system integrity or security by the Employer, or a failure on the part of the Employer to comply with established procedures or legal requirements. Some or all SSA and Department of Homeland Security responsibilities under this MOU may be performed by contractor(s), and SSA and the Department of Homeland Security may adjust verification responsibilities between each other as they may determine.

Nothing in this MOU is intended, or should be construed, to create any right or benefit, substantive or procedural, enforceable at law by any third party against the United States, its agencies, officers, or employees, or against (Employer), its agents, officers, or employees.

 Each party shall be solely responsible for defending any claim or action against it arising out of or related to E-Verify or this MOU, whether civil or criminal, and for any liability wherefrom, including (but not limited to) any dispute between the Employer and any other person or entity regarding the applicability of Section 403(d) of IIRIRA to any action taken or allegedly taken by the Employer.

The employer understands that the fact of its participation in E-Verify is not confidential information and may be disclosed as authorized or required by law and Department of Homeland Security or SSA policy, including but not limited to, Congressional oversight, E-Verify publicity and media inquiries, and responses to inquiries under the Freedom of Information Act (FOIA).

The foregoing constitutes the full agreement on this subject between the SSA, the Department of Homeland Security, and the Employer.

The individuals whose signatures appear below represent that they are authorized to enter into this MOU on behalf of the Employer, SSA, and the Department of Homeland Security respectively.

To be accepted as a participant in E-Verify, you should only sign the Employer's Section of the signature page. If you have any questions, contact E-Verify at 888-464-4218.

Employer

_____   _____
Name (Please type or print)   Title

_____   _____
Signature   Date

Social Security Administration

_____   _____
Name (Please type or print)   Title

_____   _____
Signature   Date

Department of Homeland Security - Verification Division

_____   _____
Name (Please type or print)   Title

_____   _____
Signature   Date

Social Security No-Match Letters

Since 2006, ICE has been trying to put in to force a Social Security "no-match" rule. The No-Match rule describes the obligations of employers when they receive no-match letters from the SSA or receive a letter regarding employment verification forms from the DHS. The rule also provides "safe harbors" employers can follow to avoid a finding that the employer had constructive knowledge that the employee referred to in the letter was an alien not authorized to work in the United States. Employers with knowledge that an immigrant worker is unauthorized to accept employment are liable for both civil and criminal penalties.

Almost immediately upon the release of the no-match final rule in August 2007, it was challenged in court and the rule was barred from taking effect by a federal judge. That court battle has continued through publication of this book in 2009.

Though the rule is *not* in effect while the litigation proceeds, most expect that a no-match rule will eventually come into force and that it will closely resemble the rule as originally released. This chapter is included in order to educate readers on what to expect if and when the DHS succeeds in its efforts.

The challenged rule describes the obligations of employers when they receive no-match letters from the SSA or receive a letter regarding employment verification forms from the DHS. The rule also provides safe harbor procedures that employers can follow to avoid a finding the employer had constructive knowledge that the employee referred to in the letter was an alien not authorized to work in the United States. Employers with knowledge that an immigrant worker is unauthorized to accept employment are liable for both civil and criminal penalties.

The regulation finalized a proposed rule released on June 14, 2006. The DHS, ICE's parent department, received nearly 5,000 comments on the rule from a variety of interested parties including employers, unions, lawyers, and advocacy groups. According to the DHS, the opinions were highly varied with both strong opposition and support being enunciated. The DHS also held a meeting with business and trade associations to discuss the proposed rule.

12.1 Why did the court block the rule from taking effect?

The rule was challenged in court prior to taking effect in September 2007 and a judge issued a preliminary injunction on three grounds:

- The DHS failed to supply a reasoned analysis justifying what the court thought was a change in the DHS' position — i.e., that a no-match letter may be sufficient, by itself, to put an employer on notice that its employees may not be work authorized.
- The DHS exceeded its authority (and encroached on the authority of the DOJ) by interpreting antidiscrimination provisions in IRCA.
- The DHS violated the Regulatory Flexibility Act (RFA) by not conducting a regulatory flexibility analysis.

12.2   How has the DHS attempted to address the court's objections?

On March 21, 2008, the DHS released a supplemental proposed rule designed to address the court's concerns. The DHS hoped that the court would overturn the preliminary injunction and allow the agency to implement the proposed rule. That did not happen and the agency decided on October 23, 2008, to release the rule anyway, claiming that it had the authority to issue a new rule that met the court's objections.

In the new rule, the DHS first addressed the court's concern that that agency had failed to provide a detailed analysis explaining the agency's new position that no-match letters are an indicator of unauthorized status.

The DHS first cited a number of sources indicating that SSNs are being used to gain employment authorization by people unauthorized to work. It included quotes from the 1997 report of the U.S. Commission on Immigration Reform and also cited reports issued by the Government Accountability Office and the Inspector General of the SSA. It also noted that the industries most affected by the rule have admitted that much of their workforce is unauthorized and millions of employees have used false numbers. Finally, the agency cited public and private studies confirming that a sizeable portion of employees identified by no-match letters are working illegally in the United States.

The DHS cited two other justifications for the law. First, many employers fail to respond to no-match letters because they fear being accused of violating anti-discrimination rules if they react inappropriately to them. The no-match rule would provide protection from such liability if the employer follows the requirements of the regulation. Second, many U.S. citizens and aliens would benefit by being notified of problems in the Social Security database and being able to get proper credit for their earnings. U.S. citizens would also benefit, according to the DHS, by seeing an expansion of employment opportunities as a result of unauthorized employees being terminated for not providing a valid SSN.

The DHS then described a series of rulings and opinions by the agency that it believes show the agency has had a consistent position on no-match letters. But the agency stated that even if it conceded that it was taking a new position, it met the requirement to show a reasoned analysis justifying the chance in policy. In this case, it stated that the "most basic justification for issuance of this rule – and for the "change" in policy found by the district court – is to eliminate ambiguity regarding an employer's responsibilities upon receipt of a no-match letter. Absent this rule, employers have been taking very different positions based on the DHS' ambiguous statements.

The DHS also defended the rule by pointing out that only employers with more than 10 employees identified with no-matches get SSA no-match letters and only if the percentage of no-matches exceeds 0.5 percent of the employer's work force.

With regard to the question of usurping the DOJ's anti-discrimination enforcement authority, DHS insisted that its rule does not interfere with "the authority of DOJ to enforce anti-discrimination provisions of the INA or adjudicate notices of intent to fine employers."

It also specifically rescinded statements from the August 2007 rule's preamble describing employers' obligations under anti-discrimination law or discussing the potential for anti-discrimination liability. That includes the statement "employers who follow the safe harbor procedures … will not be found to have violated unlawful discrimination."

In the October 2008 final rule, the DHS also addressed the concerns about a conflict with the Justice Department's anti-discrimination rules by citing a Justice Department memorandum published at http://www.usdoj.gov/crt/osc/htm/ Nomatch032008.htm that included the following assurance:

> *An employer that receives an SSA no-match letter and termi-*
> *nates employees without attempting to resolve the mismatches, or*
> *who treats employees differently or otherwise acts with the purpose*
> *or intent to discriminate based upon national origin or other*
> *prohibited characteristics, may be found by OSC to have engaged*
> *in unlawful discrimination. However, if an employer follows all*
> *of the safe harbor procedures outlined in DHS's no-match rule but*
> *cannot determine that an employee is authorized to work in the*
> *United States, and therefore terminates that employee, and if that*
> *employer applied the same procedures to all employees referenced in*
> *the no-match letter(s) uniformly and without the purpose or intent*
> *to discriminate on the basis of actual or perceived citizenship status*
> *or national origin, then OSC will not find reasonable cause to*
> *believe that the employer has violated section 1324b's anti-discrim-*
> *ination provision, and that employer will not be subject to suit by*
> *the United States under that provision.*

With respect to the regulatory flexibility analysis, the DHS took the position that the rule is a voluntary safe harbor rather than a mandate. Hence, the rule does not require a showing that employers will not be significantly impacted economically.

However, the agency claimed it would comply with the judge's ruling by providing an initial regulatory flexibility analysis (IRFA). In the March 2008 proposed rule, they provided a very cursory summary of the analysis in the proposed regulation. In the October 2008 final rule, a more detailed analysis was included.

The DHS claimed that it has been stymied to some extent in providing a highly specific analysis because the SSA had denied its request for the names and addresses of the companies already identified by the SSA in its preparation to release no-match letters pursuant to the August 2007 regulation. The SSA reminded the DHS that this disclosure would actually be illegal under taxpayer privacy laws. In the March 2008 proposed rule, SSA did, however, provide more general information including a table showing the distribution of employers slated to receive no-match letters in 2006. The DHS estimated it would cost employers anywhere from $3,009 to $33,759 depending on the size of the employer and the percentage of current no-match employees assumed to be unauthorized. The DHS does not believe these costs constitute a "significant economic impact."

The DHS noted that the costs associated with losing an employee as a result of the rule are due to the INA itself and not the new rule. However, the agency did not mention "false positives" where employees authorized to work are incorrectly identified in a no-match letter. The agency did not account for costs associated with losing employees unable to resolve problems within 90 days, something that critics fear will become common as hundreds of thousands of people attempt to resolve problems at the same time under the new rule.

The DHS did cite the following costs: labor costs for human resource personnel, certain training costs, legal services, and lost productivity.

12.3 Did the DHS mention any changes to the August 2007 rule in the new October 2008 rule?

The DHS made only two relatively minor changes. First, DHS changed the rule requiring that employers "promptly" notify affected employees after they are unable to resolve a mismatch through internal checks. Employers will now be given five business days to notify employees.

Second, the DHS made clear that employees hired before November 1, 1986, are not covered by the no-match rule since these workers are not subject to IRCA.

12.4 Why did ICE issue this rule?

All employers in the U.S. are required to report Social Security earnings for their workers. Those W-2 form reports listing an employee's name, Social Security number and the worker's earnings are sent to the SSA. In some cases, the Social Security number and the name of the employee do not match. In some of these cases, the SSA sends an employer a letter informing the employer of the no-match.

In some cases, the no-match is the result of a clerical error or a name change. In other cases, it may indicate that an employee is not authorized to work.

ICE issues similar letters to employers after they conduct audits of an employer's Employment Eligibility Verification forms (the I-9s) and find evidence that an immigration status document or employment authorization document does not match the name of the person on the I-9 document.

To date, there has been considerable confusion and debate over an employer's obligations after receiving a letter like this as well as whether an employer would be considered to be on notice that an employee is not unauthorized to work. This rule clarifies both issues albeit in a way that will be very unfriendly to employers and workers.

The DHS cites the *Mester Manufacturing* case from the 9th Circuit Court of Appeals to remind employers that if they will have "constructive" knowledge that an employee is out of status, they are in violation of IRCA, the statute that punishes employers for knowingly hiring unlawfully present workers or violating paperwork rules associated with the I-9 employment verification form.

12.5 When was the rule to become effective?

It became effective publication in the *Federal Register* (expected to take place within a few workdays of the announcement of the rule on October 23, 2008). However, DHS is still enjoined from implementing the rule until the court lifts the injunction.

12.6 How has the definition of "knowing" changed in the rule?

Two additional examples of "constructive knowledge" are added to the list of examples of information available to employers indicating an employee is not authorized to work in the United States. First, if an employer gets a written notice from the SSA that the name and SSN do not match SSA records. And second, written notice is received from the DHS that the immigration document presented in completing the I-9 was assigned to another person or there is no agency record that the document was assigned to anyone.

However, the question of whether an employer has "constructive knowledge" will "depend on the totality of relevant circumstances." So this rule is just a safe harbor regulation telling how an employer can avoid a constructive knowledge finding, but not guaranteeing that an employer will be deemed to have constructive knowledge if the safe harbor procedure is not followed.

12.7   What steps must an employer take if it gets a no-match letter?

First, an employer must check its records to determine if the error was a result of a typographical, transcription, or similar clerical error. If there is an error, the employer should correct the error and inform the appropriate agency — either the DHS or the SSA, depending on which agency sent the no-match letter. The employer should then verify with that agency that the new number is correct and internally document the manner, date, and time of the verification. ICE indicated in the preamble to the regulation that 30 days is an appropriate amount of time for an employer to take these steps.

If these actions do not resolve the discrepancy, the employer should request that an employee confirm the employer's records are correct. If they are not correct, the employer needs to take corrective actions which would include informing the relevant agency and verifying the corrected records with the agency. If the records are correct according to the employee, the reasonable employer should ask the employee to follow up with the relevant agency (such as by visiting an SSA office and taking the original or certified copies of the required identity documents). Just as noted above, 30 days is a reasonable period of time for an employer to take this step.

The rules provide that a discrepancy is only resolved when the employer has received verification from the SSA or the DHS that the employee's name matches the record.

When 90 days have passed without a resolution of the discrepancy, an employer must undertake a procedure to verify or fail to verify the employee's identity and work authorization. If the process is completed, an employer will not be deemed to have constructive knowledge that an employee is not work authorized, if the system verifies the employee (even if the employee turns out not to be employment authorized). This assumes that an employer does not otherwise have actual or constructive knowledge that an employee is not work authorized.

If the discrepancy is not resolved and the employee's identity and work authorization are not verified, the employer must either terminate the employee or face the risk that the DHS will find it had constructive knowledge of the lack of employment authorization.

12.8   What is the procedure to reverify identity and employment authorization when an employee has not resolved the discrepancy as described above?

Sections 1 and 2 of the I-9 form need to be completed within 93 days of receiving the no-match letter. So, if an employer took the full 90 days to try to resolve the problem, the employer would then have three more days to complete the new I-9. And, an employee may not use a document containing the disputed SSN or alien number, or a receipt for a replacement of such a document. Only documents with a photograph may be used to establish identity.

12.9   Does an employer need to use the same procedure to verify employment authorization for each employee who is the subject of a no-match letter?

Yes, the antidiscrimination rules require the employer to apply these procedures uniformly. The DHS is also reminding employers about the document abuse provisions which bar employers from failing to honor documents that, on their face, appear reasonable. But employers now have the safe harbor of a new regulation stating that this provision does not apply to documents that are the subject of a no-match letter.

The DHS notes that if employers require employees to complete a new I-9 form, the employer must not apply this discriminatorily but rather should require I-9 verification for all employees who fail to resolve the SSA discrepancies and apply a uniform policy to all employees who refuse to participate in resolving discrepancies and completing new I-9s. *Note that employees hired before November 6, 1986, are not subject to this rule. This reflects a change in the October 2008 rule from the 2007 rule.*

12.10 **What if the employer has heard that an employee is unlawfully present aside from hearing from the SSA or the DHS in a no-match letter?**
Employers who have *actual* knowledge that an alien is unauthorized to work are liable under the INA even if they have complied with the I-9 and no-match rules. But the government has the burden of proving actual knowledge. The DHS also notes that constructive knowledge may still be shown by reference to other evidence.

12.11 **Does the DHS have the authority to regulate the treatment of notices received by the SSA?**
A number of comments on the rule questioned this issue, but they were dismissed by the DHS. Presumably, the issue could be the source of litigation.

12.12 **Why did the DHS issue this rule when the Bush White House supported comprehensive immigration reform that would give employers legal options for hiring these employees?**
The DHS indicated in the preamble to the rule that, while it wants to work with Congress on such legislation, there is no way to predict when it will pass and interior enforcement needs to be conducted. Others argued that the White House was interested in demonstrating to Congress that it was getting tough on illegal immigration in order to increase the likelihood that members of Congress would support comprehensive immigration reform in the future.

12.13 **Will following the procedures in this rule protect an employer from all claims of constructive knowledge, or just claims of constructive knowledge based on the letters for which the employers followed the safe harbor procedure?**
An employer who follows the safe harbor procedure will be considered to have taken all reasonable steps in response to the notice, and the employer's receipt of the written notice will not be used as evidence of constructive knowledge. But if other independent evidence exists that an employer had constructive knowledge, the employer is not protected.

12.14 **Are there any special rules for circumstances such as seasonal workers, teachers on sabbatical, and employees out of the office for an extended period due to excused absence or disability?**
The no-match rule is not entire clear on the issue, but the DHS does state that with respect to seasonal workers and others out of employment for an extended period, employers may not be able to comply with the new rule and that compliance in such a case is voluntary.

12.15 **What are the time frames required under the rule to take each necessary action after receiving the no-match letter?**
- Employer checks its own records, makes any necessary corrections of errors, and verifies corrections with the SSA or the DHS *(0 – 30 days)*.
- If necessary, employer notifies employee and asks employee to assist in correction *(0 - 90 days)*. (Note that under the March 2008 proposed rule, employers have five days to notify employees of the no-match if the employer conducts its internal review.)

- If necessary, employer corrects its own records and verifies the correction with the SSA or the DHS *(0 - 90 days)*.
- If necessary, the employer performs special I-9 procedure *(90 - 93 days)*.

12.16   May an employer continue to employ a worker throughout the process noted above?

Yes. The only reason an employer would have to terminate an employee prior to 93 days would be if the employer gained actual knowledge of unauthorized employment. The DHS notes that it is not requiring termination by virtue of this rule; rather, it is just providing a safe harbor to avoid a finding of constructive knowledge. Employers may be permitted to terminate based on their own personnel files, including an employee's failure to show up for work or an employee's false statement to the employer. Employers are advised to consult labor counsel before terminating employees for such reasons during the no-match process.

Employers may terminate as well if they notify an employee of the no-match letter and the employee admits that he or she is unauthorized to work.

12.17   What if the no-match letter is sent to the employee, not the employer?

The new rule only applies in cases where the written notice is sent to the employer.

12.18   Does it matter which person at the employer receives the letter?

No, the DHS will not allow a designated person to receive these letters despite concerns raised about a no-match letter not making it to the appropriate party or taking too long. The DHS has noted that an employer can designate an office within a company to be the recipient of all mail from the DHS and the SSA.

12.19   Does verification through systems other than that described in this rule provide a safe harbor?

No, and this includes instances where the SSA provides options for SSN verification as well as the USCIS electronic employment verification system. But the DHS does note that it may choose to use prosecutorial discretion when employers take such steps.

12.20   Does an employer filing a labor certification or employment-based "green card" application have constructive knowledge that an employee is unauthorized?

The new rule includes language stating "an employee's request that the employer file a labor certification or employment-based visa petition on behalf of the employee" may be an example of a situation that may, depending on the totality of relevant circumstances, require an employer to take reasonable steps in order to avoid a finding of constructive knowledge. But the DHS notes that some employees are work authorized and are not necessarily unauthorized to work just because they request such sponsorship from an employer.

12.21   Does an employer have to help an employee resolve the discrepancy with the SSA or the DHS?

No. An employer merely needs to advise the employee of the time frame to resolve the discrepancy. Employers are not obligated to help resolve the question or share any guidance provided by the SSA.

12.22   In what manner must employers retain records required under the new rule?

The rule is flexible in this regard and employers may use any manner they choose. The rule permits employers to keep records alongside the I-9 form. Employers are encouraged to document telephone conversations as well as preserve all written correspondence.

12.23   If a new I-9 is prepared based on this rule, does that affect the amount of time the I-9 must be retained?

No. The original hire date remains the same even though the safe harbor procedure is used. So, for example, if an employee was hired several years ago, has the I-9 form prepared again, and then moves on to a new employer, the original date of hire applies for purposes of determining the one-year retention requirement.

12.24   Doesn't requiring an employee to fill out a new I-9 form per this rule constitute document abuse?

The DHS does not believe this is the case because any presented document that contained a suspect SSN or alien number would not be facially valid and it is proper for employers to require new documentation.

12.25   Won't this rule lead to massive firings across the country?

Many people are certainly worried that employers won't bother to go through the safe harbor procedures and will just panic and fire all employees who are the subject of these notices, or will simply decide not to expend the effort complying. The DHS denies that this is likely to be the case and has said the rule is in response to confusion under the current process.

12.26   Will an employer be liable for terminating an employee who turns out to be work authorized if they get a no-match letter?

If the employee is authorized to work and an employer does not go through the various safe harbor steps in the rule, then the employer might be liable in an unlawful termination suit.

12.27   What if the employee is gone by the time the no-match letter arrives?

An employer is not obligated to act on a no-match letter for employees no longer employed by them.

Mergers and Acquisitions

13.1   Generally speaking, how does immigration law factor into a merger, acquisition, or other major corporate transaction?

While U.S. immigration laws have been a factor in corporate transactions for decades, a massive increase in the enforcement of immigration laws and the proliferation of new rules should certainly have raised the profile of this subject amongst lawyers handling major corporate transactions. But survey transactional lawyers regarding how many address immigration issues in their due diligence inquiries, including adding immigration provisions to their agreements and dealing with immigration in their due diligence and pre-closing activities, and you're likely to get a very scant response.

Perhaps the lack of attention to immigration issues is the result of so many large law firms and in-house legal departments lacking immigration lawyers in their offices to educate them on the immigration issues. It may also be due to the fact that most immigration lawyers, even those at large law firms, focus their practice on filing visa petitions and simply lack a background in corporate law.

In any case, the community of lawyers working on these deals will need to quickly get up-to-speed and address these issues if they are to avoid an immigration "train wreck." Inheriting immigration problems is no longer a mere inconvenience for a company. Consider these developments:

- At the federal level, employers are suddenly being aggressively targeted by the DHS for worksite raids as well as compliance audits. Both can result in significant fines and even jail time.
- At the state level, new laws allow authorities to revoke business licenses and access to state contracts if employers are found to have immigration law violations.
- Employees on work visas are now suing companies for negligence in handling their immigration matters when actions of the company result in the employees falling out of legal status, having problems pursuing permanent residency, and potentially facing bars on coming back to the United States.
- Major companies like Wal-Mart are now including strong immigration compliance provisions in their vendor contracts, and having a history of immigration law violations can jeopardize doing business with such firms.
- Immigration is a major topic being covered by the media, and any companies with immigration law violations risk facing front-page coverage.

In some cases, companies pick up immigration problems that occurred prior to closing. In other instances, the actual closing of the deal triggers the immigration violations that create exposure. In other words, at the moment the transactional documents are signed, employees may find themselves converted into an illegal status and subject to deportation. And, unfortunately, these consequences are ticking time bombs that are frequently not discovered until long after the celebration of the closing has occurred and it is too late to reverse the damage.

If these concerns are not enough to convince the corporate attorney of the need to routinely deal with immigration in corporate transactions and warn clients of the immigration consequences, perhaps the threat of being found liable for legal malpractice will.

13.2   What are the major immigration risks associated with a merger, acquisition, or other major corporate transaction?

There are three major immigration risks associated with the closing of a transaction. First, the visas or pending applications of the employees could potentially be affected by the deal. Do petitions need to be transferred prior to closing? Are amendments required? Are any employees no longer eligible in the category under which they were petitioning?

Second, all employers in the U.S. are, of course, barred from hiring unauthorized employees and are required to maintain documentation (the I-9 form and supporting paperwork) demonstrating that each of their employees is legally permitted to work in the United States. Companies may also be required to file new paperwork regarding the status of all employees, and this paperwork may need to be completed on the actual day of closing or before.

13.3   What immigration law concepts come into play when discussing mergers and acquisitions?

Before assessing the immigration law implications of a transaction, a review of a few basic immigration and corporate law concepts is necessary.

Employees coming to the U.S. for employment normally hold either nonimmigrant or immigrant status. Nonimmigrant employees at corporations normally are in the H-1B, L, E, and TN visa categories as well as on training tied to J-1 and F-1 visas. Immigrant visas are held by those who have obtained lawful permanent residency. In the corporate transaction context, only nonimmigrant visa holders are considered since the transaction will not affect the status of "green card" holders. However, those in various stages of "green card" processing short of completion of the process could be impacted.

Employers are also federally mandated to verify the employment eligibility of all their employees via Form I-9, Employment Eligibility Verification. The Form I-9 must be completed on the day of hire and employees are required to present documents from a specific official list of documents deemed to demonstrate one's identity and employment authorization. Some employers also participate in the E-Verify system where an employee's work authorization is verified electronically by the DHS. Finally, some employers receive "no-match" letters from the SSA when the SSN and employee name do not match. Under a rule set to take effect soon, employers may be deemed to have knowledge that an employee is in the United States illegally when they receive such a letter and the name and number do not match.

The most common employment visa, the H-1B, is used for an "alien who is coming to perform services in a specialty occupation" in the United States. L visas are used for intracompany transferees who enter the U.S. to render services "in a capacity that is managerial, executive, or involves specialized knowledge," while E-1 and E-2 visas are used for "treaty traders and investors," and E-3s are used by Australians working in specialty occupations. The TN category includes "Canadian and Mexican citizens seeking temporary entry to engage in business activities at a professional level" as listed in the North American Free Trade Agreement (NAFTA). F-1 visas are held by students, many of whom are entitled to employment authorization for periods up to a year during and after completion of their studies. J-1 visas are held by exchange visitors in many categories including one that permits internship and training opportunities of 12 and 18 months.

Corporate changes that typically have immigration consequences are stock or asset acquisitions, mergers, consolidations, initial public offerings, spin-offs, corporate name changes, changes in payroll source, and the relocation of an employer or its employees.

Acquisitions involve the purchase of assets or stock. In an asset acquisition, the purchaser may not accept the liabilities of the seller. In a merger, two or more legal entities combine all their assets in what is called the "surviving entity." Other entities, which are called the "merged entities," cease to exist. The surviving entity assumes all of their liabilities. In a consolidation, however, two or more legal entities combine all their assets to form a new entity. The new entity assumes their liabilities, and they cease to exist. An initial public offering (IPO) changes the ownership structure of a corporation, similar to an acquisition. A spin-off involves the creation of a new company from a divestiture of shares or assets of an existing company.

There is no one-size-fits-all approach to advising clients regarding the immigration consequences of a merger or acquisition. Rather, there are a number of important questions to ask as the due diligence process begins. They include:
- How is the deal to be structured? Is it a merger or spin-off where employees will have a new employer with a different taxpayer identification number? Is it a stock purchase? Is it an asset acquisition where no liabilities are being assumed (or where just immigration liabilities are assumed)? Or is it a successor in interest where liabilities are to be assumed?
- What are the timing issues in the case? Is there enough time to file new petitions? Are employees going to suffer adverse consequences as a result of the timing? Is it possible to lease employees to the successor entity until the necessary transfer paperwork can be filed? Can filings be deferred until after the closing without a penalty or risk?
- For I-9 forms and E-Verify filings, will the documentation of the post-transaction entities survive? And, if so, does the convenience of not being required to have employees prepare new I-9s or to have to refile in E-Verify outweigh the risk of assuming liabilities associated with the old employer's prior filings?

These questions should initially be addressed in the due diligence request and in early discussions between the lawyers involved in the transaction. In most cases, immigration is not addressed in due diligence and many lawyers may not know where to begin in requesting documentation. Box 13.1 provides a sample immigration due diligence checklist.

The impact of a corporate change will vary from employee-to-employee depending on the type of visa or status they have and at what stage they are in their immigration process.

One goal of the due diligence process will be to determine whether the company that is the subject of the due diligence has complied with immigration laws and the scope of any potential liability. Another goal will be to identify what pre-closing and post-closing activities are required to ensure a smooth transition.

To meet those objectives, the due diligence review will cover the visa history of employees potentially affected by the transaction. The review will also test the I-9 compliance of the company that is the subject of the due diligence. This may take the shape of a full review of the I-9s or a sample audit if a full review is not practical. If a sampling determines that there are many problems, a full audit may be warranted.

Box 13.1 Sample: Immigration Due Diligence and Boilerplate Language

Below is a sample due diligence query that can be included with a request in a merger, acquisition, or other major corporate transaction.

1. Provide a list of all employees who are not U.S. lawful permanent residents or citizens. The list should break down employees by visa category, work authorization expiration date, number of years in a particular visa category, the employee's work site and whether any non-immigrant visa applications or extension petitions or permanent residency petitions are pending or promised. Also note any changes in job duties, location or salary that will occur as a result of the transaction.

2. For all employees listed above, please provide a copy of all documents relating to such employees' immigration status including, but not limited to:
    a. Nonimmigrant visa applications and extension petitions
    b. EADs
    c. I-9 forms
    d. Labor certification and immigrant visa applications and supporting documentation
    e. Approval notices and correspondence with any government agencies
    f. I-94 forms and passport visa stamps
    g. Visa documentation for the employees' spouses and minor children
    h. H-1B public access files

3. Provide copies of all correspondence with the SSA relating to the "mismatch" of SSNs for any employees.

4. Provide copies of any correspondence with agencies of the DHS, DOL, DOJ, or State Department regarding compliance with the country's immigration laws.

5. I-9s – [Provide a copy of all I-9s required to be kept by the employer] [Provide a list of all employees of the company employed since 1986. Counsel will select ____ employees from the list and request their I-9s be provided]

13.4   How are H-1B visas affected by mergers and acquisitions?

In an H-1B visa case, the questions to analyze are whether a corporate change results in a new employer and, if so, to what extent are the interests of the target corporation being assumed.

An H-1B visa requires separate applications to the DOL and the USCIS. A petitioner should first obtain an approved Labor Condition Application (LCA) from the DOL, and then should get its Form I-129, Petition for a Nonimmigrant Worker, approved by the USCIS.

Prior to December 2000, the DOL considered a change in an employer's federal Employer Identification Number (EIN) enough to trigger a need to file a new LCA. Under the rules adopted December 22, 2000, a new LCA will not be required merely because a corporate reorganization results in a change of corporate identity, regardless of whether there is a change in the EIN, provided that the successor entity, prior to the continued employment of the H-1B employee, agrees to assume the predecessor's obligations and liabilities under the LCA with a memorandum to the "public access file" kept for LCA purposes.

Material changes in the employee's duties and job requirements and the relocation of the employee may also require a new LCA. Therefore, if employees are relocated due to a merger or sale, new LCAs will be required for H-1B employees. (The DOL uses the Standard Metropolitan Statistical Area (SMSA) as criteria in determining the need for a new LCA. If the employee is relocated outside the SMSA, then a new filing is required.) However, a simple name change will not trigger the need for a new LCA.

The rules governing when a new I-129 petition must be filed are similar to the LCA rules, but not identical. The need to file a new I-129 can be a fairly expensive requirement. For each new employment petition, the employer must pay the American Competitiveness and Workforce Improvement Act fee, which was recently increased to $1,500 for companies with more than 25 employees (though it was dropped to $750 from $1,000 for smaller companies). Couple this with a new $500 fraud fee, a $320 base filing fee, and a $1,000 premium processing fee for fast adjudication and employers are looking at over $3,300 per employee.

The INA contains an exemption from filing a new I-129 petition in cases of corporate structuring where the new employer is a successor in interest that assumes the interests and the obligations of the prior employer. This is a restatement of the existing USCIS policy stating that if an employer, for H-1B purposes, "assumes the previous owner's liabilities which include the assertions the prior owner made on the labor condition application" then there is no need for a new or amended petition. If a new or amended petition is not needed, then the employer may wait until filing an extension petition for the employee to notify the USCIS.

One potential pitfall involving H-1B employees relates to the dependency provisions in the H-1B statute. Employers with over a certain number or a certain percentage of H-1B employees are considered "H-1B dependent" and such companies face tight restrictions in terms of documenting recruiting efforts and hiring H-1Bs before and after lay offs. The numbers will need to be recalculated for a company after a transaction and this could dramatically affect a company's bottom line. Companies that are H-1B dependent should also signal further scrutiny since it may be the result of prior H-1B violations, and this could mean a company may be inheriting a company with a poor history of compliance.

An issue likely to affect only a small number of employers (particularly in the health care sector) involves loss of eligibility for cap-exempt status. If an employer's status as exempt from the quota limitations on H-1B visas was the basis for an employee's H-1B status, the corporate practitioner will want to examine whether cap-exempt status is lost after the closing. This may happen, for example, when a nonprofit entity is replaced by a for-profit entity as a sponsoring employer. A loss of H-1B cap-exempt status could make it impossible for an employee to continue being employed by the succeeding entity as an H-1B status holder.

13.5   What impact do mergers, acquisitions, and other major corporate transactions have on TN visas?

Since LCAs are not required for obtaining a TN visa or status for a citizen of Canada or Mexico, a basic successor-in-interest analysis is required to determine how to proceed here. If the new company succeeds to the interests of the prior company, new petitions are not required. The fact that a company may change nationality won't matter in these cases because the TN visa is tied to the employee's nationality, not the company's.

13.6   How are L-1 intracompany transfers affected by mergers, acquisitions, and other major corporate transactions?

For an L-1 visa, the law requires a qualifying relationship between the U.S. entity and the foreign entity from which the employee will be transferring. This relationship must be within the definitions of a "parent, branch, affiliate or subsidiary" as defined by the USCIS. Obviously, changes in the ownership structure of either one of the entities may terminate the qualifying relationship and, consequently, invalidate the underlying L visas. However, if the petitioner, after a corporate change, can document that the qualifying relationship survives, then only an amended petition will be necessary.

For affiliated companies, if the ownership breakdown of the overseas entity and the U.S. entities changes, the qualifying relationship may no longer be there. Also, if the U.S. company is sold to another international company, the L-1 may survive even if the original foreign entity is no longer part of the corporate family. The key will be whether the company still maintains an overseas office.

Finally, companies will want to look at issues pertaining to the "blanket L." Blanket L-1s are available to companies who prequalify with the USCIS and can show they are large multinational operations with a large volume of L-1 filings. A transaction may render a company too small or suddenly large enough to qualify for a blanket L filing. From a strategic point of view, if a company can qualify for a blanket L under a merged entity's qualification after a transaction, it may be possible to add the new entity and then employees can be covered under the blanket.

13.7   How are E visas affected by mergers, acquisitions, or other major corporate transactions?

Under the E-1 and E-2 visas, certain investors and traders may be admitted to and employed in the U.S., if a treaty-qualifying company petitions and obtains status for them. A company is qualified based on its nationality. A corporate change may change a corporation's nationality and, therefore, result in the termination of the qualification. The USCIS regulations specifically state that prior USCIS approval must be obtained when there has been a "fundamental change" in a company's characteristics, including in the case of a merger, acquisition, or sale.

The new E-3 visa for nationals of Australia is similar in many respects to the H-1B including in the requirement for the filing of a LCA. The same considerations applicable to the H-1B apply here. Note that E-3 status is tied to the nationality of the employee, not the company. In that respect, it is similar to the TN visa in not being affected per se by a change of a company's nationality.

13.8   How are permanent residency applications affected by mergers, acquisitions, and other major corporate transactions?

A lawful permanent residency (LPR) application normally consists of three steps. First, the employer usually must prove that, despite reasonable recruitment efforts, it has not been able to find a domestic employee to fill the alien's position. This is called the "labor certification" and is handled through the DOL. Second, the employer files a Form I-140, Immigrant Petition for Alien Worker, with the USCIS. After the I-140 petition is approved, the employee files a petition for the adjustment of his or her immigration status to the status of a lawful permanent resident with the USCIS.

The DOL takes a liberal view of when a new labor certification petition must be refiled. If after an acquisition, a new owner remains the employee's employer and has assumed all of the past owner's obligations, the new owner should qualify as a successor in interest and a labor certification will survive.

In LPR cases, the USCIS traditionally used a stricter version of the successor-in-interest theory and permitted an employer to continue with the prior employer's petition, only if the new employer assumed all of the prior employer's liabilities. Without successorship, a new I-140 petition may be necessary even when an adjustment of status application is already pending.

The LPR process may take several years and, until recently, unless the case did fit under certain exceptions, beneficiaries of immigrant petitions were not able to change employers until the completion of the entire process. Therefore, corporate changes that created a new employer potentially caused further delays. Legislation now makes it possible in many instances to change employers while an adjustment application is pending. An adjustment application pending six months or more will survive if an employee finds new employment in the same or a very similar occupation. The sponsoring employers may, in some cases, want to consider leasing an employee to the new entity for a period of time in order to ensure that the portability rule is available.

Unfortunately, because of long "green card" backlogs, many applicants are not in a position to file a Form I-485, Application to Register Permanent Resident or Adjust Status. Hence, the applicant may find that a petition becomes worthless if the original job offer disappears.

Aside from labor certification cases, some employees pursue permanent residency through an intracompany transfer-based I-140 petition. In these cases, a labor certification is not required. In these cases, many of the same issues regarding maintaining a qualifying relationship as apply in an L-1 case will arise. However, if a case has advanced far enough, the portability rule noted above may apply as well.

Some permanent residency petitions are based on self-sponsorship by an applicant. These include national interest petitions and EB-1 extraordinary ability cases. These matters are normally not affected by a major transaction except that in some cases, an employment relationship is how an applicant demonstrates that he or she will work in the field upon approval of permanent residency. If the transaction will result in an employee losing the position, this could, in theory, affect qualifying for EB-1 or EB-2 status.

13.9   How are Form I-9s affected by a merger, acquisition, or other major corporate transaction?

Finally, a successor also assumes the I-9 liabilities of a corporation. Failure to comply with I-9 requirements may result in serious sanctions running into thousands of dollars per employee. Therefore, before a corporate restructuring, the transition team should examine the I-9 compliance of the entity by either a sample I-9 audit or a review of the alien employees' I-9s.

If a company does not assume the liabilities of the acquired corporation, I-9 forms are generally required of all the employees and in the case of a merged entity which is completely new, I-9s may be needed for all employees of both entities.

The good news here may be that a successor in interest can assume the I-9s in place at the time of closing. But many companies will want to consider, as a matter of course, requiring that all employees of an acquired or merged entity complete new I-9s on the date of closing in order to ensure that past violations are not continued and also to ensure that they have a handle on which employees have a temporary EAD that will require reverification at a later time. Of course, the employer needs to be careful to require that all employees fill out a new I-9, as opposed to singling out some.

13.10 What are some general tips from employers going through a merger, acquisition, or other major corporate transaction?

- Ensure visas are transferred to a new employer prior to closing, when a closing will affect their validity.
- File amendments before or shortly after closing (unless regulations specifically require filing before closing).
- Move employees to new visa categories before the closing when they will no longer be eligible in a particular category post-closing.
- In cases where a closing will void a visa status, employ an employee in an employee-leasing arrangement in order to continue the employer-employee relationship.
- Start "green card" processing early in order to minimize the number of nonimmigrant visas requiring attention.

Immigration queries should be incorporated into the due diligence inquiry, and representations and warranties (see Box 13.2) addressing immigration issues should be incorporated into the transaction documents.

Box 13.2 Sample: Contract Representation and Warranty

Below is sample language that can be adapted for inclusion in agreement language associated with a merger, acquisition, or other major corporate transaction.

Immigration. All necessary visa or work authorization petitions have been timely and properly filed on behalf of any employees requiring a visa stamp, I-94 status document, EAD, or any other immigration document to legally work in the United States. All paperwork retention requirements with respect to such applications and petitions have been met. No employees have ever worked without employment authorization from the Department of Homeland Security or any other government agency that must authorize such employment and any employment of foreign nationals has complied with applicable immigration laws. I-9 Forms have been timely and properly completed for all employees hired since the establishment of the company or the effective date of the Immigration Reform and Control Act of 1986, whichever is earlier. I-9 Forms have been lawfully retained and re-verified. There are no claims, lawsuits, actions, arbitrations, administrative or other proceedings, governmental investigations or inquiries pending or threatened against the Company relating to the Company's compliance with local, state or federal immigration regulations, including, but not limited to, compliance with any immigration laws except for employees named in schedule __.

There have been no letters received from the Social Security Administration (SSA) regarding the failure of an employee's SSN to match their name in the SSA database. There have been no letters or other correspondence received from the Department of Homeland Security or other agencies regarding the employment authorization of any employees. If the Company operates in a state or has contracts with a state of Federal agency that requires or provides a safe harbor if an employer participates in the Department of Homeland Security's e-Verify electronic employment verification system, the Company has been participating in e-Verify for the entire period such participation has been required or available as a safe harbor or as long as the company has been operating in such state or contracting with such agency.

Criminal Law and Employer Immigration Law Compliance (with Jonathan L. Marks)

In fiscal year 2007, ICE dramatically imposed more than $30 million in fines against employers while making 863 criminal arrests and 4,077 administrative arrests. This is a dramatic increase from prior years and all signs point to even more enforcement in the coming years (see Figure 14.1).

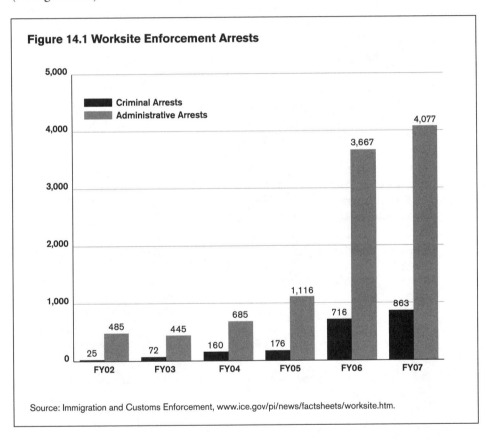

Figure 14.1 Worksite Enforcement Arrests

Source: Immigration and Customs Enforcement, www.ice.gov/pi/news/factsheets/worksite.htm.

In the past, employers largely worried about simply being fined for violations of IRCA and had little else with which to be concerned. However, the dramatic increase in criminal enforcement actions has changed the dynamic and employers need to be more concerned about avoiding criminal sanctions. (See Appendix A.)

14.1 Which agency is responsible for worksite enforcement operations?

ICE is primarily responsible for employer enforcement actions. Depending on the facts of the case, enforcement actions can also involve the DOJ and local U.S. Attorney's Offices, the IRS, the SSA, the DOL, other federal agencies, various state agencies, and local law enforcement.

14.2 **On what grounds are criminal arrests being made and criminal charges being brought in worksite enforcement operations?**

Companies and company officials can be charged under a variety of statutes in an immigration enforcement case. They include:

- Criminal sections of IRCA.
- Racketeer Influenced and Corrupt Organizations Act (RICO).
- Statutes that prohibit false statements and false identity documents.
- Mail fraud and wire fraud.
- Money laundering.

These charges can lead to, among other things:

- Tax evasion charges.
- Charges for structuring of monetary transactions.
- Forfeitures of assets and proceeds of the conduct.

14.3 **What types of employers are more likely to be targeted?**

Any employer may be targeted for worksite enforcement. However, there are factors that may increase the odds of being the subject of a criminal or administrative action. They include:

- The employer has previously been the subject of an audit.
- The employer provides services in an area connected to "critical infrastructure" or national security.
- The employer is in an industry known to have a high rate of employing unauthorized immigrants (e.g., construction trades, restaurants, and warehouses).
- The employer has received Social Security no-match letters.

Critical infrastructure and national security sites would include military bases, defense facilities, nuclear power plants, chemical plants, airports, and ports. Obviously terrorism threats since September 11, 2001, have dramatically increased surveillance work at facilities of this type.

14.4 **What is the difference between an administrative arrest and a criminal arrest?**

An administrative arrest in the immigration context refers to the detaining of an individual on suspicion of being an unauthorized immigrant. The person will be placed in deportation proceedings. A criminal arrest can result in criminal charges which, if they result in conviction, can lead to prison sentences, supervised release (the equivalent of probation), fines, and forfeiture of assets and proceeds.

14.5 **Are employees of a company who are not owners potentially liable for criminal violations?**

Yes. In many cases, nonowners have been held liable, including human resource managers, plant managers, supervisors, union stewards, and corporate officers. Also, the company itself can be held criminally liable.

14.6 **What is the offense of "unlawfully employing illegal aliens"?**

IRCA makes it unlawful "to hire, or to recruit or refer for a fee, for employment in the U.S., an alien knowing the alien is an unauthorized alien." It is also unlawful to continue to employ someone if an employer later finds out that an employee is unauthorized.

14.7 **What are the penalties for "unlawfully employing illegal aliens"?**

Violators can be punished with criminal penalties and injunctions. Unlawfully employing illegal aliens would be considered a misdemeanor, as opposed to a felony. Anyone engaged in a "pattern or practice of violations" can be fined up to $3,000 for each unauthorized alien and imprisoned up to six months for the entire pattern or practice.

14.8   What defenses may be available to the charge of "unlawfully employing illegal aliens"?

Employers may avoid criminal liability under IRCA if they can demonstrate that they lacked knowledge that an employee was unauthorized to work or that they acted in a good-faith manner to comply with IRCA's requirements.

14.9   What is the crime of "bringing in and harboring" unauthorized immigrants?

The INA makes it a crime for anyone who:

- Knowing that a person is an alien, brings to or attempts to bring to the U.S. the person at a place other than a designated port of entry regardless of whether the alien previously received authorization to enter the United States.
- Knowing or in reckless disregard of the fact that an alien has come to the United States illegally, transports such alien within the U.S. in furtherance of such violation of the law.
- Knowing or in reckless disregard of the fact that an alien has come to the U.S. in violation of the law, "conceals, harbors, or shields from detection" such alien in any place, including any building or any means of transportation.
- Encourages or induces an alien to come to, enter, or reside in the U.S. knowing or in reckless disregard of the fact that coming to the U.S. is a violation of law.
- Knowing or in reckless disregard of the fact that an alien has not received prior official authorization to enter or reside in the U.S., brings to or attempts to bring to the U.S. such alien.

In some circumstances, individuals who conspire with or aid or abet others in committing these offenses can be charged as well. In addition, charges can also be brought for attempting these prohibited acts depending on the situation. Employers can be guilty of these offenses if they had actual knowledge of an employee's immigration status or, depending on the situation, if they "recklessly disregarded" the fact that the person was an alien. Reckless disregard has sometimes been construed to mean circumstances in which an employer is aware of, but consciously disregards facts and circumstances that the person was an alien.

14.10   What are the potential penalties for "bringing in and harboring" unauthorized immigrants?

For anyone bringing someone into the U.S. illegally, the penalty is up to 10 years imprisonment and a fine of up to $250,000, or both.

For transporting, concealing, harboring, shielding from detection, or encouraging or inducing, the penalty is up to five years imprisonment and a fine of up to $250,000, or both. If a person is found guilty of any of these offenses and it was done "for the purpose of commercial or private financial gain," the maximum prison sentence rises to 10 years.

For aiding and abetting any of these kinds of offenses, the maximum prison sentence is five years and a fine of up to $250,000, or both.

For conspiring to commit any of these offenses, the maximum prison sentence is 10 years and a fine of up to $250,000, or both.

If anyone is seriously injured or anyone's life is endangered, the maximum jail sentence will increase to 20 years. If someone is killed, the penalty can be death or up to life in prison.

If a person is found guilty of bringing or attempting to bring into the U.S. an alien who has not received prior official authorization to enter or reside in the U.S., the maximum penalty is one year. But if that act is committed "for the purpose of commercial advantage or private financial gain," a sentence of 3-to-10 years for a first or second violation may be imposed and 5-to-15 years for subsequent violations.

Maximum jail times for each of these offenses can be increased by another 10 years if the offense was part of an ongoing commercial organization, immigrants were transported in groups of 10 or more, the aliens were transported in a very dangerous manner, or the aliens presented a life-threatening health risk to people in the United States.

Punishment can also include the forfeiture of the proceeds of the violation.

14.11 What is the crime of hiring more than 10 unauthorized immigrants?

The INA makes it a crime to hire at least 10 individuals with actual knowledge that the individuals are unauthorized aliens illegally brought into the United States.

14.12 What is the penalty for hiring more than 10 unauthorized immigrants?

Violators can be punished by up to five years imprisonment, a fine, and forfeiture of the proceeds of the violation.

14.13 What crimes involving false statements have been used to charge employers in cases involving unauthorized immigrants?

It is a crime to knowingly and willfully make a materially false statement or representation in any matter within the jurisdiction of any branch of the U.S. government. It is also a crime to make or use in such matters a document knowing that the document contains any materially false statement. Additionally, it is a crime to falsify, conceal, or cover up by any trick, scheme, or device a material fact in such matters. A statement has been considered material if it has the tendency to influence or is capable of influencing a governmental entity. Though this prohibition is not uniquely applied to instances of unauthorized immigrants, it has been used by the government to charge employers in connection with information communicated or presented to the government.

14.14 What is the penalty for making false statements?

Violators can be imprisoned for up to five years and fined up to $250,000, or both.

14.15 What fraud and identity theft offenses potentially apply to employers of unauthorized immigrants?

It is a federal crime to:

- Knowingly and without lawful authority produce an identification document.
- Knowingly transfer such a document knowing it was stolen or produced without lawful authority.
- Possess such a document with the intent that it will be used to defraud the United States.
- Possess an identification document of the U.S. knowing that the document was stolen or produced without lawful authority.

It is also a crime to knowingly transfer, possess, or use without lawful authority another person's identification with the intent to violate federal law, commit a felony under state or local law, or to aid and abet such wrongdoing. The prohibition applies to documents issued by the U.S. or, if the offense involves or affects interstate commerce, documents issued by a state or political subdivision of a state.

Employers in several cases around the country have been accused of violating these provisions, including circumstances in which employers assisted employees in obtaining false documents. Such employers can be viewed as assisting workers in making it appear that an employee is authorized.

It should be noted that states are also tightening document fraud and identity theft rules and employers could face prosecution under these rules as well.

14.16   What penalties may be imposed on employers convicted of document fraud and identity theft?

Employers violating these rules may be imprisoned for up to five years and fined up to $250,000, or both. The potential penalty increases up to 15 years if the offense involved a fraudulent identification document that is a federal document (e.g., a passport), birth certificate, driver's license, or personal identification card, the production or transfer of five or more documents, or the transfer, possession, or use of a document with the intent to violate federal law or commit a felony under state law, and the offense resulted in obtaining anything of value worth $1,000 or more.

14.17   What is the crime of mail fraud?

It is a crime for a person to devise, or participate in, a scheme to defraud, or to obtain money or property by false representations, if the person does so with the intent to defraud and if, for the purpose of carrying out or attempting to carry out the scheme or misrepresentation, the person used or caused another person to use the U.S. mails or a commercial interstate carrier (e.g., Federal Express). The item mailed or sent by interstate carrier need not itself be fraudulent as long as the use of the mails or interstate carrier furthered the wrongdoing.

14.18   What is the crime of wire fraud?

It is a crime for a person to devise, or participate in, a scheme to defraud, or to obtain money or property by false representations, if the person does so with the intent to defraud and if, for the purpose of carrying out or attempting to carry out the scheme or misrepresentation, the person transmitted or caused another person to transmit by wire, radio, or television in interstate commerce some communication. As with mail fraud, the communication sent by interstate wire need not itself be fraudulent as long as the use of an interstate wire transmission furthered the wrongdoing.

14.19   What are the potential penalties for mail fraud and wire fraud?

Violators of either the mail fraud or wire fraud statutes can be imprisoned for up to 20 years and fined up to $250,000, or both. If a violation of these statutes affects a financial institution, the penalties can be increased up to 30 years' imprisonment and a $1 million fine, or both.

14.20   What is the crime of money laundering and how does it apply to employers?

The federal crime of money laundering punishes a person who conducts a financial transaction with property that represents the proceeds of "specified unlawful activity" with the intent to promote the carrying on of "specified unlawful activity." It is also a crime to conduct a financial transaction with property that represents the proceeds of specified unlawful activity, knowing that the transaction was deigned to conceal or disguise the nature, the location, the source, the ownership, or the control of the proceeds of specified unlawful activity. Money laundering also involves a person knowingly engaging in a monetary transaction with property derived from specified unlawful activity and having a value of more than $10,000. "Specified unlawful activity" includes the crimes of harboring unauthorized aliens, employing 10 or more unauthorized aliens, mail fraud, and wire fraud. Thus, for example, if an employer were to knowingly employ 10 or more unauthorized aliens and such employment generated funds, the employer could be guilty of money laundering if the employer engaged in a financial transaction with those funds with the intent to carry on the crime of employing unauthorized aliens or in order to hide the source of the funds. Similarly, a employer could be charged with money laundering if that employer engaged in a monetary transaction involving more than $10,000 derived from employing 10 or more unauthorized aliens.

The government has been aggressively pressing money-laundering charges in enforcement cases under a theory that employers who knowingly employ unauthorized immigrants are often using the money gained from such illegal employment to further a criminal enterprise that continues to hire illegally such employees.

14.21   What are the penalties for money laundering?

Depending on which money-laundering statute is charged, violators can be imprisoned for up to 10 years and fined up to $250,000 or both, or imprisoned for up to 20 years and fined up to $500,000 or twice the value of the property involved in the transaction. Additionally, the government can seek forfeiture of any property involved in the offense or any property traceable to such property.

14.22   What is the crime of fraud and misuse of visas and permits?

It is a federal crime to use or attempt to use, possess, obtain, accept, or receive a forged immigrant or nonimmigrant visa, permit, border-crossing card, alien registration receipt card, or other document prescribed for entry into the U.S. or for employment in the U.S., knowing that the document is forged, altered, or obtained by fraud. It is also a federal crime to, under oath, knowingly subscribe as true any false statement about a material fact in any application or other document required by the immigration laws or regulations or to knowingly present such a document which contains a false statement. Also criminal would be for a person to use an identification document, knowing or having reason to know, that the document was not lawfully issued to the possessor or that the document is false, for the purpose of meeting the employee verification requirements under the INA.

14.23   What are the penalties for fraud and misuse of visas and permits?

Violators of these provisions can be fined up to $250,000 or, depending on which provision is involved, imprisoned for up to five years or 15 years, or both.

14.24   What is "misuse of an SSN"?

It is unlawful for any person to falsely represent, with intent to deceive, that an SSN assigned to one person is, in fact, assigned to another person. It is also a crime to use an SSN obtained based on submitting false information to the Commissioner of Social Security.

14.25   What is the penalty for "misuse of an SSN"?

Anyone found to have unlawfully misused an SSN can be fined up to $250,000 or imprisoned for up to five years, or both.

14.26   What is RICO?

The Racketeer Influenced and Corrupt Organizations Act (RICO) was originally enacted to address organized crime, though it has been used in a wide variety of circumstances to punish repeated criminal acts typically carried out through an entity, organization, or group. Thus, it is criminal for any person employed by or associated with an enterprise to conduct or participate in the conduct of the affairs of that enterprise through a pattern of racketeering activity. An "enterprise" can include a partnership, a corporation, an association, or other legal entity, or even a group of associated individuals. A "pattern of racketeering activity" typically involves two or more violations of certain identified laws. Among the offenses that can lead to RICO charges would be repeated acts of harboring unauthorized aliens, employing 10 or more unauthorized aliens, mail fraud, and wire fraud.

14.27   What are the penalties for violation of the RICO Act?

Persons convicted of criminal RICO violations can be fined up to $250,000, imprisoned for up to 20 years, and subject to civil forfeiture of property.

14.28   What types of penalties are typically being imposed on employers convicted in connection with unauthorized immigrants?

While the statutes under which employers are charged usually set a maximum term of incarceration, judges imposing sentences have greater flexibility and sentences are almost always considerably below the maximum. A recent sampling of prison terms imposed reflects sentences ranging from two months to five years, with an average sentence of two years in cases in which a prison term was actually imposed. Terms of imprisonment are often followed by a term of supervised release which is similar to probation. Some cases, however, have involved probation rather than imprisonment. A recent sampling of terms of probation in cases in which probation was imposed rather than imprisonment reflects probation terms from one-to-five years, with an average of two years. Forfeiture of assets and fines are also being imposed. There have been instances of fines as high as $175,000 and of forfeiture of assets as high as $12 million.

14.29   What is "seizure and forfeiture"?

Employers found to be liable for certain criminal offenses can be subject to having seized any assets that are deemed to be the fruits of such wrongdoing. While IRCA fines typically have not amounted to more than $100,000, seized assets in harboring and money-laundering cases have involved millions of dollars.

14.30   Is it more likely ICE will pursue a worksite enforcement charge or a criminal investigation?

While criminal prosecutions were rare in the past, over the last two years, ICE has clearly moved to favoring criminal charges over administrative fines alone. The numbers reflect this shift. The General Accounting Office (GAO) reported that the number of notices of intent to fine dropped from 417 in 1999 to three in 2004, while the number of criminal arrests rose from 25 in fiscal year 2002 to 863 in fiscal year 2007. ICE also obtained more than $31 million in fines in 2007.

14.31   What should you do if an ICE agent arrives at your place of business in connection with an investigation of immigration violations?

There is no one-size-fits-all answer to this question and to some extent the answer depends on whether the investigator is seeking to conduct an on-site inspection immediately, where your I-9 forms are kept, how careful your company has been with respect to I-9 compliance, whether the ICE officer has a notice of inspection and subpoena or a search warrant, and other factors. The best approach is to consult with immigration counsel and develop a set of protocols for reacting to such a visit or raid ahead of time. Employers and their counsel will need to balance a variety of considerations including antagonizing an ICE officer and unnecessarily leading to more hostile treatment versus protecting the employer's rights.

But there are some basic items to put on the protocol list in most cases, including:

- Instructing the receptionist and other employees to immediately contact a designated manager or company official and inform him or her which agency is conducting the inspection.
- Contacting immigration counsel immediately.
- Trying to note the names of officials and any comments made including any references to alleged violations.
- Not consenting to a search until counsel is consulted.
- Not destroying or tampering with Form I-9s.

- Not consenting to the removal of Form I-9s or the copying of Form I-9s by ICE officials without consulting with counsel.
- Insisting on three days' notice for an inspection as required by law.
- Designating one person to communicate with an inspector.

Layoffs and Downsizing

15.1 **What are the immigration related consequences of layoffs on alien employees in nonimmigrant status?**

For employers that employ foreign nationals, the company's alien workforce consists of two separate groups of employees: nonimmigrant workers and immigrant workers. Nonimmigrant workers usually fall under the H-1B, L, E, and TN temporary visa categories. The most common nonimmigrant employment visa, H-1B, is used for an "alien who is coming to perform services in a specialty occupation" in the United States. L visas are used for intra-company transferees that enter the U.S. to render services "in a capacity that is managerial, executive, or involves specialized knowledge," while E visas are used for "treaty traders and investors" as well as Australian specialty occupation workers. Finally, the TN category includes "Canadian and Mexican citizens seeking temporary entry to engage in business activities at a professional level" as listed in the North American Free Trade Agreement. As compared to nonimmigrant workers, immigrant workers are those who have obtained or are in the process of obtaining lawful permanent residency.

Nonimmigrant work visas are generally issued for the specific purpose of employment with a particular employer. Thus, a nonimmigrant residing in the U.S. under one of the temporary work visa categories is legally authorized to remain in the U.S. only as long as they are employed with the particular employer noted in their visa application. If the employee is laid off, they immediately lose their visa status. As a result, employers that lay off nonimmigrant employees with little or no notice put these individuals in the difficult situation of having to quickly find an alternative visa status in order to remain legally in the United States. If the nonimmigrant employee cannot secure an alternative status, he or she must choose between remaining in this country illegally or leaving everything behind and returning to their home country to possibly seek a new visa status from abroad.

If the nonimmigrant is married, or has children, his or her dependants must also leave the country as their legal status is derived from the visa status of the nonimmigrant worker. This can be particularly hard when, for example, children must be pulled out of school in the middle of the school year or someone in the family is receiving regular treatment for a medical condition. And returning to legal status once an employee becomes illegally present can be extremely difficult.

Securing an alternative visa status without notice, or with only a little notice, is not easy, but the employee needs to act very quickly once he or she learns of the termination. Even if the nonimmigrant is fortunate enough to secure an alternate employment offer, he or she will not be permitted to begin work for the new employer under most nonimmigrant work visa categories until a new visa petition is actually approved, something which could take up to several months. An exception is available to those working under the H-1B visa category. Those workers may normally start work for a new employer immediately upon filing a new visa petition.

A more likely scenario is for the employee to file to change to visitor status. This strategy will allow the worker to remain legally in the U.S., though not authorized to work. As long as the application is filed while the worker remains employed, the worker will remain in status for up to 120 days while the visitor change of status application is pending. The worker will also have to file a new nonimmigrant application once a new position is found.

For those previously holding an H-1B filing for a new H-1B, H-1B "portability" remains available in most cases and work for the new employer can begin immediately upon filing the new H-1B change of status petition. One additional good piece of news for H-1B visa holders, however, is that if a worker was counted against the H-1B cap for the prior position, the worker should not need to be counted again and the new employer does not need to go through the H-1B lottery.

L-1, E-1, and E-2 applicants very often need to find a new visa category to remain in the United States. Because L-1s are intracompany transfers and must be working for an employer that employed them for a year outside the U.S. within the prior three, the odds are pretty low that they will qualify to work for a different employer in the same status. So changing to another nonimmigrant category will likely be necessary. E-1 and E-2 status is tied to working for an employer with the same nationality as the employee. In order to remain in the E-1 or E-2 status, the worker must find another employer from his or her country and be employed in a managerial, executive or essential skills position. Like the L-1 employee, a laid off E-1 or E-2 worker will probably need to switch to another nonimmigrant visa category. TN and E-3 workers are in better shape because if they can find a job in the same occupation and, in the case of an E-3, are paid the prevailing wage, their status can continue with a new employer.

In situations where the nonimmigrant remains in the U.S. in a visa category that prohibits employment or while an employment-based visa is pending, the individual is generally not eligible to collect any type of unemployment compensation under most states laws because unemployment statutes usually require that an individual must be available to work and authorized to accept work to be eligible for unemployment compensation. Thus, unlike their U.S. counterparts, these alien workers must get by without any supplemental income during this interim period even though unemployment taxes were deducted from their wages while they were employed.

15.2 What should a nonimmigrant employee do if they fall out of legal status?

If the nonimmigrant employee is unable to secure a legal visa status after being laid off, any time spent out of status has the potential to create significant future problems that the nonimmigrant often does not realize. Even minor periods of time spent out of legal status can render the nonimmigrant ineligible for certain immigration benefits. For example, in the final stage of the green card process, an individual usually has the choice of completing the process from within the U.S. (referred to as adjustment of status) or at the U.S. Consulate located in their home country. However, individuals who have spent any period of time out of status are potentially not eligible to adjust status and must endure the disruption of having to return home to complete their green card process. Furthermore, USCIS has recently begun cracking down on workers who engage in any unlawful employment even after an adjustment application has been filed. An adjustment applicant must therefore be very careful to make sure that he or she has a valid employment authorization card just in case he or she loses their nonimmigrant work status.

Individuals who spend longer periods of time out of status are faced with considerably more serious consequences. Under immigration law, individuals who are unlawfully present in the U.S. for a period of six months to one year are barred from reentering the U.S. for three years. Individuals unlawfully present in the U.S. for over one year are barred for 10 years.

Persons in this situation may be able to convince an examiner to exercise discretion and approve a late-filed change of status petition based on extraordinary circumstances beyond the control of the alien. But a prudent person should assume the decision will be no and should be cognizant of the fact that the longer a person remains out of status, the harder it will be convince a consular officer to approve a visa.

15.3   Is there a grace period allowing a period of time for an H-1B worker to find a new position without being considered out of status?

No. Workers terminated from their positions are considered out of status immediately upon their termination unless they have a change of status petition filed before they are terminated. During the recession in 2001, USCIS announced that the agency did not provide or recognize any "grace period" for maintaining H-1B status. While USCIS suggested it was considering allowing a 60 day grace period in a June 2001 memorandum, nothing ever came of the proposal and no grace period is available to laid off H-1B workers.

There is a 10 day grace period following the expiration of the admission period noted on the Form I-94, but this would not apply to prematurely terminated workers.

Note, however, that when employees are given a notice of termination from employment, but the employee continues to receive salary and benefits after the employee is no longer coming in to the place of employment, the rules are more liberal. For example, under the WARN Act, some employees are given 60 days notice prior to a layoff or plant closing. The salary may appear on the pay stub as a lump sum paid up front, but it is based upon a pro rata salary until a future date.

According to an American Immigration Lawyers Association/USCIS liaison meeting from February 25, 2009, if an employee finds a new position and the new employer files an H-1B petition after the worker has stopped coming in to the first employer, the employee would be considered to still be in status. The employee would need to provide pay statements with documentation from the previous employer documenting that the employee's final date of pay and benefits.

15.4   What are the immigration related consequences of layoffs on alien employees with pending green card applications?

For employees with pending green card applications, a layoff can present different problems. Often, after having an opportunity to evaluate an alien employee's skills and future potential, an employer will agree to sponsor the alien for lawful permanent residency status, commonly referred to as "green card" status. A lawful permanent residency (LPR) application generally consists of three steps. First, through a process called labor certification or PERM, the employer must prove to the satisfaction of the DOL that it has not been able to find a domestic employee to fill the alien's position. Second, after the labor certification is complete, the employer files an immigrant petition with the USCIS. Finally, after the immigrant petition is approved, the employee files a petition for the adjustment of his or her immigration status to the status of a lawful permanent resident with the USCIS. The entire LPR process may take several years.

The LPR process is predicated on the idea of granting an alien permanent work authorization to work for a particular employer in a particular position. Thus, alien employees who are laid off during the first two steps of the LPR process cannot continue with their application, and must restart the entire process with another employer if they remain interested in securing LPR status. Alien employees laid off during the third step of the process may or may not be able to continue the LPR process depending on their situation.

Historically, alien employees could not switch employers before their status was adjusted without risking invalidation of their underlying immigrant petition. However, under a law passed in October 2000, an alien employee whose adjustment of status application has been pending for over six months can now switch employers without validating his or her immigrant petition as long as they will be working in a position similar to the position noted in their labor certification and immigrant petition. Obviously, during a recession, finding work in one's occupation may not be easy and if a worker accepts employment in field not closely related to the field that served as the basis for the green card application, adjustment portability may not be available. Note also that the worker must be working in the new position at the time the adjustment petition is adjudicated.

15.5   What are the immigration related consequences of layoffs on alien employees who are already permanent residents?

For alien workers who have already secured LPR status, the impact of being laid off is not much different from that of a U.S. worker. The alien green card holder would continue to be in lawful permanent residency status while he or she looks for new employment. Many immigrants who have recently obtained their green card status may be rightfully concerned about leaving their positions too quickly after getting permanent residency. The USCIS will sometimes accuse an individual of not having appropriate intentions when they got permanent residency. However, an involuntary termination of employment will not trigger that type of problem since the applicant presumably did not intend to leave the employer. Also, depending on the applicable state law, the alien LPR might be eligible for unemployment compensation because he or she is lawfully present in the U.S. and is available and authorized to accept employment.

15.6   What are the immigration related consequences of layoffs on employers employing foreign nationals?

When downsizing includes laying off a company's alien workers, the employer must be cognizant of its affirmative duties under immigration law with respect to those workers. For most employment-related visa types, the employer has an affirmative responsibility to notify the USCIS when an alien's employment has been terminated so that USCIS can revoke the individual's visa. In the case *Administrator, Wage & Hour Div. v. Help Foundation of Omaha, Inc. et al.*, the court held that an employer was liable for back wages to a worker when the employer failed to notify USCIS of the termination in employment. With respect to H-1B employees, the employer also must provide the H-1B worker return transportation to their home country at the employer's expense.

In the H-1B context, these affirmative responsibilities are particularly important because employers that do not comply with these obligations run the risk of being subject to continuing wage obligations for the H-1B employee. Under the anti-benching provisions of the H-1B regulations, an employer must continue to pay an H-1B employee their normal wages during any time spent in nonproductive status "due to the decision of the employer." In a layoff situation, the employer's payment obligation ends only if there has been a "bona fide" termination of the employment relationship, which the DOL will deem to have occurred when the employer notifies the USCIS of the termination, the H-1B petition is canceled, and the return fare obligation is fulfilled.

In addition to complying with its affirmative immigration obligations when laying off alien workers, an employer must also be aware of other possible consequences of its downsizing strategy, particularly with respect to the H-1B visa program. One possible issue that could arise in a layoff scenario concerns severance benefits provided by the employer. Under H-1B regulations, all employers employing H-1B workers are required to provide these workers with fringe benefits equivalent to those of its US workers. While the DOL has not said whether severance benefits would fall under the definition of "fringe benefits," DOL could possibly interpret the failure to provide similar severance benefits to both U.S. and H-1B workers as a violation of the H-1B regulations.

Another possible issue that may arise with downsizing relates to how the resulting change in the employer's workforce impacts its calculation of "H-1B dependency," a concept outlined in the final H-1B regulations issued by the DOL in December 2000. Under these regulations, an employer with 25 or fewer employees is considered "H-1B dependent' if it has more than 7 H-1B employees. Employers with between 26 and 50 employees are considered "H-1B dependent" if they have more than 12 H-1B employees. An employer with over 50 employees is "H-1B dependent" if more than 15 percent of its employees are H-1B visa holders.

When an employer lays off a significant number of workers, regardless of whether they are U.S. or H-1B workers, it is important that the employer recalculate if it is an H-1B dependent employer. Non-dependent employers that become dependent will become subject to a myriad of additional legal requirements applicable to H-1B dependent employers such as additional recruiting requirements. Likewise, an H-1B dependent employer could become non-dependent following a downsizing, thus relieving itself from many burdensome obligations.

If you are an H-1B dependent employer, downsizing can present even more issues to consider. Under a new immigration law, H-1B dependent employers filing a visa petition must attest under oath that they have not displaced a U.S. worker for a period of 90 days before and 90 days after the petition is submitted. A "displacement" occurs when an employer lays off a U.S. worker from a job essentially equivalent to that offered the H-1B worker. A U.S. worker that accepted an offer of voluntary retirement is not considered to have been "laid off." Also, a lay off does not result when the employer offers the U.S. worker a similar employment position at equivalent or higher terms in lieu of termination. To comply with these anti-displacement provisions, H-1B dependant employers are required to keep detailed records relating to all layoffs impacting U.S. workers.

H-1B dependent employers that place their H-1B employees with secondary employers where there are "indicia of employment" between the secondary employer and the H-1B worker can also sustain displacement liability when the secondary employer lays off U.S. workers. Under the new H-1B regulations, U.S. workers at secondary employers are also protected from displacement by H-1B workers. Thus, if an H-1B dependent employer is placing an H-1B employee with a secondary employer, the H-1B dependent employer must use due diligence to make sure the secondary employer has not displaced any U.S. workers in a position equivalent to that offered the H-1B worker for a period of 90 days before and after filing the H-1B petition. Secondary employers who lay off workers are not subject to any liability, so the H-1B dependent employer is obliged to make inquiries as to the secondary employer's layoffs and cannot ignore constructive knowledge that the layoffs have occurred.

Employers that violate either the primary or secondary employer displacement prohibitions can be subject to both monetary penalties and/or be barred from using the H-1B program. This being the case, H-1B dependent employers who have laid off U.S. workers or place employees with secondary employers who have laid off U.S. workers must be extremely careful when hiring new H-1B employees.

Employers that lay off workers could also jeopardize permanent residency applications pending for the company's workers. With USCIS and DOL examiners now regularly searching the Internet for information on petitioners and beneficiaries, practitioners are already reporting more and more denials of PERM and immigrant visa petitions based on examiners' finding media reports of downsizing at the employer. Employers will need to be prepared to document that the sponsored worker is not employed in an occupation where U.S. workers have found themselves terminated.

15.7   What are some proactive strategies for preventing negative immigration consequences for employers and employees during downsizing?

With careful planning, employers can protect themselves and their employees from most of the immigration problems associated with corporate downsizing discussed above. Here are some general guidelines to keep in mind when developing your company's layoff strategy:

1. Try to provide alien employees who will be laid off as much advance notice as possible. With advance notice, alien employees are in a better position to take steps to secure an alternate visa status, allowing them to remain legally in the U.S. without having to spend time out of status, or being required to leave the country. Also, employers should try to fully understand each individual's immigration situation. Often, employers may learn through this exercise that by keeping an alien employee employed for a few more weeks or months, the alien employee can secure immigration benefits that would take several years to reprocess if the employee had to start over. If you feel you do not fully understand the immigration issues facing your alien employees, you should work with an immigration attorney to help develop a comprehensive transition plan.

   Some progressive employers will provide laid off workers with access to an immigration lawyer to assist the worker in maintaining status. The cost associated with this may be offset for some workers by not having to reimburse the workers for transportation costs to their home country since proper counseling may result in the worker not having to leave the country at all.

2. Laid off workers should be very careful not to allow themselves to fall out of status even for a day. If a new work status application cannot be filed before being terminated, the worker should consider filing an application to change to visitor status. Interviewing for a new job is an acceptable visitor visa activity.

3. Make sure you are aware of all of the affirmative immigration-related obligations that apply to you based on the types of alien employees you are laying off. Different visa categories have different requirements when terminating employment, and a failure to comply with these requirements could result in considerable financial liability on the part of the employer.

4. As layoffs occur, make sure you constantly reassess whether the resulting change in the makeup of your workforce impacts the "H-1B dependency" determination. A change in your company's classification could result in a substantial increase or decrease in legal compliance obligations.

5. If you are an H-1B dependent employer, carefully consider how layoffs at your company, or at companies where you place your employees, impact the prohibition against displacing U.S. workers.

CHAPTER 16.

State Employer Immigration Laws

As of the time of the publication of this book, 23 states have enacted employer sanctions laws that impose additional restrictions on employers beyond federal requirements. This chapter's chart and state law summaries contain a complete overview of state level immigration legislation. Note that while nearly half the states now have legislation, a number of additional states are still considering various employer sanctions proposals. Just two years ago, almost no state legislation existed. For information on new legislative proposals working their way through state legislatures, go to the I-9, E-Verify, and Employer Immigration Compliance Blog at http://www.visalaw.com/blog_i9/blog_i9.html.

16.1 What types of immigration laws and compliance requirements are in my state?

See Table 16.1.

Arizona

On January 1, 2008, Arizona H.B. 2779, the Legal Arizona Workers Act (LAWA), took effect. The law requires the Arizona attorney general or the county attorney to investigate employers that "knowingly employ an unauthorized alien." Also, beginning on January 1, 2008, all employers are required to verify the employment eligibility of their employees using the federal government's E-Verify program. All Arizona employers participating in E-Verify will be publicly listed on a state web site.

On May 2, 2008, Arizona Governor Janet Napolitano signed H.B. 2745 which made significant changes to H.B. 2779.

AZ.1 How are complaints investigated in Arizona?

Complaints are investigated by the Arizona attorney general (AG) or a county attorney (CA). Under the changes passed in May 2008, the AG is required to create a complaint form for alleging violations. The form may not require the complainant's SSN or require notarization. Complaints will also be accepted that are not on the prescribed form and the complaints may be submitted anonymously. Complaints made using the form must be investigated. Complaints made not using the form may be investigated depending on the discretion of the AG.

Complaints submitted to a CA must be submitted to the CA in the county where the alleged unauthorized employment occurred. The CA may be assisted in the investigation by the county sheriff or any other local law enforcement agency.

The AG or the CA must check with the federal government to determine if the employee is an unauthorized alien. State, county, and local officials are not to independently attempt to verify employment authorization. Persons who knowingly file false complaints can be charged with a misdemeanor. The statute does not say who can file a complaint, but presumably

Table 16.1 Type of Law

Type of Law	States
General bar on employers knowingly hiring unauthorized immigrants	AZ, CO, MS, MO, NH, SC, TN, WV
Revocation of business licenses of employers knowingly hiring unauthorized employees	AZ, MS, MO, SC, TN, VA, WV
Requires all employers in the state to use E-Verify	AZ, MS, SC
Requires all public employers in the state to use E-Verify	AZ, GA, MN, MO, MS, NC, RI, SC, VA
Requires all public employers to use either E-Verify *or* an equivalent government or third-party status verification	OK, UT
Requires employers contracting with public employers to use either E-Verify *or* an equivalent government or third-party status verification	OK, UT
Requires employers contracting with public employers to use either E-Verify *or* possess a qualifying state driver's license	SC
Bars employers in the state from using E-Verify	IL
State agencies are barred from contracting with employers who knowingly employ unauthorized immigrants	AR,CO, ID, MA, MO, SC, TN
Requires businesses contracting with state agencies to certify employees are legal	AR, CO, MA, MO, OK, SC, TN, VA
Requires business contracting with state to use E-Verify	AZ, CO, GA, MN, MO, MS, RI
Requires companies receiving subsidies or economic incentives from state agencies to certify all employees are authorized to work	CO, IA, MN, MO, PA, TX
Requires companies receiving economic incentives to use E-Verify	AZ
Employers using E-Verify gave favorable treatment in securing subsidies or economic incentives from state agencies	MN
Requires that public employer's employees by US citizens, permanent residents or have the right to work in the US for any employer	HI
E-Verify is a safe harbor protecting employers from prosecution for knowingly hiring unauthorized immigrants	AZ, MS, MO, OK, SC, TN
Employers requesting more or different documents than required under IRCA's Form I-9 are committing a civil rights violation	IL
Requires employers using E-Verify to sign a state law attestation	IL
Requires employers post a notice about state laws if they use E-Verify	IL
In considering a bid, a state agency may consider a potential contractors' use of non-citizens employees and whether the use of such employees would be detrimental to state residents or the state economy.	MI
Employers are required to maintain file copies of all documents reviewed as part of the Form I-9 process	CO
Employers subject to fines and jail sentences for violating state law	CO, NV, OK, WV
State harboring and transporting laws targeting employers	MO, NV, OK, SC, UT
Wages paid to unauthorized immigrants may not be deducted on employers' state income tax returns	CO, GA, MO, SC, WV
Requires employers to certify to the state that all employees are authorized	CO
Requires employers to withhold income tax payments for independent contractors who provide a taxpayer identification number	CO, GA
Creates a private cause of action for US employees when employer terminates to hire an unauthorized employee	OK, MS, SC, UT
Makes it a felony to accept unauthorized employment	MS

it will be interpreted broadly, given the provision allowing for prosecution of false claims.

Complaints made solely on the basis of race, color, or national origin are expressly barred under the May 2008 changes. Also under that law, the AG must determine that a complaint is not false as well as not frivolous. Prior to the change, the AG would only have to determine that the complaint is not frivolous.

If the AG determines the complaint is not frivolous, the AG or the CA shall notify ICE, local law enforcement, and the appropriate CA. The CA will then bring an action against an employer.

AZ.2   What are the penalties if an employer is found to have violated the Arizona law?

For a first violation where an employer is guilty of a "knowing violation," the court:

- Shall order the employer to terminate the employment of all unauthorized aliens.
- Shall order the employer to be subject to a three-year probationary period where the employer will file quarterly reports with the CA on all new hires on a form to be created for this purpose. (The May 2008 changes specify that this order will only apply to the business location where the unauthorized employee performed work.)
- Shall order the employer to file a signed affidavit with the CA within three business days after the order is issued stating that the employer has terminated all unauthorized aliens in Arizona and that the employer will not intentionally or knowingly employ any unauthorized aliens in Arizona.
- May, depending on the severity of the violations and all of the factors in the case, order the appropriate agencies to suspend the business license of the employer for up to 10 business days for the business location that is the subject of the complaint (unless the employer does not hold a license specific to that location). The license shall be reinstated as soon as the employer signs the affidavit noted above.

The court may consider the following factors in determining whether to suspend the business license including:

- The number of unauthorized employees.
- Prior misconduct.
- The degree of harm caused by the violation.
- Whether the employer made good-faith efforts to comply.
- The duration of the violation.
- The role of the directors, officers, or owners in the violation.
- Any other factors the court deems appropriate.

For a second violation occurring during a probationary period, the court shall order the appropriate agencies to permanently revoke the business license specific to the business location where the unauthorized employment occurred (unless the employer does not hold a license specific to that location).

Employers who are found to be violators are to have their names listed on the AG's web site.

AZ.3   Are there any safe harbors in the bill?
Yes. If an employer has complied in good faith with the federal I-9 rules, the employer will have an affirmative defense that it did not knowingly employ an unauthorized alien. This includes technical or procedural violations that are isolated, sporadic, or accidental.

Employers also benefit from a rebuttable presumption that they did not knowingly employ an unauthorized alien if they have verified the status of an employee using E-Verify, DHS' electronic employment eligibility verification system (formerly called the Basic Pilot Program).

The May 2008 changes also create a "voluntary enhanced employer compliance program" for companies not already in a probationary period. The program has a sunset date in 2018. Employers participating in this voluntary program shall not be subject to the state's employer sanctions penalties. Program participants must submit a signed affidavit to the AG stating the employer shall perform all of the following in good faith:
- Verify new employees in E-Verify.
- Run the employee's SSN through the SSNVS.
- Provide the AG documents indicating the employee has been run through E-Verify or SSNVS.

Participants in the voluntary program shall be listed on a publicly available state web site.

AZ.4   How does Arizona define "knowingly"?
The new law uses the same definition of "knowingly" as the federal I-9 statute (8 U.S.C. §1324a). Federal law defines "knowing" to include both actual and constructive knowledge. Because constructive knowledge triggers liability, employers need to be very careful that the actions of managers and supervisors are monitored since their knowledge of violations can be imputed to the whole company.

"Knowing" is not actually defined in §1324a, but the DHS does have pertinent regulations, including a new one that was to take effect in September 2007, but which, at the time of this book's publication, was still the subject of an injunction barring its implementation. Under the current regulation, an employer will be considered to have "constructive knowledge" if it fails to properly complete I-9 forms, has information that would indicate the alien is not authorized to work, or acts recklessly for the legal consequences of an alien.

The enjoined regulation added receiving a no-match letter to the list of circumstances where a person would be held to know an employee's unauthorized status. It would also permit punishment of employers that act with reckless and wanton disregard for the legal consequences of pending employees. Constructive knowledge can be avoided by following the no-match rule's procedures, including notifying employees of violations and requiring employees to refile an I-9 form at 90 days.

AZ.5   Who is an "unauthorized alien"?
Arizona law states that this includes an alien who does not have the legal right under federal law to work in the U.S. as described in 8 U.S.C. §1324a(h)(3). This is the section of the U.S. Code containing the I-9 rules.

AZ.6   Is an employer liable for work performed by independent contractors?
The statute originally defined "employee" to mean anyone who performs employment services for an employer pursuant to an employment relationship between the employee and employer. This language was modified in the May 2008 revisions to make clear that when contract labor is used, "employer" means the independent contractor and not the entity using the contract labor. Whether an organization is actually an independent contractor or not is determined based on several factors including:

- Who supplies the tools or materials.
- Whether the services are available to the general public.
- Whether the contractor works for a number of clients at the same time.
- Whether the contractor can actually make a profit as a result of the labor.
- Whether the contractor invests in the facilities for work.
- Who directs the order or sequence in which the work is done.
- Who determines when the work is finished.

However, an employer is still liable if it knows that the contract employees are not authorized to work.

AZ.7   Do existing employees need to be run through E-Verify to satisfy the Arizona law?
No. The law only covers employees hired on or after January 1, 2008.

AZ.8   What steps can a company take to reduce the likelihood of being found to have violated the new Arizona law?
Aside from using E-Verify, which is required beginning January 1, 2008, companies should consider the following actions:

- Conduct regular I-9 training for employees responsible for the function.
- Centralize I-9 recordkeeping.
- Establish a nondiscriminatory system to reverify I-9s with expiring work authorization documents.
- Switch to an electronic I-9 system rather than a paper-based one.
- Purge I-9s which employers are legally permitted to purge.
- Have an outside firm conduct an internal I-9 audit to identify and remediate violations before a government audit occurs.
- Develop a government audit response plan and train employees thoroughly in how to respond to a surprise audit.

AZ.9   The May 2008 revisions to the Arizona employer sanctions law made changes to the state's identity theft rules that relate to the employment of unauthorized employees. What were those changes?
H.B. 2745 adds using a false identity to obtain or continue employment as one of the elements that may constitute identity theft, a felony in Arizona. It also makes it a crime to hire a person knowing that the person is providing false identification and using that identification information to meet IRCA's employment authorization requirements. Trafficking in false identification documents to enable someone to obtain or continue employment now is a felony as well.

AZ.10   What penalties do employers receiving economic development incentives face for violating the Arizona sanctions laws?
The May 2008 changes specify that an employer receiving economic development incentives must provide proof to the agency providing the incentive that it is registered in E-Verify. Employers not participating will be required to repay all monies received under the incentive.

AZ.11 **What are Arizona's special sanctions rules for employers paying employees in cash?**

Employers with two or more employees who pay their employees in cash are required to comply with income tax withholding rules, employer reporting laws, employment security law, and workers' compensation rules. The law is not specific to employers of unauthorized immigrants, but it is included in the sanctions law because many employers of unauthorized employees pay such employees with cash in order to keep them off the books and avoid complying with IRCA. Employers violating this rule are subject to triple damages or $5,000 for each employee, whichever is greater. Fines shall be used to help the state offset moneys appropriated for education and health care expenses for unauthorized aliens. Note that this does not affect imposing penalties under other statutes.

AZ.12 **How does Arizona regulate government procurement contracts for employers with IRCA violations?**

Beginning October 1, 2008, governmental agencies in Arizona are not permitted to award contracts to any contractors or subcontractors that are not registered in E-Verify. Each contractor and subcontractor also will be required to certify their compliance with federal immigration laws and will be required to include contract language that states that such violations will be considered a material breach of the contract. The contract must also state that the contractor agrees to allow the governmental agency to inspect the documents of the contractor to ensure compliance with federal immigration laws and agrees to be subject to random audits by the governmental agency.

Arkansas

In 2007, legislation passed in Arkansas prohibiting state agencies from contracting with businesses that employ "illegal immigrants."

AR.1 **What does the Arkansas law bar?**

No state agency may enter into or renew a public contract for services with a contractor who knows that the contractor or a subcontractor employs or contracts with an "illegal immigrant" to perform work under the contract.

AR.2 **When did the Arkansas law take effect?**

The law took effect on August 1, 2007.

AR.3 **Who is an "illegal immigrant" under the law?**

An "illegal immigrant" is any person who is not a U.S. citizen and who has:

- Entered the U.S. in violation of federal immigration laws.
- Legally entered the U.S. but is not authorized to work.
- Legally entered the U.S. but has overstayed the time limit on their status.

AR.4 **Who is a "contractor" under the Arkansas law?**

"Contractor" includes any person having a public contract with an Arkansas state agency for professional services, technical and general services, or any category of construction.

AR.5 **Are all contracts covered?**

All "professional service contracts" where there is a relationship between the contractor and state agency is an independent contractor relationship and not an employee relationship. The services offered must be professional in nature and the state may not exercise direct managerial control of the day-to-day activities of the individual providing the services. The contract must specify the results expected from the rendering of the services and the services are rendered to the state agency itself or to a third-party beneficiary. Contracts must have a total value of $25,000 or more to be covered by this law.

AR.6   Are all agencies in Arkansas covered?

"Covered agencies" include any agency, institution, authority, department, board, commission, bureau, council, or other agency of the state supported by state or federal funds.

Some institutions are exempt from the new law including all constitutional departments of the state, the elected constitutional offices of the state, the General Assembly and its supporting agencies, the Arkansas Supreme Court and related courts.

AR.7   How do contractors show they have not hired unauthorized employees?

Before signing a public contract, a prospective contractor must certify in a manner that doesn't violate federal law that the contractor, at the time of certification, does not employ or contract with an illegal immigrant.

AR.8   What if it is determined that a contractor has hired illegal immigrants?

If a contractor violates the law, the state must give a contractor 60 days to remedy the violation. If the violation is not remedied by that point, the state is to terminate the contract. The contractor shall then be liable to the state for actual damages for violating the contract.

AR.9   Does it matter if a contractor is using the services of individuals hired by a subcontractor?

If a contractor uses a subcontractor, the subcontractor must certify that it does not employ or contract with an illegal immigrant and it must submit the certification within 30 days of execution of the subcontract. Contractors who learn that a subcontractor is violating the rule may terminate the contract and not be liable for a breach of contract.

AR.10   Does the law require employers that have contracts with the state to use E-Verify?

No. Unlike other states, the Arkansas law does not require employers contracting with the state to use E-Verify, the government's electronic employment eligibility verification system.

Colorado

Colorado has passed five separate pieces of legislation affecting employers. They are the following:

- H.B. 06-1343 requires employers contracting with the state to use E-Verify.
- H.B. 06S-1001 bars employers from receiving access to state economic development incentives if they are not complying with IRCA.
- H.B. 06S-1017 requires employers to attest that all employees have been verified to determine their legal status and that the employer has kept copies of federally required documentation. It also requires the state to conduct random audits of employers.
- H.B. 06S-1015 requires the state to set up an employment verification web site that will enable a person to access a database to determine the validity of a taxpayer identification number.

- H.B. 06S-1020 passed in a statewide ballot initiative and bars employers who cannot verify that an employee is a legal U.S. resident from claiming an employee's wages as a deductible business expense.

CO.1   What does H.B. 06-1343 bar?

H.B. 06-1343 bars state agencies and local governmental agencies from entering into or renewing public contracts for services with contractors who knowingly employ or contract with an illegal alien to perform work under the contract or contractors who contract with subcontractors who knowingly employ or contract with an illegal alien to perform work under the contract.

CO.2   When did H.B. 06-1343 take effect?

H.B. 06-1343 went into effect on August 7, 2006.

CO.3   Who is an "illegal alien" under the law?

Unlike other similar state laws, "illegal alien" is not defined under the Colorado statute.

CO.4   Who is a "contractor" under the Colorado law?

A "contractor" is a person having a public contract for services with a state agency.

CO.5   Are all contracts covered?

No. Only public contracts are covered. These are agreements between a state agency and a contractor for the provision of services (as opposed the provision of goods). "Services" covers the furnishing of labor by a contractor or subcontractor and not the delivery of goods.

CO.6   Are all agencies in Colorado covered?

Yes. The statute provides no exemptions from complying with the new Colorado rule.

CO.7   How do contractors show they have not hired unauthorized employees?

Contractors are required to include language in their contract with the state certifying that they do not knowingly employ illegal aliens and that the contractor has participated in E-Verify.

C0.8   What if it is determined that a contractor has hired illegal aliens?

If a contractor violates this law, a state agency may terminate its contract with the contractor. The contractor would be liable for any damages to the state agency. The state agency shall also inform the secretary of state of the breach. The secretary of state shall keep a list including the name of the contractor and the state agency that terminated the public contract and shall not remove the contractor from the list until two years have passed. And the list shall be available to the public.

CO.9   Does the law require employers contracting with the state to use E-Verify?

Yes. Employers are required to include a provision in their contracts with state agencies that states that the employer participates in E-Verify.

C0.10   Does it matter if a contractor is using the services of individuals hired by a subcontractor?

Yes. First, if a contractor obtains actual knowledge that a subcontractor performing work under a public contract knowingly employs an illegal alien, the contractor must notify the subcontractor and the contracting agency within three days of gaining actual knowledge. And, the contractor must terminate the subcontract if the subcontractor does not stop employing or contracting with the illegal alien, unless the subcontractor shows that it has not knowingly employed an illegal alien.

CO.11 **If an employer is found to have violated the law, how long will the employer remain on the list of employers barred from doing business with the state?**
Two years.

CO.12 **What type of investigative authority does the state have under this law?**
The Department of Labor and Employment (DLE) has the authority to investigate whether a contractor is complying with the terms of a public contract. It may conduct on-site inspections where a public contract is being performed. The DLE shall receive complaints of suspected violations and shall have the discretion to determine which complaints, if any, are to be investigated.

CO.13 **What does H.B. 06S-1001 require?**
Employers must be in compliance with IRCA's rules in order to be eligible to receive a grant, loan, performance-based incentive, or other economic development incentive offered by the Colorado Economic Development Commission.

CO.14 **How does the Colorado Economic Development Commission (CEDC) determine that an employer is in compliance with IRCA?**
The CEDC has the discretion to determine when to verify that an employer is in compliance with IRCA.

CO.15 **What happens when the CEDC determines an employer is out of compliance?**
When the CEDC determines that an employer is out of compliance or the employer cannot prove compliance, the CEDC shall notify the employer of noncompliance and the employer shall repay the total amount of money received as an economic development incentive within 30 days of receipt of notice. Furthermore, an employer will be barred from receiving an economic development incentive for five years after the date that the employer has repaid the CEDC in full.

CO.16 **Do employers have any right to argue against the determination of the CEDC?**
Yes. Employers can appear at a hearing before the CEDC to present proof that the employer is in compliance with IRCA.

CO.17 **What does H.B. 06S-1017 do?**
The law requires all employers in Colorado to affirm that they have examined the legal work status of newly hired employees within 20 days of hire. They shall also retain file copies of all documents presented by employees under Section 2 of Form I-9. Under IRCA, employers are not required to retain copies. The employer must keep a written or electronic copy of the affirmation for the term of employment of each employee.

CO.18 **What facts must the employer state in its affirmation?**
The employer must affirm that:
- The employer has examined the legal work status of all newly hired employees.

- It has retained file copies of the documents required to be presented by employees under Section 2 of Form I-9.
- The employee has not altered or falsified the employee's identification documents.
- The employer has not knowingly hired an unauthorized immigrant.

CO.19 **When did the law go into effect?**
The law went into effect on January 1, 2007.

CO.20 **What enforcement powers does the state have under this law?**
The director of the Division of Labor in the DLE may request employers to present documentation that the employer is in compliance with IRCA and with this law's requirements concerning affirmations and copies. The director may conduct random audits of employers to obtain the required documentation.

CO.21 **What penalties are faced by an employer who violates the law?**
An employer who, with reckless disregard, fails to submit the documentation required under this law shall be subject to a fine of not more than $5,000 for the first offense and not more than $25,000 for the second and any subsequent offense. The money is to go into a state fund to underwrite enforcement of this law.

CO.22 **What does H.B. 06S-1015 do?**
The law requires Colorado to create a "work eligibility verification portal" that will enable a person to access a database to verify whether a taxpayer identification number is valid. Persons providing a 1099 to persons who fail to provide a valid taxpayer identification number are required to withhold state income taxes presumably because it is assumed that an undocumented immigrant is not as likely to pay taxes on their own.

CO.23 **When does the law take effect?**
The portal described in the bill must be online by January 1, 2008. If the portal is not ready, the law will take effect on the first January after the portal comes online.

CO.24 **What does H.B. 06S-1020 do?**
This law was passed by the legislature and then as a statewide referendum. It bars employers from taking a state income tax deduction for wages greater than $600 paid to unauthorized aliens if the business knew the unauthorized status of the alien.

CO.25 **Are there exceptions to the law?**
Yes. It does not apply to individuals hired before the effective date of the bill. It does not apply to persons who hold and present a valid license or identification card issued by the Colorado Department of Revenue. And it does not apply where the individual being paid is not directly compensated or employed by the taxpayer.

Georgia

The Georgia Security and Immigration Compliance Act of 2006 (S.B. 529) requires public employers and employers doing business with state agencies to participate in E-Verify, the federal electronic employment verification system.

In 2007, Georgia passed S.B. 184 which bars deductions by employers for wages paid to employees unlawfully present in the United States.

GA.1   What does Georgia do with respect to E-Verify?

All public employers are required to use the E-Verify system, and all contractors working with state agencies must participate as well.

GA.2   What is a "public employer"?

A "public employer" includes all departments, agencies, or instrumentalities of the state of Georgia.

GA.3   When did this change take effect?

The law took effect generally on July 1, 2007. Contractors with 500 or more employees were required to be using E-Verify by July 1, 2007. Contractors with between 100 and 500 employees were required be using E-Verify by July 1, 2008. All other employers must be using E-Verify by July 1, 2009.

GA.4   What does the bill do with respect to deduction of wages paid by employers to unauthorized employees?

Employers who pay more than $600 to an employee may not deduct as a business expense the amount if an individual is not an authorized employee. Independent contractors receiving a 1099 form are covered by this provision as well. Individuals hired before January 19, 2008, are not covered, nor are individuals not directly compensated or employed by an employer. And, individuals who present a valid license or identification card issued by the Georgia Department of Driver Services are exempted.

GA.5   What are the changes made with respect to withholding state income tax?

Employers must withhold state income tax at the rate of six percent for individuals receiving a 1099 form if the individual has failed to provide a taxpayer identification number, provided an incorrect taxpayer identification number, or provided an IRS-issued taxpayer identification number for nonresident aliens. Employers failing to withhold shall be liable for the taxes.

Idaho

Idaho Governor James E. Risch has issued Executive Order No. 2006-40 addressing the subject of illegal immigration.

ID.1   What does the executive order do?

The executive order, which is very short and contains few details, directs that policies be implemented to ensure that all state employees in Idaho are authorized to work legally. Also, agencies must set procedures to ensure that businesses contracting with state agencies are employing workers legally.

Illinois

Illinois has passed two bills, H.B. 1743 and H.B. 1744, which move in the opposite direction of other states. The first bill provides state-level protections for employees from employers that discriminate. The second actually bars employers from using E-Verify until the number of false positives falls below a prescribed rate. *Note: A federal district court has ruled that the Illinois law is invalid based on the Supremacy Clause of the Constitution. As of publication, it is not clear whether the case will be appealed or not.*

IL.1   What are H.B. 1743's antidiscrimination rules?

H.B. 1743 creates a series of new state civil rights violations for discrimination against employees. These include:

- Employers who refuse to hire, segregate, or otherwise treat employees adversely on the basis of unlawful discrimination or citizenship status.
- Employers who impose restrictions on a language (excluding slang or profanities) being spoken by an employee if the communication is unrelated to the employee's duties.
- Employment agencies which refuse to accept or refer applicants or which make or have the effect of making unlawful discrimination or discrimination on the basis of citizenship status a condition of referral.
- Unions that limit membership or employment opportunities on the basis of unlawful discrimination or citizenship status.

IL.2   What types of immigration-related practices does H.B. 1743 bar?

Employers are barred from requiring more or different documents than are required in the Form I-9 rules. Employers participating in E-Verify are also barred from refusing to hire, to segregate, or to act with respect to recruitment, hiring, promotion, renewal of employment, selection for training or apprenticeship, discharge, discipline, tenure, or other privileges without following the E-Verify rules. Employers who follow IRCA's rules are not considered to be violating H.B. 1743.

IL.3   When did H.B. 1743 go into effect?

H.B. 1743 went into effect on January 1, 2008.

IL.4   H.B. 1744 prohibits participating in the E-Verify program. When will this prohibition be lifted?

Employers are barred from enrolling in the E-Verify system until the DHS databases are able to make a determination on 99 percent of tentative nonconfirmation notices issued to employers within three days.

IL.5   The DHS is fighting Illinois on this legislation. What is the status of that court fight?

In September 2007, the DHS challenged Illinois' new law to prevent it from taking effect as scheduled on January 1, 2008. As of February 2008, the state of Illinois agreed to hold off on implementing H.B. 1744 until the lawsuit is over. Employers already using E-Verify are permitted to continue using the system and new businesses may continue to enroll. As part of this agreement with the DHS, Illinois has agreed that it will not punish such employers should it win the suit. Also note that the E-Verify requirements in H.B. 1743 discussed above are not affected by this lawsuit.

IL.6   What type of attestation must employers make once they are permitted to participate in E-Verify?

Assuming the DHS is able to meet the 99 percent test noted above, employers who sign up for E-Verify are still barred from using the system unless the employer attests on a form to be provided by the Illinois Department of Labor (IDOL) that the employer has received the E-Verify training materials and has completed the requisite training in using E-Verify, and that the employer has posted the notice from DHS indicating that the employer is enrolled in E-Verify, as well as the antidiscrimination notice issued by the OSC and the antidiscrimination notice issued by the Illinois Department of Human Rights (IDHR).

IL.7   Where are these notices to be posted?

These three notices (mentioned in IL. 6) must be posted in a prominent place that is clearly visible to prospective employees.

IL.8 **What are an employer's responsibilities in Illinois if they use E-Verify?**

- The employer must prominently post the notices supplied by the DHS, the OSC, and the IDHR.
- The employer must require all employer representatives to complete computer-based training on E-Verify.
- The employer must become familiar with the E-Verify manual.
- The employer must notify all prospective employees that it uses E-Verify.
- The employer must provide all employees who receive a nonconfirmation notice with a referral letter and contact information for the agencies that can help clear up the discrepancy.
- The employer must comply with the Illinois Human Rights Act and applicable federal discrimination rules.
- The employer must use information it receives from the SSA or the DHS only to confirm employment eligibility and that all information is safeguarded to ensure the information remains confidential.

IL.9 **Which employees must complete the computer-based tutorial on using E-Verify?**

All employer representatives performing employment verification services must complete the computer-based training and the employer must attest on a form to be provided by the IDOL that the employer representatives completed the training.

IL.10 **What other responsibilities do employers who use E-Verify have under the Illinois law?**

Employers must become familiar with the E-Verify manual, must notify all employees at the time of application for employment that the employer uses E-Verify, and must provide employees who receive a tentative nonconfirmation under E-Verify with a referral letter and contact information for the agency that can resolve the discrepancy.

IL.11 **Are state agencies affected by the new law?**

State agencies may not require contractors to use E-Verify in order to have access to receiving a government contract or a business license.

Iowa

IA.1 **What does Senate File 562 do?**

Businesses receiving economic development assistance are now subject to contract provisions stating that new and retained jobs shall be filled by people who are U.S. citizens or those otherwise authorized to work in the United States. Employers may be required by the state to provide "periodic assurances" that employees are authorized to work in the United States.

IA.2 **When did the law take effect?**

The law went into effect on July 1, 2007.

Massachusetts

On February 23, 2007, Massachusetts Governor Deval L. Patrick signed Executive Order No. 481 regarding the use of undocumented employees on state contracts.

MA.1 **What does the executive order do?**

Under the executive order, all state agencies are prohibited from using "undocumented workers" in connection with the performance of state contracts.

MA.2 **Are employers subjected to any new requirements under the executive order?**

Yes. Employers must certify, as a condition to receiving Massachusetts government funds, that they shall not knowingly use undocumented workers in connection with the performance of the contract and that the employer has lawfully verified the immigration status of all workers assigned to the contract. Also, employers must certify that they have not knowingly or recklessly altered, falsified, or accepted altered or falsified documents from any workers.

MA.3 **What provisions must be added to contracts between employers and state agencies?**

All contracts must now specify that a breach of the new immigration terms of the agreement may be regarded as a material breach and the employer will be subject to sanctions, monetary penalties, withholding of payments, and contract suspension or termination.

Michigan

MI.1 **How does Michigan regulate state government contractors?**

On October 31, 2007, Michigan's governor signed Public Act No. 127, which orders state agencies to consider a business' use of employees, contractors, subcontractors, or others who are not citizens of the U.S., legal resident aliens, or individuals with valid visas, in determining whether to contract with that business. If contracting with such an employer would be detrimental to the people of Michigan, that fact may be considered when deciding to contract with the employer.

Minnesota

On January 7, 2008, Minnesota Governor Tim Pawlenty signed an executive order that requires employers entering into contracts with the state that are valued at more than $50,000 to participate in the E-Verify program.

MN.1 **What does the executive order do?**

The executive order directs the Minnesota Department of Employee Relations, Department of Administration, and Department of Employment and Economic Development to use E-Verify to screen all new state employees and requires all contractors and subcontractors doing business with the state or who receive state business incentives to use E-Verify.

MN.2 **Are there new rules for business licenses under the executive order?**

Yes. Employers risk losing their business license if they knowingly hire unauthorized immigrant employees. As part of the process of seeking a business license, employers must certify that they do not knowingly hire unauthorized employees.

MN.3 **Are employers who use E-Verify treated differently with respect to being punished for hiring unauthorized employees?**

Yes. The executive order recommends that employers who use E-Verify should be able to use that as evidence that they did not knowingly employ an illegal immigrant.

MN.4 **How does the executive order deal with ensuring the order is carried out?**

The order requires annual random audits of the executive branch agencies to ensure compliance.

For employers, contract language is to be developed that allows the state to terminate the contract and/or debar the contractor if the state determines that the contractor or subcontractor under the contractor's control knowingly employed unauthorized employees.

MN.5 **What other provisions are in the executive order that affect employers?**
- Employers that get government subsidies will have to certify compliance with IRCA.
- The Commissioner of Employment and Economic Development will require employers to certify compliance with IRCA and will also set up a system to give extra credit to employers in competitive programs that use E-Verify.

Mississippi

On March 17, 2008, Mississippi Governor Haley Barbour signed a major immigration bill. The bill mandates using E-Verify for all employers in the state, calls for the revocation of business licenses of employers violating immigration laws, and creates a new felony for persons illegally accepting employment.

MS.1 **What is the new law regarding employing workers unauthorized to work?**

Employers in Mississippi are only permitted to hire employees who are legal citizens of the U.S. or are legal aliens. "Legal aliens" are those lawfully present in the country at the time of employment and for the duration of employment.

MS.2 **What is the state's new E-Verify mandate?**

All employers, both public and private, are going to have to use E-Verify, the electronic employment verification system. The law is being phased in as follows:
- Employers required to use E-Verify by July 1, 2008:
  - » State agencies.
  - » Contractors and subcontractors doing business with Mississippi governmental agencies.
  - » Companies with more than 250 employees.
- Employers required to use E-Verify by July 1, 2009:
  - » Employers with between 100 and 250 employees.
- Employers required to use E-Verify by July 1, 2010:
  - » Employers with between 30 and 100 employees.
- Employers required to use E-Verify by July 1, 2011:
  - » All employers.

MS.3 **What penalties do employers face for violating the Mississippi law?**

Employers are subject to the cancellation of any state or public contract and face a bar of up to three years on accessing state contracts. Employers also face the loss of any license, permit, certificate, or other document granted by any agency in Mississippi. This includes a business license and the revocation of the license may be for up to one year. The Department of Employment Security, State Tax commission, Secretary of State, Department of Human Services, and the Attorney General shall have the authority to seek penalties for noncompliance.

MS.4   **Are there any safe harbors for employers?**
Yes. Employers in the following circumstances are exempted from liability:

- Employers hiring employees through a state or federal work program requiring verification of the employee's SSN and verifying employment authorization.
- Any candidate referred by the Mississippi Department of Employment Security (MDES), if the MDES has verified the employee's SSN and verified employment authorization.
- Individual homeowners who hire workers on their private property for noncommercial purposes unless required by federal law to do so.

MS.5   **What are the obligations of out-of-state employers who send workers into the state?**
All employers employing workers in Mississippi are required to register to do business in Mississippi with the MDES before placing employees into the workforce in Mississippi.

MS.6   **How are U.S. citizen workers affected by the new law?**
Mississippi now makes it a discriminatory practice if an employer discharges a U.S. citizen or permanent resident employee and replaces him or her with an employee not authorized to work. This provision takes effect July 1, 2008. Employers using E-Verify are protected from liability. Employees who can demonstrate they were unlawfully terminated shall have the right to sue an employer for damages.

MS.7   **What is the new felony provision in Mississippi applicable to those accepting unauthorized employment?**
Mississippi now makes it a felony for any person to accept employment if they know they are unauthorized. Violators are subject to imprisonment from one-to-five years and a fine of between $1,000 and $10,000.

Missouri
Missouri's legislature has recently passed H.B. 1549, a tough employer sanctions bill. It also has the governor-issued Executive Order 87-02. Under Executive Order 87-02, the Missouri Housing Development Commission (MHDC) is required to prohibit owners of a project which receives federal or state tax credits from using "undocumented workers" in the construction of MHDC-funded projects.

MO.1   **What does the new law in Missouri say generally with respect to hiring "unauthorized aliens"?**
H.B. 1549 bars business entities and employers from knowingly employing, recruiting, hiring for employment, or continuing to employ unauthorized aliens.

MO.2   **What is a "federal work authorization program" under H.B. 1549?**
A "federal work authorization program" is an electronic employment verification system run by the DHS as authorized by IRCA. Currently, that would only include E-Verify.

MO.3   **Who is a "public employer"?**
Every department and agency in the state or any political subdivision of the state is a "public employer."

MO.4   **How does H.B. 1549 affect public employers?**
Public employers are required to enroll in a federal work authorization program.

MO.5   **How does H.B. 1549 affect employers contracting with state agencies?**
As a condition to any contract worth more than $5,000, employers are required to certify and document that it is enrolled in a federal work authorization program. The certification is limited to employees working in connection with the contracted services. Businesses must also certify that they do not knowingly employ unauthorized aliens in connection with contracted services.

MO.6   **Is there a safe harbor in H.B. 1549?**
Yes. Employers who enroll in a federal work authorization program shall have an affirmative defense against claims under H.B. 1549 related to hiring unauthorized aliens.

MO.7   **Are businesses liable for the actions of contractors and subcontractors?**
No, as long as the contract with the contractor or subcontractor states that the contractor or subcontractor has not hired unauthorized aliens and is enrolled in a federal work authorization program. A signed affidavit swearing that the contractor's or subcontractor's workers are not unauthorized aliens shall also be acceptable.

MO.8   **How are complaints filed and handled under H.B. 1549?**
Any state official, business entity, or resident of Missouri can file a written complaint alleging the actions constituting the violation as well as the date and location of the violation. Complaints based on national origin, race, or ethnicities are invalid. Within 15 days, the Missouri Attorney General (AG) will request identity information from the employer and if the employer fails to respond, the AG will direct the municipality or county to suspend the employer's licenses or permits.

Once the AG gets the identifying information, he or she shall check the names with the federal government to determine if the workers are authorized to be employed. If the federal government says the workers are authorized or that it is unable to make a determination, then the AG will drop the investigation. State officials are not to make independent determinations of work authorization status and the law explicitly states that only the federal government can make such a determination.

If the federal government indicates that an employee is not work authorized, the AG shall bring an action in a court in Cole County.

MO.9   **What penalties may a court impose when the attorney general brings an action under H.B. 1549?**
If an employer did not knowingly violate the law against hiring unauthorized aliens, the employer shall have 15 business days to terminate the unauthorized alien or get new documentation that the employee is authorized. The employer shall provide an affidavit swearing that the violation has ended and that it has enrolled in a federal work authorization program.

If the employer knowingly violated the law, the applicable municipality or county shall suspend any license or permit held by the employer for 14 days or one day after the employer provides an affidavit that it no longer has unauthorized workers and is enrolled in a federal work authorization program.

Municipalities and counties that fail to suspend a license or permit as directed by the court shall be considered "sanctuary cities" and subject to penalties.

Second violations shall result in a one-year suspension of a license or permit. Subsequent violations will result in a permanent revocation.

Businesses contracting with the state that are found to have hired unauthorized aliens will be deemed to be in breach of the contract and the state may break the contract and debar the employer from doing business with the state for up to three years for first violations. The debarment may be permanent for subsequent violations. The state may also withhold up to 25 percent of the money due the employer under the contract.

MO.10   What happens if someone files a frivolous complaint?
Anyone who submits a frivolous complaint shall be liable for actual, compensatory, and punitive damages to the alleged violator.

MO.11   How are employer tax deductions for the wages paid to unauthorized aliens affected?
Employers are not allowed to deduct wages paid to unauthorized aliens.

MO.12   Does the new law contain transporting provisions?
Yes. It is now a state crime to knowingly move or transport an illegal alien for the purposes of employment and violators shall be subject to jail for not less than a year and at least a $1,000 fine.

MO.13   When did H.B. 1549 become effective?
H.B. 1549 became effective on January 1, 2009.

MO.14   What does Executive Order 87-02 do?
Owners of MHDC-funded projects must require their contractors to obtain a Form I-9 from each employee and also require that contractors, in turn, require subcontractors to obtain a Form I-9 for their employees. The owner is required to collect copies of these Form I-9s, to keep the Form I-9s at the project site, and to require their contractors to assemble a list of all employees completing Form I-9 (and to update the list regularly). The owner must provide MHDC with a list each month of all employees employed by the contractor or subcontractor. Violators are subject to sanctions, though they are not specified in the order.

Nevada
On June 2, 2007, Nevada's governor signed Assembly Bill 383, a bill that regulates various aspects of immigration in Nevada. The bill has an employer sanctions provision.

NV.1   How does Nevada regulate employer compliance?
A.B. 383 permits the Nevada Tax Commission to impose administrative fines on employers with business licenses that "willfully, flagrantly or otherwise egregiously" engage in the unlawful hiring or employment of an unauthorized alien in violation of federal law. Employers are permitted to submit proof that they have attempted to verify the SSN of the unauthorized alien within six months from the date on which the unauthorized

alien was allegedly employed. The proof may include a printout from the Internet. The statute does not specify the amount of the fines.

The bill also contains a provision penalizing harboring of unauthorized aliens, a charge that has been used against employers at the federal level.

New Hampshire

NH.1 **How does New Hampshire regulate employer compliance?**
Since 1976, New Hampshire has had in force a law (N.H. Rev. Stat. Ann. §275-A:4-a) that bars employers from employing any alien whom the employer knows is not a U.S. citizen and who is not in possession of either a permanent residency card or other documentation showing the individual is authorized to work. Employers violating this provision are subject to fines of up to $2,500 per day.

North Carolina

In 2006, North Carolina passed S.B. 1523 and all public employers in the state now must use E-Verify.

NC.1 **When did S.B. 1523 go into force?**
The law covers all employees hired on or after January 1, 2007. Local education agencies were covered for new hires after March 1, 2007.

NC.2 **What does the law do?**
Public employers in the state are required to use E-Verify to verify their employees' legal status or authorization to work in the United States.

NC.3 **Which employers are covered?**
The North Carolina law covers each state agency, department, institution, university, community college, and local education agency.

Oklahoma

The Oklahoma Taxpayer and Citizen Protection Act (OTCPA) was passed in 2007 and includes, among a variety of measures targeting illegal immigration, several that affect employers. In June 2008, a U.S. District Court judge issued an injunction preventing the enforcement of the employer sanctions provisions of the OTCPA. That injunction was appealed to the Tenth Circuit Court of Appeals and as of publication of this book, a decision in the case has not been issued.

OK.1 **What are OTCPA's transporting and harboring provisions?**
The Oklahoma law makes it unlawful for any person to transport, conceal, harbor, or shelter from detection in any place, including any building or means of transportation, any alien that is in violation of the law. This provision could be used against employers knowingly employing unauthorized immigrants.

OK.2 **What are the penalties for violating the transporting and harboring provisions?**
Violating these provisions constitutes a felony punishable by a year in jail and a fine of not less than $1,000, or both.

OK.3 **What are OTCPA's "status verification system" provisions?**
All public employers are required to use a "status verification system" to verify the work authorization of all new employees.

A status verification system includes:

- E-Verify.
- Any equivalent federal program designated by the federal government.
- Any other independent, third-party system with an equal or higher degree of reliability.
- The SSNVS or a similar online service implemented by the SSA.

Beginning July 1, 2008, no public employer shall enter into a contract for the performance of services within the state unless the employer participates in a status verification system. Contracts entered into prior to July 1, 2008, are not affected.

OK.4   What is OTCPA's unfair trade practices provision?

The firing of any U.S. citizen or permanent resident alien employee by an employer who, at the time of the firing, employed an unauthorized immigrant shall be considered an unfair trade practice. Fired employees shall have a private right to sue for such an unfair trade practice. This would only cover situations, however, where the terminated employee is working in a job category requiring equal skill, effort, and responsibility. and which is performed under similar working conditions. This provision took effect July 1, 2008.

OK.5   Is there a safe harbor provision under the Oklahoma law?

Yes. Employers using a status verification system for employees hired after July 1, 2008 shall be exempt from liability.

Pennsylvania

PA.1   How does Pennsylvania regulate employers who fail to comply with immigration law?

Pennsylvania H.B. 2319, passed in 2006, bars employers from knowingly employing the labor services of an illegal alien on any project. The law requires employers that receive any state grants or loans to repay such grants or loans if they are found under federal law to have knowingly used labor provided by an illegal alien. Employers can avoid liability if they can show that contractors who provided the labor to the employer provided a certification regarding compliance with IRCA.

Rhode Island

On March 27, 2008, Rhode Island Governor Donald Carcieri signed Executive Order 08-01 governing illegal immigration in his state.

RI.1   What does the executive order require of state employers?

The order requires the Rhode Island Department of Administration to register in E-Verify and use the program to verify all new state employees.

RI.2   What does the executive order state with regard to private employers doing business with state agencies?

All businesses, including grantees, contractors and their subcontractors, and vendors, doing business with Rhode Island should register with and use E-Verify.

South Carolina

On May 29, 2008, the South Carolina legislature passed the South Carolina Illegal Immigration Reform Act (SCIIRA).

SC.1   **What obligation does the new law impose on government employers?**
Beginning January 1, 2009, all public employers are required to register and participate in E-Verify.

SC.2   **What obligations does the new law impose on employers engaged in contracts with state agencies?**
Contractors and subcontractors seeking to do business with state agencies must register for E-Verify or only employ workers with a valid South Carolina driver's license or an out-of-state driver's license if the license requirements are as strict as South Carolina's. The provision does not apply to contracts worth less than $15,000 for political subdivisions and $25,000 for other public employers (and employers may not divide work in order to avoid the applicability of the section). It also does not apply to contracts for the acquisition of an end product and contracts predominantly for professional or consultant services. Contractors must provide a written statement verifying compliance, though the public employer need not audit or independently verify compliance by the contractor.

SC.3   **Are there requirements applicable to all private employers?**
All employers with more than 100 employees (and their contractors and subcontractors) must, by July 1, 2009, either use E-Verify and verify employment authorization within five days or employ only workers possessing a valid South Carolina driver's license or a license from a state with requirements at least as strict as South Carolina. The state is required to have published a list of states with equivalent driver's licenses no later than January 1, 2009. This provision of the new law will apply to employers with less than 100 employees beginning July 1, 2010.

Employers who elect to use E-Verify must provisionally employ a new employee until the employee's work authorization has been verified. A private employer who elects to verify a new employee's work authorization must submit a new employee's name and information for verification even if the new employee's employment is terminated less than five days after becoming employed. If a new employee's work authorization is not verified by the federal work authorization program, a private employer must not employ, continue to employ, or re employ the employee.

There is now a general requirement stating that a private employer shall not knowingly or intentionally employ a person who is not lawfully present in the United States.

SC.4   **How are complaints against private employers investigated and violations punished?**
After the director of the State Budget and Control Board receives a written complaint against a private employer or the state begins its own investigation based on good cause or under random auditing, the director must conduct an investigation. If the director believes "substantial evidence exists" to support a finding of a violation of the South Carolina law, the director shall notify ICE, notify local and state law enforcement agencies enforcing state immigration laws, and assess a penalty as follows:
- A fine for between $100 and $1,000 for each violation (though a first offense will not be assessed with a penalty if the employer complies within 72 hours of being notified of a violation.) Fines may vary based on the number of employees for whom the employer failed to verify status, the violation history of the employer, the size of the employer, the steps the employer has taken to remediate the problem, and the duration of the violation.

- Employees must be terminated if the director notifies the employer that the work authorization of an employee was not verified during the director's investigation.
- The employment license shall be suspended 10-30 days for a first offense and the employer may not employ any workers during the suspension period. After the period of suspension, the private employer's license may be reinstated if the employer demonstrates that the unauthorized employee has been terminated, and a reinstatement fee equal to the cost of investigating and enforcing has been paid (not to exceed $1,000).
- For a second offense, the suspension of the employment license shall be for 30 to 60 days with reinstatement being permitted based on the same terms as above.
- For a third or later offense, the employment license is revoked and the employer may seek a provisional license only after 90 days. The employer would have to provide quarterly reports to the director demonstrating compliance and that unauthorized employees have been terminated. Also, a reinstatement fee must be paid.
- If an employer engages in business or employs a new employee during the suspension period, the employer is subject to a revocation of the employment license and reinstatement shall not be permitted for at least five years.

The director shall maintain a list of violators and publish it on the agency's web site.

SC.5 **What is the new "employment license" created by the new law?**
All private employers in South Carolina on or after July 1, 2009, will be deemed to have an employment license which permits the employer to employ a person in the state. After July 1, 2009, the employer may not employ a person in South Carolina unless the employment license is in effect and is not suspended or revoked. The employment license will remain in effect only as long as the employer is in compliance with the new law.

SC.6 **When does the new law take effect?**
Under the provisions of the law relating to contractors with public employers, subcontractors with 500 or more employees must comply by January 1, 2009. For those with 100 to 500 employees, the new law takes effect July 2009. For everyone else, the law takes effect on and after January 1, 2010.

SC.7 **Is there a safe harbor for employers in the new law?**
Yes. Employers complying with the E-Verify or driver's license requirements may not be sanctioned under the contractor section of the new law. Private employers subject to the general section applicable to all private employers with 100 or more employees are also provided a safe harbor if they are in compliance with the I-9 rules.

SC.8 **Are there penalties for those filing false complaints?**
Those making false reports shall be guilty of a felony and imprisoned for up to five years.

SC.9 **What is the new requirement for reporting violations?**
The State's Commissioner for Minority Affairs is required to set up a 24-hour hotline to receive allegations of federal work authorization pro-

gram violations and the department shall, in turn, relay the information to the appropriate law enforcement agency.

SC.10   **What does the new law change with respect to deducting wages paid to unauthorized employees?**

The new law bars after January 1, 2009, the deduction of wages paid to persons not authorized to be working in the U.S. except where, after a reasonable investigation, the employer did not know or should not have known the worker was unauthorized. The provision only applies to individuals hired after January 1, 2009, and does not apply to any individuals with a valid South Carolina driver's license or license issued by a state with license requirements as strict as South Carolina's.

SC.11   **What is the new transporting bar contained in the new law?**

It is now a state-law felony to transport, shelter, harbor, or conceal unauthorized individuals knowingly or in reckless disregard of the fact that the person is illegally present in the United States. Fines range from $3,000 to $5,000 and guilty parties may be subject to imprisonment for up to five years. Also, persons convicted under the law are barred from receiving a professional license in South Carolina.

SC.12   **What does the new law change with regard to identity theft?**

Individuals who engage in identity theft for the purpose of working in the U.S. must pay restitution to the state for any benefits received under any state programs and individuals suffering any harm as a result of such identity theft may now bring a private cause of action and seek triple damages and attorney's fees.

SC.13   **Does the law give any rights to discharged U.S. workers?**

Yes. Employees who are replaced by unauthorized workers when the employer knows the replacement worker is unauthorized shall have a civil right of action for wrongful termination. The replacement must have occurred within 60 days of the termination, the replacement worker must not have been authorized at the time of the replacement, the employer must have known the replacement worker's status, and the replacement worker must perform the same duties and have the same responsibilities as the terminated employee. Employees successful in such a lawsuit can seek reinstatement in the position, actual damages, and attorney's fees. The claim must be made within a year of the date of the alleged violation.

Tennessee

On January 1, 2008, Tennessee H.B. 729 (Public Chapter No. 529) took effect. The bill created a new version of Tenn. Code Ann. §50-1-103. The new §50-1-103 permits the Tennessee Commissioner of Labor and Workforce Development (LWD) to order the suspension of a business license of any employer found to "knowingly employ, recruit or refer for a fee for employment, an illegal alien."

In 2006, Tennessee passed H.B. 111 (Public Chapter No. 878) which bars state agencies from contracting with employers that have knowingly hired illegal aliens.

S.B. 903 (Public Chapter 220) was signed in May 2007 and bars employers from accepting taxpayer identification numbers to prove immigration status.

TN.1 **How does Tennessee define "knowingly" in Public Chapter No. 529?**
The new law requires actual knowledge that a person is an illegal alien or, importantly, having a "duty imposed by law" to determine the immigration status of an illegal alien and failing to perform such duty.

So, aside from the obvious problem of simply hiring someone an employer knows is out of status, an employer arguably could be found to have knowingly employed an illegal alien if the employer did not follow immigration law in determining the immigration status of an employee. This could mean failing to complete an I-9 form for an employee, failing to examine the identity and work authorization documents associated with the I-9, and failing to reverify employment authorizations on I-9s for employees with expiring work documents.

TN.2 **Who is an "illegal alien"?**
While this may seem obvious, the definition in the bill is broad. All persons who are neither permanent residents nor authorized to work are "illegal aliens." So someone legally in the U.S. who is not a permanent resident would be considered an illegal alien under the law. This might include a nonimmigrant, like a student, a legally admitted refugee, or a person with a pending adjustment application who is awaiting "green card" status and is legally allowed to remain in the U.S. while he or she waits. The catch is that if such a person is not authorized to work, for purposes of the law, they are illegal aliens. This is because the law is designed to prevent employers from hiring individuals barred from working in the U.S. and not just those who are out-of-status.

TN.3 **How does the commissioner of Labor and Workforce Development (LWD) determine when to go after a company?**
In order for an investigation to occur of an alleged violation of the new law, a complaint must be filed. The complaint may be lodged by a state or local governmental agency, an "officer" (a term not defined), an employee of the company (though this presumably would cover a former employee as well), or an "entity" (this term is also not defined though it could presumably mean competitor companies as well as anti-immigration organizations).

TN.4 **If the commissioner determines there is evidence the new law has been violated, what is the process that occurs before a company's business license is affected?**
If the commissioner determines that there is substantial evidence of a violation, then a hearing shall be conducted. After a hearing, if the commissioner determines that there is "clear and convincing evidence" that a person has violated the law, then an order shall be requested to revoke, suspend, or deny an employer's business license. The commissioner is required to state whether there have been prior violations of this law.

TN.5 **If the business license is revoked, how can it be reinstated?**
For a first violation, the commissioner can only order the revocation of the business license "until the person shows to the satisfaction of the commissioner that the person is no longer in violation of subsection (b)." If the case is focused on the employment of a single individual and the individual is terminated, then the business license would presumably be reinstated. But there is no timetable in the statute providing how long the commissioner has to make this determination. Furthermore, if an investigation determined that numerous employees may be working illegally at the company because a company has been lax with respect to

its I-9s and other immigration recordkeeping, the commissioner might choose to conduct an audit to determine that a company has no other employees illegally working for it.

TN.6   What happens if a subsequent violation is found to have occurred?
If an employer is found to have committed a second or subsequent violation within three years of the first order, the business license shall be suspended for one year.

TN.7   Is there an appeals process?
The statute does not provide for an appeals process.

TN.8   Is an employer liable for work performed by independent contractors?
No, as long as labor law does not consider the work to be true employment where a W-2 must be filed for an employee.

TN.9   Are there any safe harbors in the bill?
Yes. If an employer has received an I-9 form from an employee within 14 days of hire (federal law requires such a form be received by an employee on the day of hire anyway and the documentation proving work authorization within three days of hire) and the information provided by the person is later determined to be false, an employer will not be found to have violated the new law.

Employers are also protected if they have verified the status of an employee using E-Verify, the DHS' electronic work authorization program (formerly called the Basic Pilot Program).

TN.10   What steps can a company take to reduce the likelihood of being found to have violated Tenn. Code Ann. §50-1-103?
Companies should consider the following actions:
- Conduct regular I-9 training for employees responsible for the function.
- Centralize I-9 recordkeeping.
- Establish a nondiscriminatory system to reverify I-9s with expiring work authorization documents.
- Switch to an electronic I-9 system rather than a paper-based one.
- Purge I-9s which employers are legally permitted to purge.
- Have an outside firm conduct an internal I-9 audit to identify and remediate violations before a government audit occurs.
- Develop a government audit response plan and train employees thoroughly in how to respond to a surprise audit.
- Begin using the DHS' E-Verify system.

TN.11   Are there other Tennessee laws covering employers and immigration?
The main additional law, Public Chapter No. 878, was passed in 2006. It bars employers who knowingly utilize the services of illegal immigrants in the performance of a contract from access to contracts with Tennessee state agencies. Employers are also required to sign an attestation that they will not knowingly use the services of illegal immigrants in the performance of the contract. Firms found to have used illegal employees in the performance a state contract will be barred from contracting with the state for a one-year period.

TN.12   What limits does Public Chapter No. 878 impose on state agencies?
The state is barred from contracting to acquire goods or services from any person who knowingly uses the services of "illegal immigrants" in

the performance of a contract for goods or services entered into with the state or a state agency. Contractors who employ illegal immigrants are barred from supplying goods or services to the state. Since the law took effect, employers must first sign an attestation promising not to knowingly employ illegal immigrants.

TN.13   What happens if a contractor is found to have employed an illegal alien?

Bidders to supply goods and services to the state will be prohibited for a year from entering into a contract with the state if they have knowingly employed illegal immigrants.

TN.14   How are state agencies to ensure compliance?

Each agency must require its contractors to submit attestations on compliance semiannually during the term of the contract. Subcontractors must file attestations with the contractor under this new law.

TN.15   How often must the attestation be updated?

The governor has issued an executive order related to Public Chapter No. 878 which requires that contractors update their attestations semiannually and also obtain attestations from their subcontractors semiannually.

TN.16   When did the law go into effect?

The law went into effect on October 1, 2006.

TN.17   What does Public Chapter No. 220 do?

An employer presented with an individual taxpayer identification number by a potential employee or subcontractor as a form of identification or to prove immigration status shall reject such number and request the lawful resident verification information required under federal law. This appears to be unnecessary since under IRCA a taxpayer identification number is not permitted to prove employment authorization anyway.

Texas

Under Texas H.B. 1196, which passed in 2007, employers receiving public subsidies must sign a written statement certifying the employer has not hired unauthorized immigrants.

TX.1   What does H.B. 1196 do?

All governmental agencies in Texas that provide a "public subsidy" to businesses shall require that the business submit a statement with their application certifying that the business does not and will not knowingly employ an "undocumented worker."

TX.2   Does the law apply to companies related to the company receiving the subsidy?

Yes, it applies to branches, divisions, or departments of the business.

TX.3   How is "public subsidy" defined?

A "public subsidy" is a public program, benefit, or assistance designed to stimulate the economic development of a corporation, industry, or a sector of the state's economy to create or retain jobs in the state. Subsidies can include grants, loans, loan guarantees, benefits relating to an enterprise or empowerment zone, fee waivers, land price subsidies, infrastructure development and improvements designed to benefit a single business, matching funds, tax refunds, tax rebates, or tax abatements.

TX.4   How is "undocumented worker" defined?

Anyone who is not a "green card" holder or otherwise authorized to be employed in the United States is considered an "undocumented worker."

TX.5   What happens if a business violates its certification?

If a business is convicted of violating IRCA, the business must also repay the amount of the public subsidy with interest at a rate provided in the agreement between the state agency and the business. The agency providing the subsidy is entitled to sue to recover the owing amount and to recover attorney's fees.

TX.6   When did the law become effective?

The law became effective September 1, 2007.

Utah

In early 2008, Utah's governor signed legislation imposing new employment verification requirements on public and private employers.

UT.1   What is the new verification requirement for state agency employers in Utah?

Beginning immediately, all public employers are required to register with and use a "status verification system" to verify the federal employment authorization status of any new employee. Note that while most assume this means E-Verify, the legislation states that status verification system includes:

- E-Verify.
- An equivalent federal program designated by DHS as verifying work eligibility of newly hired employees.
- The SSVNS.
- An independent third-party system with an equal or higher degree of reliability as E-Verify or SSVNS.

UT.2   What new requirements are imposed on contractors doing business with state agencies?

State agencies may not enter into contracts with employers unless the employer registers and uses a status verification system to verify the contractor's new employees. The law does not apply to certain financial services industry occupations, such as securities placement or financial or investment banking services.

UT.3   When does the requirement that contractors use a status verification system take effect?

It takes effect on July 1, 2009. Contracts entered into before that date are not covered even if the contract involves the physical performance of services after July 1, 2009.

UT.4   Is the contractor responsible for the work of other contractors or subcontractors?

The contractor is responsible only if the contractor's or subcontractor's employees work under the contractor's supervision or direction.

UT.5   How are U.S. citizen workers affected by the new law?

Employers may not discharge employees who are U.S. citizen or permanent residents and replace them with employees not authorized to work. This provision takes effect July 1, 2009. Employers using a status verification system are protected from liability. Employees who can demonstrate they were unlawfully terminated shall have the right to sue an employer for damages.

UT.6   **What are the new Utah law's transporting and harboring provisions?**
The Utah law makes it unlawful for any person to transport more than 100 miles, conceal, harbor, or shelter from detection in any place, including any building or means of transportation, any alien (1) knowing or in reckless disregard of the fact that the alien is in the U.S. illegally and (2) when the act is done for "commercial advantage or private financial gain." This provision could be used against employers knowingly employing unauthorized immigrants.

UT.7   **What are the penalties for violating the transporting and harboring provisions?**
Violating these provisions constitutes a class A misdemeanor.

UT.8   **Are there exceptions to the transporting and harboring prohibitions?**
Yes. Persons providing charitable or humanitarian assistance are excepted, as well as certain religious organizations receiving volunteer services from a minister or missionary.

UT.9   **When does the transporting and harboring law take effect?**
The law takes effect on July 1, 2009.

Virginia

In March 2008, Virginia's legislature approved and its governor signed S.B. 782, an employer sanctions bill that calls for the revocation of a corporation's right to exist in Virginia. At the same time, the legislature also passed S.B. 517 which affects contractors.

VA.1   **What kinds of violations will trigger a termination of the right to do business in the state?**
Corporations engaged in serious immigration law violations are subject to having their corporate existence terminated involuntarily by Virginia. Under the statute, employers must have a conviction for violating 8 U.S.C. §1324a(f) which imposes criminal penalties for people or entities engaged in a "pattern or practice of violations" of IRCA.

VA.2   **What does S.B. 517 say with respect to contractors?**
The new law states that public agencies shall require contractors to certify in their contracts that the contractor shall not during the performance of the contract knowingly employ an unauthorized alien.

VA.3   **What changes are made regarding public agencies?**
The new Virginia law requires that every governmental agency must register for E-Verify.

West Virginia

In April 2007, West Virginia's governor signed S.B. 70, a bill making it unlawful for employers to knowingly employ an unauthorized worker. The law is one of the country's toughest, yet it has not received the publicity of other state laws.

WV.1   **What does S.B. 70 do?**
The law establishes criminal penalties separate from IRCA for employers found to have knowingly hiring unauthorized workers.

S.B. 70 makes it unlawful for any employer to knowingly employ, hire, recruit, or refer, for private or public employment in West Virginia, an unauthorized worker.

Employers are required to verify a prospective employee's legal status or authorization to work before employing the individual or contracting with the individual for employment services.

S.B. 70 also removes the ability of employers to deduct as a business expense from state income taxes any wages paid to unauthorized workers.

WV.2   What penalties are faced by employers who violate the law?

An employer violating the law is guilty of a misdemeanor and, upon conviction, can be subject to the following penalties:

- First offense — a fine of $100 to $1,000.
- Second offense — a fine of $500 to $5,000.
- Third offense — a fine of $1,000 to $10,000, or jail time of 30 days to a year, or both; revocation of business license.

Employers who knowingly provide false records regarding the employment authorization of employees to West Virginia's Labor Commission shall be guilty of a misdemeanor and subject to imprisonment of up to a year and a fine of up to $2,500.

Employers who knowingly and with fraudulent intent sell, transfer, or dispose of the employer's assets to evade recordkeeping requirements shall be guilty of a misdemeanor and can be confined up to a year and fined up to $10,000.

WV.3   How does S.B. 70 affect business deductions for unauthorized employees' salaries?

Employers normally can deduct wages paid to employees on the employers' state income tax returns. However, wages in excess of $600 paid to unauthorized employees cannot be deducted by employers under the law. This provision went into effect on January 1, 2008, and only affects wages paid after that date.

WV.4   Can a business license be revoked under S.B. 70?

Yes. If an employer is convicted under S.B. 70 for knowingly employing an undocumented employee a third time, the state's labor commissioner can issue an order imposing the following:

- Permanent revocation of any license held by the employer.
- Suspension of a license held by the employer for a specified period.

PART II:

An Overview of the U.S. Immigration System

Nonimmigrant Visas

17.1 **What are the five major immigration status/visa categories?**
- Nonimmigrant visas are for temporary visitors (workers, students, visitors, etc.)
- Immigrant visas are for lawful permanent residents ("green card" holders). (See Chapter 18.)
- Asylees and other special groups are asylum-seekers, refugees, and TPS holders. (See Chapter 19.)
- Citizens.
- Undocumented (illegal) immigrants.

17.2 **What are the major types of nonimmigrant visas and to whom are they available?**
- H-1B visas: Available to people in "specialty occupations."
- B-1 and B-2 visas: Available to short-term visitors for pleasure or business.
- F-1 visas: Available to students.
- J-1 visas: Available to exchange visitors (for example, trainees, interns, professors or research scholars, short-term scholars, foreign doctors, camp counselors, au pairs, and students in work/travel programs in the U.S.).
- O-1 visas: Available to people with extraordinary ability in the sciences, arts, crafts, education, business, athletics, or any field of "creative endeavor."
- L visas: Available to intracompany transfers.
- E visas: Available to E-2 treaty investors and E-1 treaty traders.
- R visas: Available to religious employees.
- TN visas: Available to Canadian and Mexican professionals working pursuant to the North American Free Trade Agreement (NAFTA).
- E-3 visas: Available to Australians.

17.3 **What kinds of questions are relevant for H-1B visa applicants?**
- Do you have a university degree?
- Do most people in your field in the U.S. have university degrees?
- If you lack a degree, do you have several years of work experience in your field?
- Do you have an employer in the U.S. willing to hire you?
- Does the job pay as much as similarly employed American employees?
- Does the employer typically only hire people with university degrees for the job?
- Does the employer guarantee that they will have continuous work available to you?
- If the occupation requires a license, do you have the necessary license?

17.4 **How long is the H-1B visa valid?**
An H-1B visa is valid for up to six years. The status can potentially be extended if a permanent residency application has been filed.

17.5 **Can an H-1B visa holder also apply for a "green card"?**
Yes, H-1B visa holders can simultaneously have a "green card" application pending.

17.6   Are spouses or children of H-1B visa holders permitted to work?
No, unless they secure a work status independent of the H-1B visa holder.

17.7   Are H-1B visa holders required to maintain ties to their home countries?
No.

17.8   How many H-1B visas are provided each year?
The granting of H-1B visas is limited to 65,000 people per year (but many H-1B employees are exempt from this cap and there is an additional quota of 20,000 for people holding masters degrees or higher granted by a U.S. university).

17.9   Are H-1B visa holders permitted to change employers?
H-1B holders can change employers, but they need a change-of-status approval for each new employer.

17.10   Are H-1B visas permitted for self-employment?
An individual can establish his or her own company and be employed by the business as an H-1B. The applicant must demonstrate all H-1B requirements, including demonstrating an ability to pay the prevailing wage.

17.11   What happens in the event the H-1B applicant lacks an appropriate degree?
Equivalent work experience must be demonstrated and an evaluation from an expert must be obtained.

17.12   What kinds of questions are relevant for B-1 and B-2 visa applicants?
- Do you have a job that pays well and which you can leave for a few weeks on a vacation?
- Do you have close relatives who will be remaining in your home country when you come to the United States?
- Are you coming for a short visit?
- Do you have assets in your home country?
- Do you own property in your home country?
- Do you have a set itinerary for your trip to the United States?
- Do you have a roundtrip plane ticket?
- Do you have close community ties in your home country?
- Do you have money or proof of support from friends or relatives in the U.S. to show adequate financial arrangements to carry out the purpose of the trip?
- If you are coming for business, is the work you are doing work that would typically be done by an American employee?
- If you are coming for business, is the main place where profits are earned outside the United States?
- If you are coming to the U.S. on business, is your payment going to be made abroad rather than in the United States?
- If you are coming as a B-2 visitor for pleasure, are you coming for one of the following purposes?
  » Tourist.
  » Social visits to friends and/or relatives.
  » Health purposes.
  » Participant in conventions of social organizations.
  » Participant in amateur musical, sports, or similar events with no pay.
  » Spouse and children of people in the U.S. Armed Forces.
  » Accompanying B-1 business visitors.
  » Coming to marry a U.S. citizen but the person plans on departing after the wedding.
  » Coming to marry someone on a nonimmigrant visa.

- » Nonspouse partner (regardless of gender) who accompanies an E, H, or L visa holder.
- » Parent seeking to accompany an F-1 student visa holder.
- » Language student in a course of short duration when the course of study is under 18 hours per week.
- If you are coming on a B-1 business visitor visa, are you coming for one of the following purposes?
    - » Engaging in commercial transactions not involving employment (negotiating contracts, litigation, consulting with clients or business associates).
    - » Participating in scientific, educational, professional, religious, or business conventions.
    - » Religious employees coming to do missionary work in the United States, ministers exchanging pulpits but who are paid by their own church abroad, and ministers on evangelical tours.
    - » Domestic servants accompanying returning U.S. citizens who are temporarily assigned to the U.S. or who permanently reside in a foreign country.
    - » Domestic servants accompanying nonimmigrant visa holders if the applicant has worked for the employer for a year or more.
    - » Professional athletes only receiving tournament money.
    - » Foreign medical students seeking to take "elective clerkship" without pay.
    - » Serving on a board of directors of a U.S. company.
    - » Coming to the U.S. to set up a U.S. subsidiary and explore investment opportunities.
    - » Installing equipment as part of a contract.
    - » Participating in a volunteer service program if religious only.
    - » Attending an executive seminar.
    - » Observing the conduct of business.
    - » Domestic partner of a person on a nonimmigrant visa.

17.13   How long is the B-1 or B-2 visa valid?

The approved applicant can usually get an authorized stay of up to six months, but chances of getting the visa improve if a shorter trip is requested. A border officer has the authority to approve a stay shorter than six months.

17.14   Are B-1 and B-2 visa holders allowed to work in the United States?

Generally speaking, no.

17.15   Nationals from which countries are eligible for the Visa Waiver Program (VWP)?

Nationals from Andorra, Australia, Austria, Belgium, Brunei, the Czech Republic, Denmark, Estonia, Finland, France, Germany, Hungary, Iceland, Ireland, Italy, Japan, Latvia, Liechtenstein, Lithuania, Luxembourg, Monaco, the Netherlands, New Zealand, Norway, Portugal, the Republic of Korea, San Marino, Singapore, the Slovak Republic, Slovenia, Spain, Sweden, Switzerland, and the United Kingdom are eligible under the Visa Waiver Program (VWP) to enter the U.S. for up to 90 days. VWP entrants cannot have their status extended and cannot change to other nonimmigrant categories while in the United States.

17.16   What kinds of questions are relevant for F-1 visa applicants?

- Do you have a residence in your home country that you don't intend to abandon?
- Have you been admitted to study full-time in a degree program or an English language program?
- Is the school where you intend to study approved for students to attend on student visas?
- Do you have proof of adequate financial resources to attend school full-time without the need to work in the United States?

- If you are not going to study in an English language program in the United States, are you proficient in English?
- Will the education you obtain in the U.S. improve your career prospects in your home country?

17.17   What are the requirements for the F-1 visa holder?

They must be enrolled full-time. They have limited on-campus work eligibility. Off-campus employment is prohibited unless the student fits under limited exceptions and the employment authorization is granted by the school or the USCIS.

17.18   Can an F-1 visa holder work in the United States after completing an educational program?

Yes, they can get up to a year of work authorization upon completion of a program.

17.19   What limitations are there on the spouses and children of F-1 visa holders?

Spouses and children are not entitled to work unless they secure a work status independently. Children can enroll in K-12 education. A spouse cannot study unless he or she has a separate student visa.

17.20   What kinds of questions are relevant for J-1 visa applicants?

- Are you coming to the U.S. to participate in an exchange program designed by the U.S. State Department?
- Do you have fluency in English and sufficient funds to live here if the program does not pay J-1 visa holders?
- If you are looking at the au pair program, have you registered with one of the eight designated au pair programs in the United States?
- If you are a doctor seeking to train in the U.S., are you admitted into a medical residency or fellowship program and have you obtained sponsorship from the Educational Commission on Foreign Medical Graduates?
- If you are coming for a business trainee or intern visa, have you found an employer to provide you with a training opportunity?
- If you have found a training opportunity, have you found a program sponsor?

17.21   Is there a requirement for J-1 visa holders to return home before switching to another visa?

Yes, there is often a requirement to return home for two years before switching to another visa.

17.22   What are the time requirements for J-1 visa holders?

Time limits vary depending on type of program:

- Training — 18 months.
- Interns — 12 months.
- Scholars and professors — up to three years.
- Au pairs — 12 months.
- Medical residents — up to seven years.
- Students — no limit.

Students are eligible for up to 18 months of postgraduate work authorization (36 months, if postdoctoral work), but students must be enrolled full-time.

17.23   What about employment opportunities in the United States for the spouses and children of J-1 visa holders?

Spouses and children are entitled to work authorization.

17.24   What kinds of questions are relevant for O-1 visa applicants?

- Are you one of the top people in your field in your country?
- Do you have an employer, manager, or agent in the U.S. who can sign your application?
- Is there a peer organization willing to say that they have no objection to your being granted an O-1 visa?
- Can you show that you have won a major international award or at least three of the following?
  - » Documentation of the alien's receipt of nationally or internationally recognized prizes or awards for excellence in the field of endeavor.
  - » Documentation of the alien's membership in associations in the field for which classification is sought, which require outstanding achievements of their members, as judged by recognized national or international experts in their disciplines or fields.
  - » Published material in professional or major trade publications or major media about the alien, relating to the alien's work in the field for which classification is sought, which shall include the title, date, and author of such published material, and any necessary translation.
  - » Evidence of the alien's participation on a panel, or individually, as a judge of the work of others in the same or in an allied field of specialization to that for which classification is sought.
  - » Evidence of the alien's original scientific, scholarly, or business-related contributions of major significance in the field.
  - » Evidence of the alien's authorship of scholarly articles in the field, in professional journals, or other major media.
  - » Evidence that the alien has been employed in a critical or essential capacity for organizations and establishments that have a distinguished reputation.
  - » Evidence that the alien has commanded and now commands a high salary or other remuneration for services, evidenced by contracts or other reliable evidence.

17.25   What is the time limit on the issuance of O-1 approvals?

They can be admitted for up to three years at a time.

17.26   Are O-1 visa holders required to maintain a residence abroad?

No.

17.27   May O-1 visa holders apply for a "green card"?

Yes, they can have a "green card" application pending while on O-1 status without problems.

17.28   What kinds of questions are relevant for L visa applicants?

- Are you coming to the U.S. to work for a company that has offices both in the U.S. and outside the United States?
- Have you worked for the company abroad full-time for at least one year of the last three?
- Are you coming to the U.S. as an owner, executive, manager, or an employee with special knowledge of the company's operations?

17.29   What are the time limits for L visa holders?

Seven-year stays for owners, executives, and managers and five-year stays for special knowledge employees.

17.30   Are "green cards" easy to get for L visa holders?

Yes, for owners, managers, and executives.

17.31 Are spouses of L visa holders allowed to work?
Yes.

17.32 Which type of employee has a difficult time getting an L visa?
Employees working on a contract basis at other employers have a difficult time, as do employees that claim specialized knowledge but cannot document that they bring skills not readily available in the local job market.

17.33 What kinds of questions are relevant for E-1 and E-2 visa applicants?
- If you are seeking an E-1 Treaty Trader visa, are you currently working for a business that has a substantial volume of trading business with the U.S. (more than 50 percent)?
- Are you a national of a country that has a bilateral trade treaty with the United States?
- Are you coming to the U.S. to work as an owner, executive, manager, or essential skills employee?
- Is at least 50 percent of the business owned by foreign nationals who are not U.S. citizens or permanent residents?
- For E-2 visas, are you investing a substantial amount of money in a commercial investment in the United States?

17.34 What are the time limits for E visa holders?
There are no limits on the total time in E visa status.

17.35 Are spouses of E visa holders allowed to work?
Yes.

17.36 What is the impact of permanent residency applications on E Visas holders?
Permanent residency applications do not adversely affect the granting of E visas.

17.37 What kinds of questions are relevant for R visa applicants?
- Are you coming to the U.S. to work as a minister or work in a religious vocation or occupation?
- Have you been a member of the religious denomination for at least two years?
- Is the employer a nonprofit organization (most churches, synagogues, and mosques qualify as well as institutions affiliated with them)?

17.38 What is the time limit for R visa holders?
R visas are valid for up to five years.

17.39 At what point may R visas convert to "green cards"?
R visas are convertible to a "green card" after two years of work, unless the applicant already has two years' experience in the religious occupation.

17.40 Has the USCIS changed the process to acquire an R visa recently?
Yes, change of status petitions now take several months because the USCIS conducts site visits to a petitioning religious institution.

17.41 What kinds of questions are relevant for TN visa applicants?
- Are you coming to the U.S. to work in an occupation listed within the North American Free Trade Agreement (NAFTA) occupation schedule?
- Are you a citizen or national of Canada or Mexico?
- Do you meet the minimum job requirements for that position as listed in the TN NAFTA Schedule?

17.42   **What is the time limit for TN visa holders?**
TN visas are valid for a year and can be extended in one-year increments.

17.43   **Are TN visa holders required to demonstrate an intent to immigrate to the United States?**
No. The TN visa is a nonimmigrant visa; therefore, the beneficiary cannot have immigrant intent.

17.44   **How do Canadians apply for TN visa status?**
Canadians can apply for the status at the port of entries with "TN offer letters."

17.45   **How do Mexicans apply for TN visa status?**
Mexicans can apply directly at U.S. Consulates.

17.46   **Where are TN visa extensions and change of status applications filed?**
They may be filed in the United States (only at the USCIS' Nebraska Service Center).

17.47   **Are degrees in a field required?**
Yes, most jobs require a degree in the field; however, for management consultants they are not required. Note, however, that these cases are closely scrutinized.

17.48   **What kinds of questions are relevant for E-3 visa applicants?**
- Are you Australian?
- Do you have a university degree?
- Do most people in your field in the U.S. have university degrees?
- If you lack a degree, do you have several years of work experience in your field?
- Do you have an employer in the U.S. willing to hire you?
- Does the job pay as much as similarly employed American workers?
- Does the employer typically only hire people with university degrees for the job?
- Does the employer guarantee that it will have continuous work available to you?
- If the occupation requires a license, do you have the necessary license?

17.49   **Do E-3 applicants require advanced USCIS approval?**
No. Like the E-1 and E-2, E-3 applications can be filed directly at a U.S. Consulate abroad.

17.50   **May spouses of E-3 visa holders be eligible for an EAD?**
Yes, when they accompany the E-3 visa holder to the United States.

17.51   **Is a Labor Condition Application (LCA) required of the E-3 visa holder?**
Yes, and the prevailing wage must be paid.

17.52   **What is the time limit for E-3 visa holders?**
Unlike the H-1B (and like the E-1 and E-2), there is no limit on the number of years an E-3 can hold E-3 status.

16.53   **Are the nonimmigrant visas listed in No. 17.2 above a complete listing?**
No. There are currently more than 25 major nonimmigrant visa classifications. The discussion in this chapter includes only the most common ones.

Immigrant Visas (the "Green Card")

18.1 What are the four basic categories of immigrant visas?
- Family-sponsored immigrants.
- Employment-based immigrants.
- Diversity immigrants.
- Refugees and asylees. (See Chapter 19, Asylee and Refugees.)

18.2 What kinds of questions and waiting periods are relevant for Family-Sponsored Immigrants?

18.2.1 For immediate relatives, there are no quotas and faster processing:
- Are you a spouse of a U.S. citizen?
- Are you a child of a U.S. citizen and under the age of 21?
- Are you the parent of a U.S. citizen over the age of 21?

18.2.2 For preference categories:
- First Preference: Are you the adult, unmarried child of a U.S. citizen? If so, then the wait is five-to-seven years (or more for the nationals of Mexico and the Philippines).
- Second Preference A: Are you the under 18-year-old child of a "green card" holder or the spouse of a "green card" holder? If so, then the wait is five-to-seven years (or more for the nationals of Mexico).
- Second Preference B: Are you the adult, unmarried child of a "green card" holder? If so, then the wait is nine years (or more for the nationals of Mexico and the Philippines).
- Third Preference: Are you a married child of a U.S. citizen? If so, then the wait is eight years (or more for the nationals of Mexico and Philippines).
- Fourth Preference: Are you a brother or sister of a U.S. citizen? If so, then the wait is 11 years (or more for the nationals of China, India, Mexico, and the Philippines).

18.3 How are these waiting periods determined?
The waiting periods in No. 18.2.2 above are based on the U.S. Department of State's Visa Bulletin published in August 2008 and the several bulletins published before that. These bulletins (found at www.travel.state.gov) are published monthly and announce the current waiting periods therein. The above periods should be considered as estimates and for accurate waiting periods, the current Visa Bulletin must be checked.

18.4 What's the implication of marriage to a U.S. citizen?
Marriage to a U.S. citizen is a common and expeditious way to acquire permanent residency status. The USCIS must still evaluate the marriage and determine that it was not entered into with the main purpose of acquiring a "green card."

18.5   Can a person convert from one immigrant preference or immediate relative category to another?

Cases may convert automatically from one category to another when a person's age and marital status change; certain rights and priority dates may be retained for children when they turn 21.

18.6   What kinds of questions are relevant for Diversity Visa (DV) applicants?

- Are you a high school graduate?
- Do you work in a field typically requiring two years of work experience and do you have at least two years of work experience in the field?
- Were you born in an eligible lottery country?

18.7   What kinds of issues are relevant to the DV "Green Card" lottery?

- The U.S. government allocates 50,000 visas a year for people to receive through a random computer drawing.
- Fewer than 1 in 40 applicants will succeed.
- It is easy to enter the lottery.
- The entry period is limited and usually is in the last quarter of the calendar year (October to December).
- Candidates must have a job available in the U.S. or proof of ability to support themselves financially.

18.8   What kinds of questions are relevant for the EB-1-1 "green card"?

- Are you a person of extraordinary ability in the sciences, arts, education, business, or athletics?
- Are you one of the top people in your field?
- Can you show that you have won a major international award or at least three of the following?
  » Documentation of the alien's receipt of nationally or internationally recognized prizes or awards for excellence in the field of endeavor.
  » Documentation of the alien's membership in associations in the field for which classification is sought, which require outstanding achievements of their members, as judged by recognized national or international experts in their disciplines or fields.
  » Published material in professional or major trade publications or major media about the alien, relating to the alien's work in the field for which classification is sought, which shall include the title, date, and author of such published material, and any necessary translation.
  » Evidence of the alien's participation on a panel, or individually, as a judge of the work of others in the same or in an allied field of specialization to that for which classification is sought.
  » Evidence of the alien's original scientific, scholarly, or business-related contributions of major significance in the field.
  » Evidence of the alien's authorship of scholarly articles in the field, in professional journals, or other major media.
  » Evidence that the alien has been employed in a critical or essential capacity for organizations and establishments that have a distinguished reputation.
  » Evidence that the alien has commanded and now commands a high salary or other remuneration for services, evidenced by contracts or other reliable evidence.

18.9   Is employment necessary to get the EB-1-1 "green card"?

No, but the applicant will need to demonstrate an intention to secure employment in the field if extraordinary ability.

18.10   What kinds of questions are relevant for the EB-1-2 "green card"?
- Are you recognized internationally as outstanding in a specific academic area?
- Do you have three years' experience in teaching or research in your area?
- Are you coming to the U.S. to work in a tenured or tenure-track teaching position or a long-term research position?
- Can you present evidence that you are recognized internationally in your academic field by presenting evidence of at least two of the following?
  - » Receipt of major prizes or awards of outstanding achievement.
  - » Membership in an association which requires outstanding achievement.
  - » Published material in the professional publications written by others about your work.
  - » Participation as a judge of the work of others.
  - » Original scientific research.
  - » Authorship of scholarly books or articles in the field.

18.11   Is the EB-1-3 "green card' identical to the L-1 visa?
The EB-1-3 is similar to the L-1 intracompany transfer nonimmigrant visa. There are, however, some important differences. For example, it is not available to specialized knowledge employees and the U.S. branch must be operating for at least a year. (See Chapter 17.)

18.12   What kinds of questions are relevant for the EB-2 "green card"?
- Do you have a degree beyond a bachelor's degree or do you have a bachelor's degree plus five years of work experience in your field?
- Do you meet the definition of exceptional ability by showing three of the following?
  - » Degree relating to the area of exceptional ability.
  - » Letter from current or former employer showing at least 10 years of experience.
  - » License to practice profession.
  - » Commanded a salary or remuneration demonstrating exceptional ability.
  - » Membership in professional association.
  - » Recognition for achievements and significant contributions to the industry or field by peers, governmental entities, or professional or business organization.
- Do you have a job offer and labor certification, or are you basing your "green card" application on benefiting the nation's interest?
- If you are planning on basing your "green card" application on a labor certification, do you work in a field where there is a shortage of U.S. employees in the local area where you intend to work?
- If your claim is based on a labor certification, are you going to be paid the prevailing wage for similarly employed employees in the city where you are going to work?
- If your claim is based on a labor certification, has your employer attempted to recruit employees to fill the position?
- If your claim is based on a national interest waiver, do you meet the following tests?
  - » The person seeks employment in an area of substantial intrinsic merit.
  - » The benefit will be national in scope.
  - » The national interest would be adversely affected if a labor certification were required.

18.13   What is the processing time for the EB-2 "green card"?
Processing times vary but labor certification cases typically take 1-2 years and national interest cases take 6-18 months.

18.14   Is employment a requirement for the EB-2 application?
It is not required in national interest waiver cases.

18.15 Who is eligible for the EB-3 "green card"?

The EB-3 is available to university graduates, and people working in jobs requiring an employee with at least two years experience can file under this category if the employer gets a labor certification.

18.16 What is the subcategory of the EB-3 "green card"?

It is for unskilled employees who do not have a work experience or education requirement, but still require a labor certification.

18.17 Is the EB-4 "green card" the same as the R-1 visa?

Yes, they basically have the same requirements except that the applicant must have been working in the field for at least a two-year period. (See Chapter 17.)

18.18 What kinds of questions are relevant for the EB-5 "green card"?

- Are you investing in a business in the United States?
- Is the business new or are you buying into a restructured business?
- Are you investing at least $500,000 if the business is in a rural, high unemployment area, or designated target investment area, or $1 million if located elsewhere?
- Is your investment in the form of cash, equipment, inventory, other tangible property, cash equivalents, and indebtedness secured by assets owned by the entrepreneur?
- Is the investment "at risk"?
- Can you document that the source of the funds is legitimate?
- Will the investment result in the creation of at least 10 full-time jobs for U.S. employees?

18.19 What does the USCIS consider when granting the EB-5?

The USCIS scrutinizes these cases carefully. While technically the investment and job creation need not take place until after granting the "green card," in practice the USCIS will deny unless the investment and job creation take place before the application is submitted. Applicants can avoid having to show direct job creation by investing in a preapproved regional investment center. Applicants applying through regional centers also do not need to show they are involved in management.

Asylees and Refugees

19.1 What are asylees and refugees?

There are certain protected groups of aliens in the United States. Most common are the asylees and refugees. Under the 1980 Refugee Act, a refugee is defined as "any person who is outside of any country of such person's nationality ... who is unable or unwilling to return to, and is unable or unwilling to avail himself or herself of the protection of that country because of persecution or a well-founded fear of persecution on account of race, religion, nationality, membership in a particular social group, or political opinion."

Asylees demonstrate the same well-founded fear of persecution, except that they are in the U.S. when they apply for such status.

Asylees and refugees are eligible for employment authorization and have special paths to permanent residency.

19.2 What is the difference between an asylee and a refugee?

In almost every way, the requirements for refugee status and asylum are the same. The most important difference is that an asylee makes his or her application while in the U.S., while the refugee applies outside of his or her home country, but also outside of the United States.

19.3 Are there other protected groups?

Yes, they are the TPS aliens. TPS stands for "temporary protected status" and is available to nationals of designated countries facing armed conflict, environmental disaster, and other extraordinary and temporary conditions.

Appendices

Notable ICE Worksite Enforcement Operations in 2006-2008

Company	Date	State(s)	Violations, crimes	Other notes
B&B Masonry, Inc.	2/2008	ND and TX	Owner of company sentenced to six months for harboring unauthorized documents; ordered to forfeit $45,450; 10 employees arrested at work site	B&B was a subcontractor on a construction project; B&B constructs Texas Roadhouse restaurants around the country
China Star Restaurant	2/2008	KY	Owner of Chinese restaurant indicted for harboring and for having employees work 12 hour days, six days per week; maximum sentence of 10 years and fine of $250,000; forfeiture of assets sought	
Universal Industrial Sales, Inc. (UIS)	2/2008	UT	57 unauthorized immigrant employees arrested; 30 cases referred for offenses such as ID theft, forgery and document fraud; company charged with 10 counts of harboring; and that the company concealed, harbored or shielded the employees from detection for commercial advantage; human resources manager indicted for encouraging or inducing unauthorized immigrants to remain in the U.S. unlawfully	
Micro Solutions Enterprises (MSE)	2/2008	CA	Toner cartridge manufacturer; 8 employees charged with crimes; 130 arrested on administrative immigration grounds; employees charged with providing false documents in order to obtain employment	
Buffet City Restaurant	1/2008	IL	Owner of Chinese restaurant sentenced to 18 months for harboring and employing unauthorized immigrants at his restaurant; ordered to pay $2500 fine within a year; owner will be deported because of unauthorized status; 16 employees arrested for immigration violations	
MJH Construction	12/2007	UT	Construction contractor indicted for alien smuggling and harboring tied to a scheme to bring unauthorized immigrants to the U.S. and requiring them work for his business to pay off their smuggling debts	
Progressive Builders	12/2007	KY	Contractor that provided framing services for new home construction sentenced to 18 months for using unauthorized immigrants as well as harboring). Owner's two employee children also sentenced as well as four crew chiefs	Crew chiefs also will face deportation proceedings once they complete their jail sentences

continued on next page

Company	Date	State(s)	Violations, crimes	Other notes
Pepe's Cabinets	11/2007	CA	Owner of business arrested after ICE agents executed search on premises; owner charged with unlawfully employing unauthorized immigrants and harboring them; owner faces maximum of five years in prison; owner and eight employees all placed in deportation proceedings; owner alleged to have paid employees in cash to conceal their illegal employment and that at least one employee may have been housed by the owner	
Ideal Staffing Solutions, Inc.	11/2007	IL	Corporate officer and office manager of a temporary employment agency were arrested on charges of harboring; 20 employees arrested for using fraudulent airport security badges to obtain entry to secure areas at O'Hare International Airport to obtain access to jobs loading pallets, freight and meals for commercial flights; 100 total employees in possession of the badges; company managers allegedly provided some employees with deactivated badges issued in other names; corporate secretary and office manager charged with harboring for financial gain and misuse of SSNs; 110 names did not match SSNs	Critical infrastructure site
ANNA II, Inc.	10/2007	IL	23 unauthorized immigrants administratively arrested at a staffing company that provides day laborers to warehouses around Chicago; criminal search took place at company premises; employer transported employees each day to work sites	
Nanak Hotel Group	10/2007	VT	Employer arrested on charges of employing and harboring unauthorized immigrants and making false statements (relating to the owner's immigration from Canada); company allegedly had a shell company employ unauthorized employees separate from their regular payroll; 10 employees administratively arrested and face removal	
Hedges Landscape Specialists Inc./ Exterior Designs, Inc./Performance Irrigation LLC	10/2007	KY	Owner of companies pled guilty to employing unauthorized immigrants; owner found to have knowingly employed at least 12 unauthorized immigrants and engaged in a "pattern or practice of knowingly hiring illegal aliens."; informant told ICE that company paid employees a flat rate no matter how many hours they worked; owner accused of having paid employees under the table; owner told HR official not to complete Forms I-9 and he "would just pay a fine" if he were caught; company faces a $250,000 fine and owner faces a $24,000 fine and six months in jail; owner to forfeit $147,000 in cash in corporate bank accounts	

continued on next page

Company	Date	State(s)	Violations, crimes	Other notes
Koch Foods	8/2007	OH	160 employees administratively arrested	Criminal search warrants issued at company's Chicago headquarters; part of bigger investigation of whether Koch may have knowingly hired unauthorized employees at its chicken plants
Fresh Del Monte Produce	6/2007	OR	10 former employees indicted for possession of fraudulent immigration documents or Social Security fraud; 160 employees administratively arrested	Criminal search warranted; contractor American Staffing Resources was also part of the investigation
George's Processing, Inc.	5/2007	MO	28 chicken plant employees indicted on Criminal immigration violations; 136 employees arrested on administrative charges; 27 charged with aggravated identity theft and falsely claiming to be U.S. citizens to gain employment; 18 charged with reentering the U.S. after a deportation; 1 arrested for Social Security fraud	
El Nopal	5/2007	AR	12 employees arrested for performing work at Army National Guard Base; arrests were administrative; 49 employees placed under administrative arrest	El Nopal was the dining room contractor at the base
Quality Service Integrity, Inc. (QSI)	5/2007	IL	Four managers at QSI charged with harboring unauthorized immigrants	QSI supplied cleaning services to Cargill
Tarrasco Steel	3/2007	MS and three other Southern states	77 employees arrested on construction sites; owner of Tarrasco charged with falsifying and altering information on Forms I-9	The arrested employees were involved in bridge projects
Jones Industrial Network (JIN)	3/2007	MD	ICE executed a criminal search warrant and civil warrants and conducted consent searches at 9 locations; ICE seized company's bank account with more than $636,000; administratively arrested 69 employees at companies that contracted with JIN	JIN identified by ICE as company suspected of providing undocumented immigrants to work at the Port of Baltimore, a critical infrastructure site
Michael Bianco, Inc.	3/2007	MA	Textile company owner and three managers arrested for conspiring to encourage or induce unauthorized immigrants to reside in the U.S. and conspiring to hire unauthorized immigrants; another charged with the knowing transfer of fraudulent IDs; 320 employees administratively arrested; alleged that company knew employees were using fraudulent green cards and Social Security cards; company's managers alleged to have instructed employees on how to obtain the documents	Company had contracts with U.S. Department of Defense; nicknamed "Operation United Front"
Stucco Design Inc.	3/2007	IN	Owner of company pled guilty to violations related to harboring aliens; sentenced to 18 months in prison; forfeited $1.4 million	Firm alleged to have been able to undercut bids of contractors to perform work at construction sites by using illegal labor
Rosenbaum-Cunningham International	2/2007	18 states	Three company executives charged with conspiring to defraud the US, harboring unauthorized immigrants for profit, and evading payment of federal employment taxes; 196 administrative arrests at 64 locations	Employer provided cleaning and grounds-maintenance at theme restaurants throughout U.S. such as House of Blues, Hard Rock Café, Planet Hollywood, ESPN Zone

continued on next page

Company	Date	State(s)	Violations, crimes	Other notes
Swift & Co.	12/2006	6 states	1,297 unauthorized immigrant employees arrested at Swift meat processing plants; massive identity theft operation; 274 charged criminally, 129 on federal charges and the others on state charges; rest charged as immigration status violators; 30% of Swift's Forms I-9s suspected of being fraudulent	Arrests included a human resource employee, a union official, and current or former Swift employees identified by the FTC as suspected identity thieves; company itself not charged and the company has used E-Verify
HVC	10/2006	OH and PA	Owner of company pleaded guilty to bringing in and harboring unauthorized immigrants, mail fraud, wire fraud, conspiracy and money laundering; $100,000 of property forfeited; HVC provided housing and transportation to unauthorized employees and assisted in obtaining fraudulent documents; 33 employees subjected to administrative arrest	HVC contracted with 16 companies to supply temporary employees; HVC, both in written contracts and on HVC's website, falsely represented to clients that employees were legal
Garcia Labor Companies/ABX Air	10/2006	OH	Two temporary employee companies plus the president and two corporate officers of one of the companies pled guilty to conspiring to provide hundreds of unauthorized immigrants to client site; individuals pled guilty to conspiracy to induce, aid and abet unauthorized immigrants to reside or remain in the U.S. for the purpose of commercial advantage or private financial gain; owner agreed to forfeit $12 million; executives facing up to ten years in prison and $250,000 fine	Company contracted with ABX Air, a national air cargo company; SSA had previously issued hundreds of no-match letters to company employees in 2002, 2003 and 2004, but company ignored
Kentucky Limited Liability Corporations	7/2006	KY	Two companies pled guilty to criminal charges of harboring illegal aliens and money laundering; companies agreed to pay $1.5 million in lieu of forfeiture and to create internal compliance programs; company executives sentenced to one year supervised probation and each company was fined $75,000	Company provided employees to Holiday Inn, Days Inn and other Kentucky hotels
Fischer Homes and subcontractors	7/2006	KY	Two subcontractors to Fischer Homes pled guilty to criminal charges of harboring unauthorized immigrants; ICE agents arrested four supervisors of Fischer Homes and 85 unauthorized employees at Fischer Homes under construction in Kentucky; Fischer Homes managers charged with aiding, abetting and harboring unauthorized immigrants; several contractors to Fischer Homes indicted on charges of harboring	
Stitching Post	7/2007	OH	Owner of store that sells and repairs sewing machines sentenced to six months in prison and forfeiture of $770,000 residence plus 100 hours of community service; owner pleaded guilty to "encouraging and inducing illegal aliens to come to the U.S., harboring illegal aliens, fraud and misuse of government documents, and engaging in a pattern of employing illegal aliens;" owner made regular trips to Mexico seeking employees; paid transportation costs from Texas to Ohio; took employees on a Caribbean cruise knowing the employee had to use false documents to re-enter the country	

continued on next page

Company	Date	State(s)	Violations, crimes	Other notes
El Pollo Rico Restaurant	7/2007	MD	Employers charged with employing and harboring unauthorized immigrants, money laundering and structuring deposits to avoid currency reporting requirements in connection with running a restaurant; employees paid in cash until they became legal; company only accepted cash from customers which made it easier to hide cash payments to employees; company deliberately avoided making deposits over $10,000 in order to avoid triggering a currency transaction report; defendants face 10 years for employing and harboring unauthorized immigrants, 10 years for the currency reporting violations and 20 years for money laundering; $2,000,000 in assets seized; six employees arrested on immigration violations	
New Century Roofing/LH Roofing LLP/Metro Roofing Services Inc./LHB Roofing Inc.	6/2007	MO	Several roofing companies and their owners indicted for employing unauthorized immigrants; nine criminal indictments; 34 employees arrested on immigration charges; one owner alleged to have paid to have employees smuggled back in to country after they were arrested and deported; alleged that companies used subcontractors to insulate themselves from liability and that paying through subcontractors was actually money laundering; charges include conspiracies to encourage and induce and aiding and abetting unauthorized immigrants to reside and remain in the U.S. for commercial advantage and private financial gain; conspiracies to commit money laundering; forfeiture of assets sought	
Monterey Pizza	6/2007	CA	Owner charged with hiring unauthorized immigrants from Brazil, paying them in cash to conceal their employment and avoid paying payroll taxes; charges include harboring; employees charged with identity theft	
Bee's Buffet Restaurant	1/2007	OH	Owner pled guilty to illegally inducing, transporting and harboring employees; owner also lacked authorization to be in U.S.; owner falsely stated U.S. citizenship in Small Business Administration loan; owner forfeited $100,000 in lieu of real property; $179,397 in cash seized from a safe at owner's residence, $150,050 in cash from safe deposit box and an automobile belonging to owner	
Osaka Japanese Steakhouse	1/2007	AR	Company pled guilty to harboring unauthorized immigrants and agreed to pay $45,000 fine; ICE executed search warrants at restaurant and at residence where five unauthorized immigrants were being harbored; fraudulent ID documents discovered at residence; owner admitted to not reviewing documents or completing Forms I-9; six employees administratively arrested on immigration charges	

continued on next page

Company	Date	State(s)	Violations, crimes	Other notes
Eversole, Martinez, Bocanegra	1/2007	VA	A U.S. citizen and two Mexican nationals were arrested on charges of conspiring to harbor unauthorized immigrants and hire them to work on a Marine base. 14 employees administratively arrested on immigration grounds (including three at the military base); indicted individuals alleged to have hired employees to work on construction project on the bas, leased the employees apartments and provided them transportation to the base; one of employers had previously been deported; no allegation of access to sensitive areas on the base	Base in question was Quantico Marine base; trucks used to transport employees had Department of Defense decals
Golden State Fence Company	12/2006	CA	Two executives at the company pled guilty to the hiring of unauthorized immigrants; company forfeited $4.7 million in assets; executives ordered to pay fine of $300,000 collectively; company notified initially in 1999 by INS that it had at least 15 unauthorized employees; ICE noted that some of these employees were still employed six years later; Social Security records showed hundreds of employees had mismatched names and numbers	Critical infrastructure investigation – company built fences at military sites
Sawczuk, Bogacki, Preus, Kanis, Kanis, Pikali	9/2006	Nationwide	Polish and Czech individuals pled guilty for bringing in 550 unauthorized immigrants from Eastern Europe who entered on visitor visas and then were employed illegally and contracted to farms and factories in the Midwest and Southeastern U.S.; defendants failed to pay $6 million in payroll taxes and laundering $20 million	
Skyworks Activities Incorporated	8/2006	NY	Cleaning company officers indicted for transporting unauthorized immigrants for profit to Buffalo to work as cleaners at a state fair; officers admitted knowing employees were not legal and that they arranged transportation	
Bob Eisel Powder Coatings, Inc.	8/2006	KS	Owner pled guilty to hiring and employing unauthorized immigrants, general manager and foreman indicted for making false statements to the government, misusing Social Security card numbers, accepting documents they knew were false for Form I-9 purposes, committing aggravated identify theft and harboring unauthorized immigrants; responded to Social Security no-match letters by telling employees to get new numbers; gave money to employees to help them secure new documents and then "fired" employees and re-hired them under new identity; indicted for making false statements on Forms I-9; owner and general manager paid $210,000 in fines ($175,000 for the company); jail term to be determined later	

continued on next page

Company	Date	State(s)	Violations, crimes	Other notes
Golden China Buffet	6/2006	KY	Owners of restaurant indicted for conspiring to transport, harbor and conceal illegal Chinese and Mexican aliens for financial gain and commercial advantage; owners also unauthorized immigrants; owner transported employees to work and provided housing; seven employees administratively arrested	
China Garden Restaurant/Panda Garden Restaurant	6/2006	IA	Owners of restaurant charged with harboring, encouraging, or inducing employees to reside in the U.S. knowing they were in the country illegally. Defendants face 10-year sentence and fine up to $250,000; five employee administratively arrested; employees told investigators they were paying off smuggling fees; employers did not complete Forms I-9	
Julio's Mexican Restaurants	5/2006	MO and IA	Owner of restaurant arrested for knowingly hiring unauthorized immigrants; 21 employees administratively arrested; employees never filled out Forms I-9; computer and $17,000 cash seized	
IFCO Systems North America	4/2006	Dozens of locations around U.S.	Seven current and former managers of IFCO arrested and charged with harboring aliens for financial gain; 1,187 employees apprehended at 40 of the company's locations; five current and former managers pled guilty for violations related to employment of the aliens; former general manager pled guilty to conspiracy to transport and harbor illegal aliens and possession of ID documents; corporate new market development manager pled guilty to conspiracy to transport and harbor aliens; current general manager pled guilty to conspiracy to commit the misdemeanor offense of unlawful employment of unauthorized immigrants	
Kawasaki Restaurant chain	3/2006	MD	Japanese restaurant chain; 15 unauthorized immigrants in "deplorable" conditions; owners of business arrested for money laundering and harboring; ICE seized assets including eight luxury vehicles, ten bank accounts, three safe deposit boxes and cash found during searches; owners pled guilty and forfeit $1.1 million in assets	ICE estimated that old approach of focusing on Forms I-9 would have resulted only in misdemeanor charge and $20,000 maximum fine

M-274, Handbook for Employers

U.S. Department of Homeland Security
U.S. Citizenship and Immigration Services
www.uscis.gov

M-274 (Rev. 11/01/2007) N

Handbook for Employers

Instructions for Completing the Form I-9
(Employment Eligibility Verification Form)

NOTE: AS OF PUBLICATION OF THIS BOOK, USCIS INDICATED THAT
A NEWER VERSION OF THE M.274 WOULD BE AVAILABLE SOON.

Future Expiration Dates

Future expiration dates may appear on the employment authorization documents of aliens, including, among others, permanent residents and refugees. USCIS includes expiration dates even on documents issued to aliens with permanent work authorization. The existence of a future expiration date:

1. Does not preclude continuous employment authorization;

2. Does not mean that subsequent employment authorization will not be granted; and

3. Should not be considered in determining whether the alien is qualified for a particular position.

Considering a future employment authorization expiration date in determining whether an alien is qualified for a particular job may constitute employment discrimination. (See Part Four.) However, as described below, you may need to reverify the employee's eligibility to work upon the expiration of certain List A or List C documents.

Reverifying Employment Authorization for Current Employees

When an employee's work authorization expires, you must reverify his or her employment eligibility. You may use Section 3 of the Form I-9, or, if Section 3 has already been used for a previous reverification or update, use a new Form I-9. If you use a new form, you should write the employee's name in Section 1, complete Section 3, and retain the new form with the original. The employee must present a document that shows either an extension of the employee's initial employment authorization or new work authorization. If the employee cannot provide you with proof of current work authorization (e.g. any document from List A or List C, including an unrestricted Social Security card), you cannot continue to employ that person.

NOTE: List B identity documents, such as a driver's license, should not be reverified when they expire.

To maintain continuous employment eligibility, an employee with temporary work authorization should apply for new work authorization at least 90 days before the current expiration date. If USCIS fails to adjudicate the application for employment authorization within 90 days, then the employee will be authorized for employment on Form I-766 for a period not to exceed 240 days.

NOTE: You must reverify an employee's employment eligibility on the Form I-9 not later than the date the employee's work authorization expires.

Reverifying or Updating Employment Authorization for Rehired Employees

When you rehire an employee, you must ensure that he or she is still authorized to work. You may do this by completing a new Form I-9 or you may reverify or update the original form by completing Section 3.

If you rehire an employee who has previously completed a Form I-9, you may reverify on the employee's original Form I-9 (or on a new Form I-9 if Section 3 of the original has already been used) if:

1. You rehire the employee within three years of the initial date of hire; and

2. The employee's previous grant of work authorization has expired, but he or she is currently eligible to work on a different basis or under a new grant of work authorization than when the original Form I-9 was completed.

To reverify, you must:

1. Record the date of rehire;

2. Record the document title, number and expiration date (if any) of any document(s) presented;

3. Sign and date Section 3; and

4. If you are reverifying on a new Form I-9, write the employee's name in Section 1.

If you rehire an employee who has previously completed a Form I-9, you may update on the employee's original Form I-9 or on a new Form I-9 if:

1. You rehire the employee within three years of the initial date of hire; and

2. The employee is still eligible to work on the same basis as when the original Form I-9 was completed.

To update, you must:

1. Record the date of rehire;

2. Sign and date Section 3; and

3. If you are updating on a new Form I-9, write the employee's name in Section 1.

Employers always have the option of completing Sections 1 and 2 of a new Form I-9 instead of completing Section 3 when rehiring employees.

Figure 5: *Reverification of Employment Eligibility for Current Employees and Rehires*

Section 3. Updating and Reverification. To be completed and signed by employer.	
A. New Name *(if applicable)*	B. Date of Rehire *(month/day/year) (if applicable)*

C. If employee's previous grant of work authorization has expired, provide the information below for the document that establishes current employment eligibility.

Document Title: Employment Authorization Card   Document #: 9876543210   Expiration Date (if any): 10/31/09

I attest, under penalty of perjury, that to the best of my knowledge, this employee is eligible to work in the United States, and if the employee presented document(s), the document(s) I have examined appear to be genuine and to relate to the individual.

Signature of Employer or Authorized Representative   *Jolene Doe*   Date *(month/day/year)* 10/31/07

Form I-9 (Rev. 3/26/07) N

1. Record the employee's new name, if applicable, and date of rehire, if applicable
2. Record the document title, number, and expiration date (if any) of document(s) presented
3. Sign and date

NOTE: You may also fill out a new Form I-9 in lieu of filling out this section.

Part Three
Photocopying and Retaining the Form I-9

Employers must retain completed Forms I-9 for all employees for 3 years after the date they hire an employee or 1 year after the date employment is terminated, whichever is later. These forms can be retained in paper, microfilm, microfiche, or, more recently, electronically.

To store Form I-9 electronically, you may use any electronic recordkeeping, attestation, and retention system that complies with DHS standards, which includes most off-the-shelf computer programs and commercial automated data processing systems. However, the system must not be subject to any agreement that would restrict access to and use of it by an agency of the United States. (See Electronic Retention of Form I-9 below.)

Paper Retention of Form I-9

The Form I-9 can be signed and stored in paper format. Simply reproduce a complete, blank Form I-9, and ensure that the employee receives the instructions for completing the form.

When copying or printing the paper Form I-9, you may reproduce the two-sided form by making either double-sided or single-sided copies.

You may retain completed paper forms onsite, or at an off-site storage facility, for the required retention period, as long as you are able to present the Form I-9 within 3 days of an audit request from DHS, OSC, or DOL officers.

Microform Retention of Form I-9

You may store Form I-9 on microfilm or microfiche. To do so:

1. Select film stock that will preserve the image and allow accessibility and usability for the entire retention period, which in certain circumstances could be upward of 20 years, depending on the employee and your business.

2. Use well-maintained equipment to create and view microfilms and microfiche that provides a high degree of legibility and readability, and has the ability to reproduce legible and readable paper copies. DHS officers must have immediate access to clear, readable documents should they need to inspect your forms.

3. We suggest that you place the required indexes either in the first frames of the first roll of film or in the last frames of the last roll of film of a series. For microfiche, place them in the last frames of the last microfiche or microfilm jacket of a series.

Remember: Form I-9 must be stored for 3 years after the date you hire an employee or 1 year after the date you or the employee terminates employment, whichever is later. For example, if an employee retires from your company after 15 years, you will need to store his or her Form I-9 for a total of 16 years.

Electronic Forms I-9

USCIS provides a Portable Document Format fillable-printable Form I-9 from its website, www.uscis.gov. The Form I-9 can also be electronically generated or retained, provided that:

1. The resulting form is legible;

2. No change is made to the name, content, or sequence of the data elements and instructions;

3. No additional data elements or language are inserted;

4. The employee receives the Form I-9 instructions; and

5. The standards specified under 8 CFR 274a.2(e) are met.

Electronic Retention of Form I-9

Employers may complete or retain the Form I-9 in an electronic generation or storage system that includes:

1. Reasonable controls to ensure the integrity, accuracy and reliability of the electronic storage system;

2. Reasonable controls designed to prevent and detect the unauthorized or accidental creation of, addition to, alteration of, deletion of, or deterioration of an electronically completed or stored Form I-9, including the electronic signature if used;

3. An inspection and quality assurance program evidenced by regular evaluations of the electronic generation or storage system, including periodic checks of electronically stored Form I-9, including the electronic signature if used;

4. A retrieval system that includes an indexing system that permits searches by any data element; and

5. The ability to reproduce legible and readable hardcopies.

Remember, Form I-9 must be stored for 3 years after the date you hire an employee or 1 year after the date you or the employee terminates employment, whichever is later, which can result in a long retention period.

Retaining Copies of Form I-9 Documentation

You may choose to copy or scan documents presented by an employee, which you must retain with his or her Form I-9. Retaining copies of documentation does not relieve you from the requirement to fully complete section 2 of the Form I-9. If you choose to retain copies of employee documentation, you may not just do so for employees of certain national origins or citizenship statuses, or you may be in violation of anti-discrimination laws.

Electronic Signature of Form I-9

You may choose to fill out a paper Form I-9 and scan and upload the signed Form to retain it electronically. Once you have securely stored the Form I-9 in electronic format, you may destroy the original paper Form I-9.

If you complete Form I-9 electronically using an electronic signature, you must implement a system for capturing electronic signatures that allows signatories to acknowledge that they read the attestation; and can associate an electronic signature with an electronically completed Form I-9. In addition, the system must:

1. Affix the electronic signature at the time of the transaction;

2. Create and preserve a record verifying the identity of the person producing the signature; and

3. Provide a printed confirmation of the transaction, at the time of the transaction, to the person providing the signature.

NOTE: If you choose to use electronic signature to complete Form I-9, but do not comply with these standards, DHS will determine that you have not properly completed the Form I-9, in violation of Section 274A(a)(1)(B) of the Act.

System Documentation

For each electronic generation or storage system used, you must maintain, and make available upon request, complete descriptions of:

1. The electronic generation and storage system, including all procedures relating to its use;

2. The indexing system, which permits the identification and retrieval for viewing or reproducing of relevant records maintained in an electronic storage system; and

3. The business processes that create, modify, and maintain the retained Form I-9, and establish the authenticity and integrity of the Forms, such as audit trails.

Note: Insufficient or incomplete documentation is a violation of section 274A(a)(1)(B) of the Act (8 CFR Part 274a.2(f)(2)).

Security

If you retain Form I-9 electronically, you must implement a records security program that:

1. Ensures that only authorized personnel have access to electronic records;

2. Provides for backup and recovery of records to protect against information loss;

3. Ensures that employees are trained to minimize the risk of unauthorized or accidental alteration or erasure of electronic records; and

4. Ensures that whenever an individual creates, accesses, views, updates, or corrects an electronic record, the system creates a secure and permanent record that establishes the date of access, the identity of the individual who accessed the electronic record, and the particular action taken.

Note: If an employer's action or inaction results in the alteration, loss, or erasure of electronic records, and the employer knew, or reasonably should have known, that the action or inaction could have that effect, the employer is in violation of Section 274A(a)(1)(B) of the Act.

Inspection

DHS, OSC and DOL give employers three day's notice prior to inspecting retained Form I-9. The employer must make Form I-9 available upon request at the location where DHS, OSC or DOL requests to see them.

If you store Forms I-9 at an off-site location, inform the inspecting officer of the location where you store them, and make arrangements for the inspection. The inspecting officers can perform your inspection at an office of an authorized agency of the United States if previous arrangements are made. Recruiters or referrers for a fee who designate an employer to complete employment verification procedures may present a photocopy or printed electronic image of the Form I-9 at an inspection. If you refuse or delay an inspection, you will be in violation of DHS retention requirements.

At the time of an inspection, you must:

1. Retrieve and reproduce only the Form I-9 electronically retained in the electronic storage system and supporting documentation specifically requested by the inspecting officer. This documentation includes associated audit trails that show who has accessed a computer system and

the actions performed within or on the computer system during a given period of time.

2. Provide the inspecting officer with appropriate hardware and software, personnel, and documentation necessary to locate, retrieve, read, and reproduce any electronically stored Form I-9, any supporting documents, and their associated audit trails, reports, and other data used to maintain the authenticity, integrity, and reliability of the records.

3. Provide the inspecting officer, if requested, any reasonably available or obtainable electronic summary file(s), such as a spreadsheet, containing all of the information fields on all of the electronically stored Form I-9.

Part Four
Unlawful Discrimination and Penalties for Prohibited Practices

Unlawful Discrimination

General Provisions

The anti-discrimination provision of the Act, as amended, prohibits four types of unlawful conduct: (1) citizenship or immigration status discrimination; (2) national origin discrimination; (3) unfair documentary practices during the Form I-9 process (document abuse); and (4) retaliation. The Office of Special Counsel for Immigration-Related Unfair Employment Practices (OSC), part of the United States Department of Justice Civil Rights Division, enforces the anti-discrimination provision of the INA. Title VII of the Civil Rights Act of 1964 (Title VII), as amended, also prohibits national origin discrimination, among other types of conduct. The United States Equal Employment Opportunity Commission (EEOC) enforces Title VII.

As discussed further below, OSC and EEOC share jurisdiction over national origin discrimination charges. Generally, the EEOC has jurisdiction over larger employers with 15 or more employees, whereas OSC has jurisdiction over smaller employers with between 4 and 14 employees. OSC's jurisdiction over national origin discrimination claims is limited to intentional acts of discrimination with respect to hiring, firing, and recruitment or referral for a fee, but the EEOC's jurisdiction is broader. Title VII covers both intentional and unintentional acts of discrimination in the workplace, including discrimination in hiring, firing, recruitment, promotion, assignment, compensation, and other terms and conditions of employment. OSC has exclusive jurisdiction over citizenship or immigration status discrimination claims against all employers with four or more employees. Similarly, OSC has jurisdiction over all document abuse claims against employers with four or more employees.

Types of Employment Discrimination Prohibited Under the INA

Document Abuse

Discriminatory documentary practices related to verifying the employment eligibility of employees and the Form I-9 process are called document abuse. Document abuse occurs when employers treat individuals differently on the basis of national origin or citizenship status in the Form I-9 process. Document abuse can be broadly categorized into four types of conduct: 1) improperly requesting that employees produce more documents than are required by the Form I-9 to establish the employee's identity and work authorization; 2) improperly requesting that employees produce a particular document,

such as a "green card," to establish identity or work eligibility; 3) improperly rejecting documents that reasonably appear to be genuine and belong to the employee presenting them; 4) improperly treating groups of applicants differently when completing the Form I-9, such as requiring certain groups of employees that look or sound "foreign" to produce particular documents the employer does not require other employees to produce. These practices may constitute unlawful document abuse and should be avoided when verifying employment eligibility. All work authorized individuals are protected against this type of discrimination. The INA's prohibition against document abuse covers employers with 4 or more employees.

Citizenship Status Discrimination

Citizenship or immigration status discrimination occurs when an employer treats employees differently based on their citizenship or immigration status in regard to hiring, firing, or recruitment or referral for a fee. U.S. citizens, recent permanent residents, temporary residents under the IRCA legalization program, asylees, and refugees are protected. An employer must treat all of these groups the same. Subject to limited exceptions, the INA's prohibition against citizenship or immigration status discrimination covers employers with 4 or more employees.

National Origin Discrimination

This form of discrimination occurs when an employer treats employees differently based on their national origin in regard to hiring, firing, or recruitment or referral for a fee. An employee's national origin relates to the employee's place of birth, country of origin, ancestry, native language, accent, or because he or she is perceived as looking or sounding "foreign." All work-authorized individuals are protected from national origin discrimination. The INA's prohibition against intentional national origin discrimination generally covers employers with 4 to 14 employees.

Retaliation

Retaliation occurs when an employer or other covered entity intimidates, threatens, coerces, or otherwise retaliates against an individual because the individual has filed an immigration-related employment discrimination charge or complaint; has testified or participated in any immigration-related employment discrimination investigation, proceeding, or hearing; or otherwise asserts his or her rights under the INA's anti-discrimination provision.

Types of Discrimination Prohibited by Title VII

As noted above, Title VII also prohibits employment discrimination on the basis of national origin, as well as race, color, religion, and sex. Title VII covers employers that employ 15 or more employees for 20 or more weeks in the preceding or current calendar year, and prohibits discrimination in any aspect of employment, including: hiring and firing; compensation, assignment, or classification of employees; transfer, promotion, layoff, or recall; job advertisements; recruitment; testing; use of company facilities; training and apprenticeship programs; fringe benefits; pay, retirement plans, and leave; or other terms and conditions of employment.

Avoiding Discrimination in Recruiting, Hiring and the Form I-9 Process

In practice, employers should treat employees equally when recruiting and hiring, and when verifying employment eligibility and completing the Form I-9. Employers should not:

1. Set different employment eligibility verification standards or require that different documents be presented by employees because of their national origin and citizenship status. For example, employers cannot demand that non-U.S. citizens present DHS-issued documents.

    Each employee must be allowed to choose the documents that he or she will produce from the lists of acceptable Form I-9 documents. For example, both citizens and work authorized aliens may produce a driver's license (List B) and an unrestricted Social Security card (List C) to establish identity and employment eligibility.

2. Request to see employment eligibility verification documents before hire and completion of the Form I-9 because someone looks or sounds "foreign," or because someone states that he or she is not a U.S. citizen.

3. Refuse to accept a document, or refuse to hire an individual, because a document has a future expiration date.

4. Request that, during reverification, an employee present a new unexpired employment authorization document (EAD) if he or she presented an EAD during initial verification. For reverification, each employee must be free to choose to present any document either from List A or from List C. Refugees and asylees may possess EADs, but they are authorized to work based on their status, and may possess other documents that prove work authorization from List A or List C to show upon reverification, such as an unrestricted Social Security card.

5. Limit jobs to U.S. citizens unless U.S. citizenship is required for the specific position by law; regulation; executive order; or federal, state, or local government contract. On an individual basis, an employer may legally prefer a U.S. citizen or national over an equally qualified alien to fill a specific position, but may not adopt a blanket policy of always preferring citizens over non-citizens.

Procedures for Filing Charges of Employment Discrimination

OSC

Discrimination charges may be filed by an individual who believes he or she is the victim of employment discrimination, a person acting on behalf of such an individual, or a DHS officer who has reason to believe that discrimination has occurred. Discrimination charges must be filed with OSC within 180 days of the alleged discriminatory act. Upon receipt of a complete discrimination charge, OSC will notify the employer within 10 days that a charge has been filed and commence its investigation. If OSC has not filed a complaint with an administrative law judge within 120 days of receiving a charge of discrimination, it will notify the charging party of its determination not to file a complaint. The charging party (other than a DHS officer) may file a complaint with an administrative law judge within 90 days after receiving the notice from OSC. In addition, OSC may still file a complaint within this 90-day period. The administrative law judge will conduct a hearing and issue a decision. OSC may also attempt to settle a charge or the parties may enter into settlement agreements resolving the charge.

EEOC

A charge must be filed with EEOC within 180 days from the date of the alleged violation, in order to protect the charging party's rights. This 180-day filing deadline is extended to 300 days if the charge also is covered by a state or local anti-discrimination law.

Employers Prohibited from Retaliating against Employees

An employer cannot take retaliatory action against a person who has filed a charge of discrimination with OSC or the EEOC, was a witness or otherwise participated in the investigation or prosecution of a discrimination complaint, or otherwise asserts his or her rights under the INA's anti-discrimination provision and/or Title VII. Such retaliatory action may constitute a violation of the INA's anti-discrimination provision and/or Title VII.

Additional Information

For more information about the anti-discrimination provision of the INA and the procedures of OSC, call 1-800-255-7688 (worker hotline) or 1-800-255-8155 (employer hotline); or 1-800-237-2515 (TDD for hearing impaired); or visit OSC's website at http://www.usdoj.gov/crt/osc

For more information on Title VII and policies and procedures of the Equal Employment Opportunity Commission, call 1-800-USA-EEOC; or 1-800-669-6820 (TTY for hearing impaired); or visit EEOC's website at http://www.eeoc.gov.

Penalties for Prohibited Practices

A. UNLAWFUL EMPLOYMENT

1. Civil Penalties

The Department of Homeland Security (DHS) may impose penalties if an investigation reveals that an employer has knowingly hired or knowingly continued to employ an unauthorized alien, or has failed to comply with the employment eligibility verification requirements, with respect to employees hired after November 6, 1986. DHS will issue a Notice of Intent to Fine (NIF) when it intends to impose penalties. Employers who receive a NIF may request a hearing before an administrative law judge. If an employer's request for a hearing is not received within 30 days, DHS will impose the penalty and issue a Final Order, which cannot be appealed.

a.   Hiring or continuing to employ unauthorized aliens

DHS may order employers it determines to have knowingly hired unauthorized aliens (or to be continuing to employ aliens knowing that they are or have become unauthorized to work in the United States) to cease and desist from such activity, and pay a civil money penalty as follows:

1.   First Offense: Not less than $275 and not more than $2,200 for each unauthorized alien;

2.   Second offense: Not less than $2,200 and not more than $5,500 for each unauthorized alien; or

3.   Subsequent Offenses: Not less than $3,300 and not more than $11,000 for each unauthorized alien.

DHS will consider an employer to have knowingly hired an unauthorized alien if, after November 6, 1986, the employer uses a contract, subcontract or exchange, entered into, renegotiated or extended, to obtain the labor of an alien and knows the alien is not authorized to work in the United States. The employer will be subject to the penalties set forth above.

b.   Failing to comply with the Form I-9 requirements

Employers who fail to properly complete, retain, and/or make available for inspection Form I-9 as required by law may face civil money penalties in an amount of not less than $110 and not more than $1,100 for each individual with respect to whom such violation occurred.

In determining the amount of the penalty, DHS will consider:

1.   The size of the business of the employer being charged;

2.   The good faith of the employer;
3.   The seriousness of the violation;

4.   Whether or not the individual was an unauthorized alien; and

5.   The history of previous violations of the employer.

c.   Enjoining pattern or practice violations

If the Attorney General has reasonable cause to believe that a person or entity is engaged in a pattern or practice of employment, recruitment or referral in violation of section 274A(a)(1)(A) or (2) of the Act, the Attorney General may bring civil action in the appropriate U.S. District Court requesting relief, including a permanent or temporary injunction, restraining order or other order against the person or entity, as the Attorney General deems necessary.

d.   Requiring indemnification

Employers found to have required a bond or indemnity from an employee against liability under the employer sanctions laws may be ordered to pay a civil money penalty of $1,000 for each violation and to make restitution, either to the person who was required to pay the indemnity, or, if that person cannot be located, to the U.S. Treasury.

e.   Good faith defense

If the employer can show that he or she has in good faith complied with the Form I-9 requirements, then the employer has established a "good faith" defense with respect to a charge of knowingly hiring an unauthorized alien, unless the government can show that the employer had actual knowledge of the unauthorized status of the employee.

A good faith attempt to comply with the paperwork requirements of Section 274A(b) of the Act may be adequate notwithstanding a technical or procedural failure to comply, unless the employer has failed to correct the violation within 10 days after notice from DHS, or the employer is engaging in a pattern or practice of violations.

2.   Criminal Penalties

a.   Engaging in a pattern or practice of knowingly hiring or continuing to employ unauthorized aliens

Persons or entities who are convicted of having engaged in a pattern or practice of knowingly hiring unauthorized aliens (or continuing to employ aliens knowing that they are or have become unauthorized to work in the United States) after November 6, 1986, may face fines of up to $3,000 per employee and/or six months imprisonment.

b.   Engaging in fraud or false statements, or otherwise misusing visas, immigration permits and identity documents

Persons who use fraudulent identification or employment eligibility documents or documents that were lawfully issued to another person, or who make a false statement or attestation for purposes of satisfying the employment eligibility verification requirements, may be fined, or imprisoned for up to five years, or both. Other federal criminal statutes may provide higher penalties in certain fraud cases.

B. UNLAWFUL DISCRIMINATION

If an investigation reveals that an employer has engaged in unfair immigration-related employment practices under the INA, the Office of Special Counsel for Immigration-Related Unfair Employment Practices (OSC) may take action. An employer will be ordered to stop the prohibited practice and may be ordered to take one or more corrective steps, including:

1.   Hire or reinstate, with or without back pay, individuals directly injured by the discrimination;

2.   Post notices to employees about their rights and about employers' obligations;

3.   Educate all personnel involved in hiring and in complying with the employer sanctions and antidiscrimination laws about the requirements of these laws.

The court may award attorney's fees to prevailing parties, other than the United States, if it determines that the losing parties' argument is without foundation in law and fact.

Employers who commit citizenship status or national origin discrimination in violation of the anti-discrimination provision of the INA may also be ordered to pay a civil money penalty as follows:

1.   First Offense: Not less than $275 and not more than $2,200 for each individual discriminated against;

2.   Second Offense: Not less than $2,200 and not more than $5,500 for each individual discriminated against;

3.   Subsequent Offenses: Not less than $3,300 and not more than $11,000 for each individual discriminated against.

Employers who commit document abuse in violation of the anti-discrimination provision of the INA may similarly be ordered to pay a civil money penalty as follows:

1.   Not less than $110 and not more than $1,100 for each individual discriminated against.

If an employer is found to have committed national origin discrimination under Title VII of the Civil Rights Act of 1964 (Title VII), it may be ordered to stop the prohibited practice and to take one or more corrective steps, including:

1.   Hire, reinstate or promote with back pay and retroactive seniority;

2.   Post notices to employees about their rights and about the employer's obligations; and/or

3.   Remove incorrect information, such as a false warning, from an employee's personnel file.

Under Title VII, compensatory damages may also be available where intentional discrimination is found. Damages may be available to compensate for actual monetary losses, for future monetary losses, and for mental anguish and inconvenience. Punitive damages may be available if the employer acted with malice or reckless indifference.

The employer may also be required to pay attorneys' fees, expert witness fees and court costs.

C. CIVIL DOCUMENT FRAUD

If a DHS investigation reveals that an individual has knowingly committed or participated in acts relating to document fraud (See Part One), DHS may take action. DHS will issue a Notice of Intent to Fine (NIF) when it intends to impose penalties. Persons who receive a NIF may request a hearing before an administrative law judge. If DHS does not receive a request for a hearing within 30 days, it will impose the penalty and issue a Final Order, which is final and cannot be appealed.

Individuals found by DHS or an administrative law judge to have violated Section 274C of the Act may be ordered to pay a civil money penalty as follows:

To cease and desist from such behavior; and

To pay a civil penalty as follows:

a.   First offense: Not less than $275 and not more than $2,200 for each fraudulent document that is the subject of the violation; or

b.   Subsequent offenses: Not less than $2,200 and not more than $5,500 for each fraudulent document that is the subject of the violation.

Part Five
Instructions for Recruiters and Referrers for a Fee

Under the Immigration and Nationality Act (INA), as amended, it is unlawful for an agricultural association, agricultural employer, or farm labor contractor to hire, or to recruit or refer for a fee, an individual for employment in the United States without complying with the employment eligibility verification requirements. This provision applies to those agricultural associations, agricultural employers, and farm labor contractors who recruit persons for a fee and those who refer persons or provide documents or information about persons to employers in return for a fee.

This limited class of recruiters and referrers for a fee must complete the Form I-9 when a person they refer is hired. The Form I-9 must be fully completed within three business days of the date employment begins, or, in the case of an individual hired for less than three business days, at the time employment begins.

Recruiters and referrers for a fee may designate agents, such as national associations or employers, to complete the verification procedures on their behalf. If the employer is designated as the agent, the employer should provide the recruiter or referrer with a photocopy of the Form I-9. However, recruiters and referrers are still responsible for compliance with the law and may be found liable for violations of the law.

Recruiters and referrers for a fee must retain the Form I-9 for three years after the date the referred individual was hired by the employer. They must also make Form I-9 available for inspection by a DHS, DOL, or OSC officer.

NOTE: This does not preclude DHS or DOL from obtaining warrants based on probable cause for entry onto the premises of suspected violators without advance notice.

The penalties for failing to comply with the Form I-9 requirements and for requiring indemnification, as described in Part Four, apply to this limited class of recruiters and referrers for a fee.

NOTE: All recruiters and referrers for a fee are still liable for knowingly recruiting or referring for a fee aliens not authorized to work in the United States.

Contents

Obtaining Form I-9 and the M-274

This Handbook includes one copy of the Form I-9, which can be photocopied. To order more forms or handbooks, call the U.S. Citizenship and Immigration Service (USCIS) toll-free number at 1-800-870-3676. Individuals also can order them by phoning the USCIS National Customer Service Center at 1-800-375-5283, or download PDF versions from the USCIS website at www.uscis.gov.

Part Six
E-Verify: The Web-based Verification Companion to the Form I-9

Since verification of the employment eligibility of new hires became law in 1986, the Form I-9 has been the foundation of the verification process. To improve the accuracy and integrity of this process, USCIS operates an electronic employment eligibility verification system called E-Verify.

E-Verify provides an automated link to federal databases to help employers determine the employment eligibility of new hires. E-Verify is free to employers and is available in all 50 states, as well as U.S. territories except for American Samoa and the Commonwealth of the Northern Mariana Islands.

Employers who participate in the E-Verify Program complete the Employment Eligibility Verification Form (Form I-9) for each newly hired employee as is required of all employers in the United States. E-Verify employers may accept any document or combination of documents acceptable on the Form I-9, but if the employee chooses to present a List B and C combination, the List B (identity only) document must have a photograph.

After completing the Form I-9 for a new employee, E-Verify employers must submit an electronic query that includes information from Sections 1 and 2 of the Form I-9. After submitting the query, the employer will receive an automated response from the E-Verify system regarding the employment eligibility of the individual. In some cases, E-Verify will provide a response indicating a tentative nonconfirmation of the employee's employment eligibility. This does not mean that the employee is necessarily unauthorized to work in the United States. Rather, it means that the system is unable to instantaneously confirm that employee's eligibility to work. In the case of a tentative nonconfirmation, the employer and employee must both take steps specified by E-Verify in an effort to resolve the status of the query.

Employers are also required to follow certain procedures when using E-Verify that were designed to protect employees from unfair employment actions. Employers may not verify selectively and must verify all new hires, both U.S. citizens and non-citizens. Employers may not prescreen applicants for employment; check employees hired before the company became a participant in E-Verify; or reverify employees who have temporary work authorization. Employers may not terminate or take other adverse action against employees based on a tentative nonconfirmation.

E-Verify, along with the Form I-9, protects jobs for authorized U.S. workers, improves the accuracy of wage and tax reporting, and helps U.S employers maintain a legal workforce.

Employers can register online for E-Verify at https://www.vis-dhs.com/EmployerRegistration, which provides instructions for completing the registration process. For more information about E-Verify, please contact USCIS at 1-888-464-4218.

Part Seven
Some Questions You May Have About the Form I-9

Questions about the Verification Process

1. Q. **Where can I obtain the Form I-9 and the M-274, Handbook for Employers?**

    A. Both the Form I-9 and the Employer Handbook are available as downloadable PDFs at www.uscis.gov. Employers with no computer access can order USCIS forms by calling our toll-free number at 1-800-870-3676. Individuals can also get USCIS forms and information on immigration laws, regulations and procedures by calling our National Customer Service Center toll-free at 1-800-375-5283.

2. Q. **Do citizens and nationals of the United States need to prove they are eligible to work?**

    A. Yes. While citizens and nationals of the United States are automatically eligible for employment, they too must present the required documents and complete a Form I-9. U.S. citizens include persons born in Puerto Rico, Guam, the U.S. Virgin Islands, and the Northern Mariana Islands. U.S. nationals include persons born in American Samoa, including Swains Island.

3. Q. **Do I need to complete a Form I-9 for everyone who applies for a job with my company?**

    A. No. You should not complete Form I-9 for job applicants. You only need to complete Form I-9 for people you actually hire. For purposes of this law, a person is "hired" when he or she begins to work for you.

4. Q. **If someone accepts a job with my company but will not start work for a month, can I complete the Form I-9 when the employee accepts the job?**

    A. Yes. The law requires that you complete the Form I-9 only when the person actually begins working. However, you may complete the form earlier, as long as the person has been offered and has accepted the job. You may not use the I-9 process to screen job applicants.

5. Q. **I understand that I must complete a Form I-9 for anyone I hire to perform labor or services in return for wages or other remuneration. What is "remuneration"?**

    A. Remuneration is anything of value given in exchange for labor or services rendered by an employee, including food and lodging.

6. Q. **Do I need to fill out Form I-9 for independent contractors or their employees?**

    A. No. For example, if you contract with a construction company to perform renovations on your building, you do not have to complete Form I-9 for that company's employees. The construction company is responsible for completing Form I-9 for its own employees. However, you must not knowingly use contract labor to circumvent the law against hiring unauthorized aliens.

7. Q. **What should I do if the person I hire is unable to provide the required documents within three business days of the date employment begins?**

    A. If an employee is unable to present the required document or documents within three business days of the date employment begins, the employee must produce an acceptable receipt in lieu of a document listed on the last page of the Form I-9. There are three types of acceptable receipts. See Question 23 below for a description of each receipt and the procedures required to fulfill Form I-9 requirements when an employee presents a receipt.

    By having checked an appropriate box in Section 1, the employee must have indicated on or before the time employment began that he or she is already eligible to be employed in the United States.

    NOTE: Employees hired for less than three business days must produce the actual document(s) and the Form I-9 must be fully completed at the time employment begins.

8. Q. **Can I fire an employee who fails to produce the required documents within three business days?**

    A. Yes. You can terminate an employee who fails to produce the required document or documents, or a receipt for a document, within three business days of the date employment begins. However, you must apply these practices uniformly to all employees.

9. Q. **What happens if I properly complete a Form I-9 and DHS discovers that my employee is not actually authorized to work?**

    A. You cannot be charged with a verification violation. You will also have a good faith defense against the imposition of employer sanctions penalties for knowingly hiring an unauthorized alien, unless the government can show you had knowledge of the unauthorized status of the employee, if you have done the following:

a.   Ensured that the employee fully and properly completed Section 1 of the Form I-9 at the time employment began;

b.   Reviewed the required documents which should have reasonably appeared to have been genuine and to have related to the person presenting them;

c.   Fully and properly completed Section 2 of the Form I-9, and signed and dated the employer certification;

d.   Retained the Form I-9 for the required period of time; and

e.   Made the Form I-9 available upon request to a DHS, DOL, or OSC officer.

Questions about Documents

10.   **Q. May I specify which documents I will accept for verification?**

A. No. The employee can choose which document(s) he or she wants to present from the lists of acceptable documents. You must accept any document (from List A) or combination of documents (one from List B and one from List C) listed on the Form I-9 and found in Part Eight of this Handbook that reasonably appear on their face to be genuine and to relate to the person presenting them. To do otherwise could be an unfair immigration-related employment practice in violation of the anti-discrimination provision in the INA. Individuals who look and/or sound foreign must not be treated differently in the recruiting, hiring or verification process.

NOTE: An employer participating in the E-Verify Electronic Employment Eligibility Verification Program can only accept a List B document with a photograph.

11.   **Q. If an employee writes down an Alien Number or Admission Number when completing Section 1 of the Form I-9, can I ask to see a document with that number?**

A. No. Although it is your responsibility as an employer to ensure that your employees fully

complete Section 1 at the time employment begins, the employee is not required to present a document to complete this section.

When you complete Section 2, you may not ask to see a document with the employee's Alien Number or Admission Number or otherwise specify which document(s) an employee may present.

12.   **Q. What is my responsibility concerning the authenticity of document(s) presented to me?**

A. You must examine the document(s) and if they reasonably appear on their face to be genuine and to relate to the person presenting them, you must accept them. To do otherwise could be an unfair immigration-related employment practice. If the document(s) do not reasonably appear on their face to be genuine or to relate to the person presenting them, you must not accept them.

13.   **Q. Why are certain documents listed in both List B and List C? If these documents are evidence of both identity and employment eligibility, why aren't they found in List A?**

A. Three documents can be found in both List B and List C: the U.S. citizen identification card and the U.S. resident citizen identification card – acceptable as identification cards in List B – and a Native American tribal document. Although these documents are evidence of both identity and employment eligibility, they are not found in List A because List A documents are limited to those designated by Congress in the law. An employee can establish both identity and employment eligibility by presenting one of these documents. You should record the document title, issuing authority, number, and expiration date (if any) for that document in the appropriate spaces for both List B and List C.

14.   **Q. An employee has attested to being a U.S. citizen or national on section 1 of the Form I-9, but has presented me with a DHS Form I-551 "green card". Another employee has attested to being a lawful permanent resident alien but has presented a U.S. passport. Should I accept these documents?**

A. In these situations, the employer should first ensure that the employee understood and properly completed the section 1 attestation of status. If the employee made a mistake and corrects the attestation, he or she should initial and date the correction, or complete a new Form I-9. If the employee confirms the accuracy of his or her initial attestation, the employer should not accept a "green card" from a U.S. citizen or a U.S. passport from an alien. Although employers are not expected to be immigration law experts, both documents in the question are directly and facially inconsistent with the status attested to and are therefore not documents that reasonably relate to the person presenting them.

15.   Q. May I accept an expired document?

A. Yes, in limited circumstances. An employer may accept an expired U.S. passport. An employer may also accept an expired document from List B to establish identity. Also, as explained in Question 23, an employer may accept an expired EAD from a Temporary Protected Status (TPS) recipient where DHS has granted an automatic extension. However, the document must reasonably appear on its face to be genuine and to relate to the person presenting it. An employer cannot accept any other expired documents.

16.   Q. How can I tell if a DHS-issued document has expired?

A. Some DHS-issued documents, such as older versions of the Alien Registration Receipt Card (Form I-551), do not have expiration dates. However, the 1989 revised version of the Resident Alien Card (Form I-551),which is rose-colored with computer readable data on the back, features a 2-year or 10-year expiration date. Other DHS-issued documents, such as the Employment Authorization Document (Form I-766 or I-688B) also have expiration dates. These dates can be found either on the face of the document or on a sticker attached to the back of the document.

17.   Q. Some employees are presenting me with Social Security cards that have been laminated. May I accept such cards as evidence of employment eligibility?

A. It depends. You may not accept a laminated Social Security card as evidence of employment eligibility if the card states on the back "not valid if laminated." Lamination of such cards renders them invalid. Metal or plastic reproductions of Social Security cards are not acceptable.

18.   Q. Some employees have presented Social Security Administration printouts with their name, Social Security number, date of birth and their parents' names as proof of employment eligibility. May I accept such printouts in place of

a Social Security card as evidence of employment eligibility?

A. No. Only a person's official Social Security card is acceptable.

19.   Q. What should I do if an employee presents a Social Security card marked "NOT VALID FOR EMPLOYMENT," but states that he or she is now authorized to work?

A. You should ask the employee to provide another document to establish his or her employment eligibility, since such Social Security cards do not establish this. Such an employee should go to the local SSA office with proof of their lawful employment status to be issued a Social Security card without the "NOT VALID FOR EMPLOYMENT" legend.

20.   Q. May I accept a photocopy of a document presented by an employee?

A. No. Employees must present original documents. The only exception is that an employee may present a certified copy of a birth certificate.

21.   Q. I noticed on the Form I-9 that under List A there are two spaces for document numbers and expiration dates. Does this mean I have to see two List A documents?

A. No. One of the documents found in List A is an unexpired foreign passport with an attached DHS Form I-94, bearing the same name as the passport and containing endorsement of the alien's nonimmigrant status, if that status authorizes the alien to work for the employer. The Form I-9 provides space for you to record the document number and expiration date for both the passport and the DHS Form I-94.

22.   Q. When I review an employee's identity and employment eligibility documents, should I make copies of them?

A. The law does not require you to photocopy documents. However, if you wish to make photocopies, you should do so for all employees, and you should retain each photocopy with the Form I-9. Photocopies must not be used for any other purpose. Photocopying documents does not relieve you of your obligation to fully complete Section 2 of the Form I-9 nor is it an acceptable substitute for proper completion of the Form I-9 in general.

23.   **Q. When can employees present receipts for documents in lieu of actual documents establishing employment eligibility?**

A. The "receipt rule" is designed to cover situations in which an employee is employment authorized at the time of initial hire or reverification, but he or she is not in possession of a document listed on page 4 of the Form I-9. Receipts showing that a person has applied for an initial grant of employment authorization, or for renewal of employment authorization, are not acceptable.

An individual may present a "receipt" in lieu of a document listed on the Form I-9 to complete Section 2 of the Form I-9. The receipt is valid for a temporary period. There are three different documents that qualify as receipts under the rule.

The first type of receipt that an employee may present (described above in the answer to question 7) is a receipt for a replacement document when the document has been lost, stolen, or damaged. The receipt is valid for 90 days, after which the individual must present the replacement document to complete the Form I-9. Note that this rule does not apply to individuals who present receipts for new documents following the expiration of their previously held document.

The second type of receipt that an employee may present is a Form I-94 containing a temporary I-551 stamp and a photograph of the individual, which is considered a receipt for the Form I-551, Permanent Resident Card. The individual must present the Form I-551 by the expiration date of the temporary I-551 stamp, or within one year from the date of issuance of the Form I-94 if the I-551 stamp does not contain an expiration date.

The third type of receipt that an employee may present is a Form I-94 containing an unexpired refugee admission stamp. This is considered a receipt for either an Employment Authorization Document (i.e., Form I-766 or I-688B) or a combination of an unrestricted Social Security card and List B document. The employee must present acceptable documentation to complete the Form I-9 within 90 days after the date of hire or, in the case of reverification, the date employment authorization expires.

DHS regulations provide that if it does not adjudicate an application for employment authorization within 90 days, it will grant an employment authorization document valid for a period not to exceed 240 days. To receive an interim employment authorization document, the individual should contact his or her local USCIS office.

Individuals under the Temporary Protected Status (TPS) Program whose EADs are subject to an automatic extension may continue to work with expired EADs during the automatic extension period specified in the Federal Register Notice announcing the extension.

24.   **Q. My employee's DHS-issued employment authorization document expired and the employee now wants to show me a Social Security card. Do I need to see a current DHS document?**

A. No. During both initial verification and reverification, an employee must be allowed to choose what documentation to present from the Form I-9 lists of acceptable documents. If an employee presents an unrestricted Social Security card upon reverification, the employee does not also need to present a current DHS document. However, if an employee presents a "restricted" Social Security card upon reverification, the employer must reject the restricted Social Security card, since it is not an acceptable Form I-9 document and ask the employee to choose different documentation from List A or List C of the Form I-9. A restricted Social Security card may state "not valid for employment" or "valid for work only with DHS authorization."

25.   **Q. Can DHS double-check the status of an alien I hired, or "run" his or her number (typically an A Number or Social Security Number) and tell me whether it's good?**

A. DHS can not double-check a number for an employer, unless the employer participates in E-Verify, which provides employers a way to confirm the employment eligibility of their newly hired employees. For more information about this program, see Part Six. You may also call DHS at 1-888-464-4218 or visit https://www.vis-dhs.com/employerregistration/.

An employer also may contact DHS if he or she has strong and articulable reason to believe documentation may not be valid, in which case ICE may investigate the possible violation of law.

26.   **Q. My employee presented me with a document issued by INS rather than DHS. Can I accept it?**

A. Effective March 1, 2003, the functions of the former Immigration and Naturalization Service (INS) in the U.S. Department of Justice were transferred to three agencies within the new DHS: USCIS, U.S. Customs and Border Protection (CBP), and U.S. Immigration and Customs Enforcement (ICE). Most immigration documents acceptable for Form I-9 use are issued by USCIS. Some documents issued by the former INS before March 1, 2003, such as Permanent Resident Cards, may still be within their period of validity. If otherwise acceptable, a document should not be rejected because it was issued by INS rather than DHS. It should also be noted that INS documents may bear dates of issuance after March 1, 2003, as it took some time in 2003 to modify document forms to reflect the new DHS identity.

27.   **Q. What should I do if an employee presents a Form I-20 and says the document authorizes her to work?**

A. The Form I-20 is evidence of employment eligibility in two specific situations:

- The employee works on the campus of the school where he or she is an F-1 student for an employer that provides direct student services, or at an off-campus location that is educationally affiliated with the school's established curriculum or related to contractually funded research projects at the post-graduate level where the employment is an integral part of the student's educational program.

- The employee is an F-1 student who has been authorized by the Designated School Official (DSO) to participate in a curricular practical training program that is an integral part of an established curriculum (e.g., alternative work/study, internship, cooperative education, or other required internship offered by sponsoring employers through cooperative agreements with the school). The Form I-20 must be endorsed by the DSO for curricular practical training, and list the employer offering the practical training, and the dates the student will be employed.

In both situations, the Form I-20 must accompany a valid Form I-94 or I-94A indicating F-1 status. When combined with an unexpired foreign passport, the documentation is acceptable for List A of Form I-9.

28.   **Q. May I accept Form DS-2019 as proof of employment eligibility?**

A. The Form DS-2019 can be used only by a J-1 exchange visitor for employment when such employment is part of his or her program. For J-1 students, the Responsible Officer of the school may authorize employment in writing. The Form DS-2019 must accompany a valid Form I-94 or I-94A. When combined with an unexpired, foreign passport, the documentation is acceptable for List A of Form I-9.

Questions about Completing and Retaining the Form I-9

29.   **Q. When do I fill out the Form I-9 if I hire someone for less than three business days?**

A. You must complete both Sections 1 and 2 of Form I-9 at the time of the hire. This means the Form I-9 must be fully completed when the person starts to work.

30.   **Q. What should I do if I rehire a person who previously filled out a Form I-9?**

A. If the employee's Form I-9 is the version dated June 5, 2007 or a subsequent version, you rehire the person within three years of the date that the Form I-9 was originally completed, and the employee is still authorized to work, you may reverify the employee in Section 3 of the original Form I-9.

If you used a version of the Form I-9 dated before June 5, 2007 when you initially verified the employee, you must complete a new Form I-9 upon rehire.

31.   **Q. What should I do if I need to update or reverify a Form I-9 for an employee who filled out an earlier version of the form?**

A. To update the June 5, 2007, version of the Form I-9, you may line through any outdated information and initial and date any updated information. You may also choose, instead, to complete a new Form I-9.

If you used a version of the Form I-9 dated before June 5, 2007 when you originally verified the employee, the employee must provide any document(s) he or she chooses from the current Lists of Acceptable Documents, which you must enter in Section 3 of the latest version of the Form I-9.

32. **Q. Do I need to complete a new Form I-9 when one of my employees is promoted within my company or transfers to another company office at a different location?**

A. No. You do not need to complete a new Form I-9 for employees who have been promoted or transferred.

33. **Q. What do I do when an employee's work authorization noted in either Section 1 or 2 of the Form I-9 expires?**

A. You will need to reverify on the Form I-9 to continue to employ the person. Reverification must occur no later than the date that work authorization expires. The employee must present a document from either List A or List C that shows either an extension of his or her initial employment authorization or new work authorization. You must review this document and, if it reasonably appears on its face to be genuine and to relate to the person presenting it, record the document title, number, and expiration date (if any), in the Updating and Reverification Section (Section 3), and sign in the appropriate space.

If you used a version of the Form I-9 that predates the June 5, 2007, version for the employee's original verification, you must complete Section 3 of the latest Form I-9 upon reverification.

You may want to establish a calendar call-up system for employees whose employment authorization will expire in the future.

NOTE: You should not reverify an expired U.S. passport or an Alien Registration Receipt Card/Permanent Resident Card, Form I-551, or a List B document that has expired.
NOTE: You cannot refuse to accept a document because it has a future expiration date. You must accept any document (from List A or List C) listed on the Form I-9 and in the Appendix of this Handbook that on its face reasonably appears to be genuine and to relate to the person presenting it. To do otherwise could be an unfair immigration-related employment practice in violation of the anti-discrimination provision of the INA.

NOTE: If an employee's EAD expires before the employee receives a new EAD, the employee may take the application receipt to a local USCIS office to receive temporary employment authorization IF it has been more than 90 days since the employee applied for the new EAD.

34. **Q. Can I avoid reverifying an employee on the Form I-9 by not hiring persons whose employment authorization has an expiration date?**

A. You cannot refuse to hire persons solely because their employment authorization is temporary. The existence of a future expiration date does not preclude continuous employment authorization for an employee and does not mean that subsequent employment authorization will not be granted. In addition, consideration of a future employment authorization expiration date in determining whether an alien is qualified for a particular job may be an unfair immigration-related employment practice in violation of the anti-discrimination provision of the INA.

35. **Q. As an employer, do I have to fill out all the Form I-9 myself?**

A. No. You may designate someone to fill out Form I-9 for you, such as a personnel officer, foreman, agent, or anyone else acting in your interest. However, you are still liable for any violations of employer sanctions laws.

36. **Q. Can I contract with someone to complete Form I-9 for my business?**

A. Yes. You can contract with another person or business to verify employees' identities and work eligibility and to complete Form I-9 for you. However, you are still responsible for the contractor's actions and are liable for any violations of the employer sanctions laws. Some employers contract with professional employer organizations (PEOs) to handle certain functions. If you and a PEO are "co-employers" (i.e., an employer-employee relationship exists between the employee and both you and the PEO), only one Form I-9 needs to be completed by either you or the PEO at the time the co-employment begins. However, both you and the PEO remain equally responsible for complying with the Form I-9 requirements, and DHS may impose penalties on either party for failure to do so.

37. **Q. As an employer, can I negotiate my responsibility to complete Form I-9 in a collective bargaining agreement with a union?**

A. Yes. However, you are still liable for any violations of the employer sanctions laws. If the agreement is for a multi-employer bargaining unit, certain rules apply. The association must track the employee's hire and termination dates each time the employee is hired or terminated by an employer in the multi-employer association.

38. **Q. What are the requirements for retaining Form I-9?**

A. If you are an employer, you must retain Form I-9 for three years after the date employment begins or one year after the date the person's employment is terminated, whichever is later. If you are an agricultural association, agricultural employer, or farm labor contractor, you must retain Form I-9 for three years after the date employment begins for persons you recruit or refer for a fee.

39. **Q. Will I get any advance notice if a DHS or DOL officer wishes to inspect my Form I-9?**

A. Yes. The officer will give you at least three days (72 hours) advance notice before the inspection. If it is more convenient for you, you may waive the 3-day notice. You may also request an extension of time to produce the Form I-9. The DHS or DOL officer will not need to show you a subpoena or a warrant at the time of the inspection.

NOTE: This does not preclude DHS or DOL from obtaining warrants based on probable cause for entry onto the premises of suspected violators without advance notice.

Failure to provide Form I-9s for inspection is a violation of the employer sanctions laws and could result in the imposition of civil money penalties.

40. **Q. How does OSC obtain information necessary to determine whether an employer has committed an unfair immigration-related employment practice under the anti-discrimination provision of the INA?**

A. OSC notifies employers in writing about the initiation of all investigations, and requests in writing information and documents. If an employer refuses to cooperate, OSC can obtain subpoenas to compel production of the information requested.

41. **Q. Do I have to complete Form I-9 for Canadians or Mexicans who entered the United States under the North American Free Trade Agreement (NAFTA)?**
A. Yes. You must complete Form I-9 for all employees. NAFTA entrants must show identity and employment eligibility documents just like all other employees.

42. **Q. If I acquire a business, can I rely on Form I-9 completed by the previous owner/employer?**

A. Yes. However, you also accept full responsibility and liability for all Form I-9 completed by the previous employer relating to individuals who are continuing in their employment.

43. **Q. If I am a recruiter or referrer for a fee, do I have to fill out Form I-9 on persons whom I recruit or refer?**

A. No, with three exceptions: Agricultural associations, agricultural employers, and farm labor contractors are still required to complete Form I-9 on all individuals who are recruited or referred for a fee. However, all recruiters and referrers for a fee must still complete Form I-9 for their own employees hired after November 6, 1986. Also, all recruiters and referrers for a fee are still liable for knowingly recruiting or referring for a fee aliens not authorized to work in the United States and must comply with federal anti-discrimination laws.

44. **Q. Can I complete Section 1 of the Form I-9 for an employee?**

A. Yes. You may help an employee who needs assistance in completing Section 1 of the Form I-9. However, you must also complete the "Preparer/Translator Certification" block. The employee must still sign the certification block in Section 1.

45. **Q. If I am a business entity (corporation, partnership, etc.), do I have to fill out Form I-9 on my employees?**

A. Yes, you must complete Form I-9 for all of your employees, including yourself.

46. **Q. I have heard that some state employment agencies can certify that people they refer are eligible to work. Is that true?**

A. Yes. State employment agencies may elect to provide persons they refer with a certification of employment eligibility. If one of these agencies refers potential employees to you with a job order or other appropriate referral form, and the agency sends you *a* certification within 21 business days of the referral, you do not have to check documents or complete a Form I-9 if you hire that person. However, you must review the certification to ensure that it relates to the person hired and observe the person sign the certification. You must also retain the certification as you would a Form I-9 and make it available for inspection, if requested. You should check with your state employment agency to see if it provides this service and become familiar with its certification document.

Questions about Avoiding Discrimination

47. **Q. How can I avoid discriminating against certain employees while still complying with this law?**

A. Employers should:

1. Treat employees equally when recruiting, hiring, and terminating employees, and when verifying employment eligibility and completing the Form I-9.

2. Allow all employees, regardless of national origin or immigration status, to choose which document or combination of documents they want to present from the list of acceptable documents on the back of the Form I-9. For example, an employer may not require an employee to present an employment authorization document issued by DHS if he or she chooses to present a driver's license and unrestricted Social Security card.

Employers should NOT:

1. Set different employment eligibility verification standards or require that different documents be presented by employees because of their national origin or citizenship status. For example, employers cannot demand that non-U.S. citizens present DHS-issued documents like "green cards".

2. Ask to see a document with an employee's Alien or Admission Number when completing Section 1 of the Form I-9.

3. Request to see employment eligibility verification documents before hire or completion of the I-9 Form because someone looks or sounds "foreign," or because someone states that he or she is not a U.S. citizen.

4. Refuse to accept a valid employment eligibility document, or refuse to hire an

individual, because the document has a future expiration date.

5. Reverify the employment eligibility of a lawful permanent resident ("LPR") whose "green card" has expired after the LPR is hired.

6. Request that, during reverification, an employee present a new unexpired employment authorization document. For reverification, employees are free to choose any document either from List A or from List C of the I-9 Form, including an unrestricted Social Security card.

7. Limit jobs to U.S. citizens unless U.S. citizenship is required for the specific position by law, regulation, executive order, or federal, state or local government contract.

NOTE: On an individual basis, an employer may legally prefer a U.S. citizen over an equally qualified alien to fill a specific position, but may not adopt a blanket policy of always preferring citizens over non-citizens.

48. **Q. Who is protected from discrimination on the basis of citizenship status or national origin under the anti-discrimination provision of the INA?**

A. All U.S. citizens, permanent residents, temporary residents, asylees and refugees are protected from citizenship status discrimination, except for those lawful permanent residents who have failed to make a timely application for naturalization after they become eligible.

An employer cannot discriminate against any work-authorized individual in hiring, firing, or recruitment because of his or her national origin.

Similarly, work-authorized individuals are protected from document abuse with the purpose or intent of discriminating on the basis of national origin or citizenship status in the case of a protected individual (e.g. discrimination during the Form I-9 process).

49. **Q. Can I be charged with discrimination if I contact DHS about a document presented to me that does not reasonably appear to be genuine and relate to the person presenting it?**

A. No. An employer who is presented with documentation that does not reasonably appear to be genuine or to relate to the employee cannot accept that documentation. While you are not legally required to inform DHS of such situations, you may do so if you choose. However, DHS is unable to provide employment eligibility verification services to employers other than through its E-Verify program. Employers who treat all employees the same and do not single out employees who look or sound foreign for closer scrutiny cannot be charged with discrimination.

50. **Q. I recently hired someone who checked box three on Section 1 of the Form I-9, indicating that he is an alien. However, he informed me that he does not have an employment authorization expiration date, which appears to be required by the form. What should I do?**

A. Refugees and asylees, as well as some other classes of alien such as certain nationals of the Federated States of Micronesia, the Marshall Islands, and Palau, are authorized to work incident to status. Some such aliens may not possess an employment authorization document (I-766 or I-688B) issued by DHS, yet can still establish employment eligibility and identity by presenting other documentation, including a driver's license and an unrestricted Social Security card or Form I-94 indicating their work-authorized status. Such individuals should write "N/A" in Section 1 next to the alien box. The refusal to hire work-authorized aliens because of their immigration status, or because they are unable to provide an expiration date on the Form I-9, may violate the anti-discrimination provision in the INA.

51. **Q. What should I do if I have further questions regarding the INA's anti-discrimination provision and the Form I-9 Verification Process?**

A. Employers should call OSC's employer hotline with questions:
1-800-255-8155
1-800-362-2735 (TDD); or
Visit the OSC website,
http://www.usdoj.gov/crt/osc/, for more information.

52. **Q. What if someone believes they have experienced discrimination under the INA's anti-discrimination provision?**

A. Call the Office of Special Counsel for Immigration Related Unfair Employment Practices (OSC) employee hotline:
1-800-255-7688
1-800-237-2515 (TDD); or

Visit the OSC website,
http://www.usdoj.gov/crt/osc/, for more information and to download a charge form.

53. **Q. What if someone believes he or she has experienced discrimination under Title VII of the Civil Rights Act of 1964?**

A. Call the Equal Employment Opportunity Commission (EEOC):
1-800-USA-EEOC
1-800-669-6820 (TTY); or
Visit EEOC's website at http://www.eeoc.gov.

Questions about Employees Hired Before November 6, 1986

54. **Q. Does this law apply to my employees if I hired them before November 7, 1986?**

A. No. You are not required to complete Forms I-9 for employees hired before November 7, 1986.

NOTE: This "grandfather" status does not apply to seasonal employees, or to employees who change employers within a multi-employer association.

55. **Q. What if an employee was hired before November 7, 1986, but has taken an approved leave of absence?**

A. You do not need to complete a Form I-9 for that employee if the employee is continuing in his or her employment and has a reasonable expectation of employment at all times. However, if that employee has quit or been terminated, or is an alien who has been removed from the United States, you will need to complete a Form I-9 for that employee.

56. **Q. Will I be subject to employer sanctions penalties if an employee I hired before November 7, 1986, is an illegal alien?**

A. No. You will not be subject to employer sanctions penalties for retaining an illegal alien in your workforce if the alien was hired before November 7, 1986. However, the fact that an illegal alien was on your payroll before November 7, 1986, does not give him or her any right to remain in the United States. Unless the alien obtains permission from DHS to remain in the United States, he or she is subject to apprehension and removal.

Part One
Why Employers Must Verify Employment Eligibility of New Employees

In 1986, Congress reformed U.S. immigration laws. These reforms, the result of a bipartisan effort, preserved the tradition of legal immigration while seeking to close the door to illegal entry. The employer sanctions provisions, found in Section 274A of the Immigration and Nationality Act, were added by the Immigration Reform and Control Act of 1986 (IRCA). These provisions further changed with the passage of the Immigration Act of 1990 and the Illegal Immigration Reform and Immigrant Responsibility Act of 1996. References to "the Act" in this Handbook refer to the Immigration and Nationality Act (INA), as amended.

Employment is often the magnet that attracts individuals to reside in the United States illegally. The purpose of the employer sanctions law is to remove this magnet by requiring employers to hire only individuals who may legally work here: citizens and nationals of the United States, lawful permanent residents, and aliens authorized to work. To comply with the law, you must verify the identity and employment eligibility of each person you hire, complete and retain a Form I-9 for each employee, and refrain from discriminating against individuals on the basis of national origin or citizenship. (See Part Four for more information on unlawful discrimination.)

The Form I-9 helps employers to verify individuals who are authorized to work in the United States. You should complete a Form I-9 for every new employee you hire after November 6, 1986. The law requires you as an employer to:

1. Ensure that your employees fill out Section 1 of the Form I-9 when they start to work;

2. Review document(s) establishing each employee's identity and eligibility to work;

3. Properly complete Section 2 of the Form I-9;

4. Retain the Form I-9 for 3 years after the date the person begins work or 1 year after the person's employment is terminated, whichever is later; and

5. Upon request, provide Form I-9 to authorized officers of the Department of Homeland Security (DHS), the U.S. Department of Labor (DOL), or the Office of Special Counsel for Immigration Related Unfair Employment Practices (OSC) for inspection.

NOTE: This does not preclude DHS or DOL from obtaining warrants based on probable cause for entry onto the premises of suspected violators without advance notice.

These requirements apply to all employers, including:

1. Agricultural associations, agricultural employers or farm labor contractors who employ, recruit or refer people for a fee; and

2. Those who employ anyone for domestic work in their private home on a regular basis (such as every week).

If you are self-employed, you do not need to complete a Form I-9 on yourself unless you are also an employee of a business entity, such as a corporation or partnership, in which case the business entity is required to complete a Form I-9 on you.

This Handbook will explain how to properly complete the Form I-9, and answer frequently asked questions about the law as it relates to the Form I-9.

Developments in the Law and Changes to the Form I-9

Congress enacted the Illegal Immigration Reform and Immigrant Responsibility Act of 1996 (IIRIRA), Pub. L. 104-208, on September 30, 1996. Section 412(a) of IIRIRA mandated a reduction in the number of documents that employers may accept from newly hired employees during the employment verification process. On September 30, 1997, the former Immigration and Naturalization Service (INS), published an Interim Designation of Acceptable Documents for Employment Verification that implemented the changes required by IIRIRA. See 62 FR 51001-51006 ("1997 interim rule"). However, the Form I-9 was not amended at that time to reflect the changes made by the 1997 interim rule. For this reason, DHS has updated the Form I-9 to bring it into compliance with the 1997 interim rule. DHS has also updated this Handbook for Employers as a companion to the new version of the Form I-9.

In the supplementary information accompanying the 1997 interim rule, the INS stated that it would exercise prosecutorial discretion not to penalize violations resulting from the changes made by that interim rule as a temporary transitional measure until a new Form I-9 was released in the context of a broader final rulemaking. While DHS still intends to pursue other changes to the Form I-9 in a future update, it decided to update the Form I-9 to bring it in compliance with existing law before making any further changes. Therefore, the Form I-9 has been amended to reflect those changes made by the 1997 regulations, but any changes that would have required the drafting of a new regulation are being saved for a future update of the Form I-9. Employers who do not comply with the current regulatory requirements as indicated on the new Form I-9, for example, by accepting documents no longer listed on the Form I-9 Lists of Acceptable Documents, may be subject to penalties under section 274A of the Immigration and Nationality Act.

Questions about Changes to Form I-9

57.   Q. Why was the Form I-9 updated?

A. In 1997, an interim regulation was published that removed five documents from List A on the List of Acceptable Documents and added one document to List A. Although the law changed in 1997, the Form I-9 itself was never updated to reflect those changes. The 2007 version of the Form I-9, bearing an edition date of June 5, 2007 now reflects existing regulations. Further revisions may be needed, so DHS may release another update to the Form I-9 in the future.

58.   Q. What is the difference between the June 5, 2007 version of the Form I-9 and previous versions?

A. Five documents have been removed from List A acceptable documents:
a) Certificate of U.S. Citizenship (Form N-560 or N-561)
b) Certificate of Naturalization (Form N-550 or N-570)
c) Alien Registration Receipt Card (I-151)
d) Unexpired Reentry Permit (Form I-327)
e) Unexpired Refugee Travel Document (Form I-571)

One document was added to List A acceptable documents:
f) Unexpired Employment Authorization Document (I-766)

All the Employment Authorization Documents with photographs have been consolidated as one item on List A:
g) I-688, I-688A, I-688B, I-766

One document on List A was modified as follows:

- Unexpired foreign passport with an Arrival-Departure Record, Form I-94, bearing the same name as the passport and containing an endorsement of the alien's nonimmigrant status if that status authorizes the alien to work for the employer is incident to that status.

Instructions on Section 1 of the Form I-9 now indicate that the employee is not obliged to provide the Social Security Number in Section 1 of the Form I-9, unless he or she is employed by an employer who participates in the USCIS E-Verify Program

A section on Photocopying and Retaining the Form I-9 has been added, which gives employers guidance on providing the form to employees, how long the forms must be retained and the regulations for electronic signatures and retention.

The estimated reporting burden under the Paperwork Reduction Act has been changed in keeping with the latest estimates.

59.   Q. Can I accept documents that were on previous editions of the Form I-9 but aren't now?

A. No. Employers may only accept documents listed on the Acceptable Documents list on the June 5, 2007 or any subsequent version of the Form I-9. When reverifying employees, employers also should ensure that they use the most recent version of the form

60.   Q. Is the Form I-9 available in different languages?

A. The Form I-9 is available in English and Spanish. However, only employers in Puerto Rico may use the Spanish version to meet the verification and retention requirements of the law. Employers in the 50 states may use the Spanish version as a translation guide for Spanish-speaking employees, but the English version must be completed and retained in the employer's records. Employees may also use or ask for a translator/preparer to assist them in completing the form.

61.   Q. Are employers in Puerto Rico required to use the Spanish version of the Form I-9?

A. No. Employers in Puerto Rico may use either the Spanish or the English version of the June 5, 2007 or any subsequent version of the Form I-9 to verify new employees.

62.   Q. May I continue to use earlier versions of the Form I-9?

A. No, employers must use the June 5, 2007 or a subsequent version of the Form I-9. All previous editions of the Form I-9, in English or Spanish, are no longer valid. The 1988 version of the Form I-9 in Spanish expired in 1991, and those employers using it will incur fines and penalties for continued use.

Part Eight
Acceptable Documents for Verifying Employment Eligibility

The following documents have been designated for determining employment eligibility by the Act. A person must present a document or documents that establish identity and employment eligibility. The comprehensive Lists of Acceptable Documents can be found on the next page of this Handbook and on the back of the Form I-9. Samples of many of the acceptable documents appear on the following pages.

To establish both identity and employment eligibility, a person can present a U.S passport, a Permanent Resident Card or Alien Registration Receipt Card, or one of the other documents from List A.

If a person does not present a document from List A, he or she must present one document from List B, which establishes identity, and one document from List C, which establishes employment eligibility.

To establish identity only, a person must present a document from List B, such as a state-issued driver's license, a state-issued identification card, or one of the other documents listed.

To establish employment eligibility only, a person must present a document from List C, such as a Social Security card, a U.S. birth certificate, or one of the other documents listed.

If a person is unable to present the required document(s) within three business days of the date employment begins, he or she must present (within 3 business days) a receipt. The person then must present the actual document when the receipt period ends. The person must have indicated on or before the time employment began, by having checked an appropriate box in Section 1 that he or she is already eligible to be employed in the United States. Receipts showing that a person has applied for an initial grant of employment authorization, or for renewal of employment authorization, are not acceptable.

LIST A

Documents That Establish Both Identity and Employment Eligibility

a. U.S. Passport (unexpired or expired)

b. Permanent Resident Card or Alien Registration Receipt Card (Form I-551)

c. Unexpired foreign passport with a temporary I-551 stamp

d. An unexpired Employment Authorization Document that contains a photograph (Form I-766, I-688, I-688A, I-688B)

e. Unexpired foreign passport with an unexpired Arrival-Departure record, Form I-94, bearing the same name as the passport and containing an endorsement of the alien's nonimmigrant status, if that status authorizes the alien to work for the employer

LIST B

Documents That Establish Identity

For individuals 18 years of age or older:

a. Driver's license or ID card issued by a state or outlying possession of the United States, provided it contains a photograph or information such as name, date of birth, gender, height, eye color and address

b. ID card issued by federal, state or local government agencies or entities, provided it contains a photograph or information such as name, date of birth, gender, height, eye color and address

c. School ID card with a photograph

d. Voter's registration card

e. U.S. military card or draft record

f. Military dependent's ID card

g. U.S. Coast Guard Merchant Mariner Card

h. Native American tribal document

i. Driver's license issued by a Canadian government authority

For persons under age 18 who are unable to present a document listed above:

a.   School record or report card

b.   Clinic, doctor or hospital record

c.   Day-care or nursery school record

LIST C

Documents That Establish Employment Eligibility

a.   U.S. Social Security card issued by the Social Security Administration (other than a card stating it is not valid for employment)

NOTE: This must be a card issued by the Social Security Administration: A copy (such as a metal or plastic reproduction) is not acceptable.

b.   Certification of Birth Abroad issued by the Department of State (Form FS-545 or Form DS-1350)

c.   Original or certified copy of a birth certificate issued by a state, county, municipal authority or outlying possession of the United States bearing an official seal

d.   Native American tribal document

e.   U.S. Citizen ID Card (USCIS Form 1-197)

f.   ID Card for Use of Resident Citizen in the United States (USCIS Form 1-179)

g.   Unexpired employment authorization document issued by DHS (other than those listed under List A)

List A
Documents that Establish Both Identity and Employment Eligibility

The following illustrations in this Handbook do not necessarily reflect the actual size of the documents.

U.S. Passport

Issued by the U.S. Department of State to U.S. citizens and nationals. There are several different versions that are currently valid that vary from the latest version shown here.

Permanent Resident Card (I-551)

The latest version of the Permanent Resident Card, Form I-551, began being issued in November 2004. The card shows the seal of the Department of Homeland Security and contains a detailed hologram on the front of the card. Each card is personalized with an etching showing the bearer's photo, name, signature, date of birth, alien registration number, card expiration date, and card number.

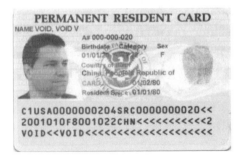

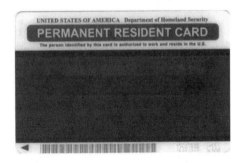

Resident Alien Card (I-551)

These cards are no longer issued, but are valid indefinitely, or until their expiration date. Recipients of this card are lawful permanent residents. This card is commonly referred to as a "green card" and is the replacement for the Form I-151.

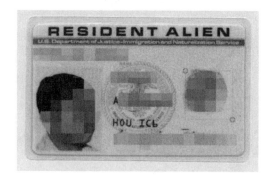

Unexpired Foreign Passport with I-551 Stamp

Employment Authorization Card I-766

Issued by USCIS to aliens granted temporary employment authorization in the United States. The expiration date is noted on the face of the card

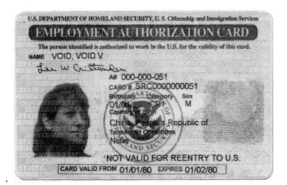

Temporary Resident Card I-688

Issued by USCIS to aliens granted temporary resident status under the Legalization or Special Agricultural Worker program. It is valid until the expiration date stated on the face of the card or on the sticker(s) placed on the back of the card.

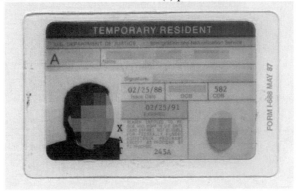

Employment Authorization Card I-688A

Issued by USCIS to applicants for temporary resident status after their interview for Legalization or Special Agricultural Worker status. It is valid until the expiration date stated on the face of the card or on the sticker(s) placed on the back of the card.

Employment Authorization Card I-688B

Issued by USCIS to aliens granted temporary employment authorization in the United States. The card has gold, interlocking lines across the front. The expiration date is noted on the face of the card.

I-94/I-94A Arrival/Departure Record

Arrival-departure record issued by DHS to nonimmigrant aliens and other alien categories. This document indicates the bearer's immigration status, the date that the status was granted, and when the status expires.

List B
Documents that Establish Identity Only

The following illustrations in this Handbook do not necessarily reflect the actual size of the documents.

Sample Driver's License

A driver's license issued by any state or territory of the United States (including the District of Columbia, Puerto Rico, the U.S. Virgin Islands, Guam, the Northern Mariana Islands, and American Samoa) or by a Canadian government authority is acceptable if it contains a photograph or other identifying information such as name, date of birth, sex, height, color of eyes, and address.

Sample State Identification Card

An identification card issued by any state (including the District of Columbia, Puerto Rico, the U.S. Virgin Islands, Guam, and the Northern Mariana Islands) or by a local government is acceptable if it contains a photograph or other identifying information such as name, date of birth, sex, height, color of eyes, and address.

List C
Documents That Establish Employment Eligibility Only

The following illustrations in this Handbook do not necessarily reflect the actual size of the documents.

U.S. Social Security card

Issued by the Social Security Administration, other than a card stating it is not valid for employment. There are many versions of this card.

Certifications of Birth Issued by the Department of State

FS-545	DS-1350
Issued by U.S. embassies and consulates overseas to U.S. citizens born abroad.	Issued by the U.S. Department of State to U.S. citizens born abroad

Sample Birth Certificates

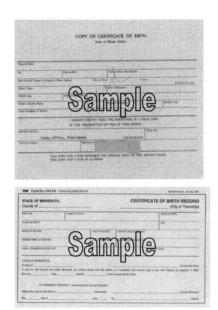

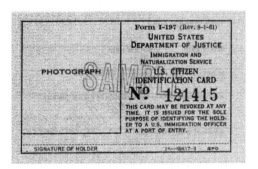

U.S. Citizen Identification Card I-197

Issued by INS to naturalized U.S. citizens. Although this card has not been issued since 1983, it is valid indefinitely.

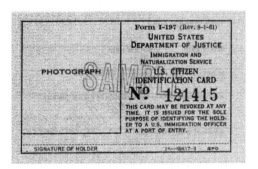

Identification Card for Use of Resident Citizen in the United States I-179

Issued by INS to U.S. citizens who are residents of the United States. Although this card is no longer issued, it is valid indefinitely.

The most significant change to the Form I-9 is a reduction in the acceptable List A documents identified on the form. Five documents are no longer listed as documents acceptable for establishing both identity and employment eligibility under List A: (1) the Certificate of United States Citizenship (Form N-560 or N-561); (2) the Certificate of Naturalization (Form N-550 or N-570); (3) the Form I-151, a long out-of-date version of the Alien Registration Receipt Card ("green card"); (4) the Unexpired Reentry Permit (Form I-327); and (5) the Unexpired Refugee Travel Document (Form I-571).

The amended Form I-9 retains four types of acceptable List A documents: (1) the U.S. Passport (unexpired or expired); (2) an unexpired Permanent Resident Card or Alien Registration Receipt Card (Form I-551); (3) an unexpired foreign passport with a temporary I-551 stamp; and (4) an unexpired Employment Authorization Document that contains a photograph (Form I-766, I-688, I-688A, I-688B). In addition, the amended Form I-9 modifies one acceptable List A document, replacing the "unexpired foreign passport with an attached Form I-94 indicating unexpired employment authorization" with "an unexpired foreign passport with an unexpired Arrival-Departure Record, Form I-94, bearing the same name as the passport and containing an endorsement of the alien's nonimmigrant status, if that status authorizes the alien to work for the employer." All of these acceptable List A documents were carried over from the previous Form I-9, with the exception of the Form I-766, which is a new version of the Employment Authorization Document that has been added to List A. The order and organization of List A also have been revised for ease of use. For example, the various Employment Authorization Documents are listed together as one category, and the unexpired foreign passport with temporary I-551 stamp is a separate entry from the unexpired passport with Form I-94 indicating an employer-specific work-authorized nonimmigrant status.

This updating of List A on the Form I-9 will help streamline the hiring process by providing employers a better means to conform their document acceptance practices to the requirements of the law. As discussed above, the 1997 regulatory List A on the Form I-9 was not enforced pursuant to the prosecutorial discretion policy described in the supplementary information to the interim rule. With a Form I-9 now available that includes the correct List A, the prosecutorial discretion policy is no longer necessary, and Immigration and Customs Enforcement (ICE) has confirmed that it will no longer be in effect 30 days following publication of the Federal Register Notice.

The amended Form I-9 also informs employees that providing their Social Security number is voluntary, pursuant to section 7 of the Privacy Act (8 U.S.C. 552a(note)). However, employees must provide their Social Security number if their employer participates in E-Verify (the employment eligibility verification program formerly known as Basic Pilot Program or Electronic Employment Verification (EEV)), as provided by Section 403(a)(1)(A) of IIRIRA. The Form I-9 also includes changes to its organization and formatting that are more consistent with standard DHS practices, such as including a clarification that there is no filing fee associated with the Form I-9.

The Homeland Security Act

The Homeland Security Act of 2002 created an executive department combining numerous federal agencies with a mission dedicated to homeland security. On March 1, 2003, the authorities of the former INS were transferred to three new agencies in the Department of Homeland Security: U.S. Citizenship and Immigration Services (USCIS), U.S. Customs and Border Protection (CBP), and U.S. Immigration and Customs Enforcement (ICE). The two DHS immigration components most involved with the matters discussed in this Handbook are USCIS and ICE. USCIS is responsible for most documentation of alien work authorization, for the Form I-9 itself, and for the E-Verify employment eligibility verification program. ICE is responsible for enforcement of the penalty provisions of section 274A of the Act, and for other immigration enforcement within the United States.

Under the Homeland Security Act, the Department of Justice retained certain important responsibilities related to the Form I-9 as well. In particular, the Office of Special Counsel for Immigration Related Unfair Employment Practices (OSC) in the Civil Rights Division is responsible for enforcement of the anti-discrimination provisions in section 274B of the Act, while the Executive Office for Immigration Review (EOIR) is responsible for the administrative adjudication of cases under sections 274A, 274B, and 274C (civil document fraud) of the Act.

I-20 ID Card Accompanied by a Form I-94

Form I-94 for F-1 nonimmigrant students must be accompanied by an I-20 Student ID endorsed with employment authorization by the Designated School Official for off-campus employment or curricular practical training. USCIS will issue Form I-766 (Employment Authorization Document) to all students (F-1 and M-1) authorized for a post-completion practical training period. (See page 37 for Form I-94/I-94A)

Front

Back

IF YOU NEED MORE INFORMATION CONCERNING YOUR F-1 NONIMMIGRANT STUDENT STATUS AND THE RELATING IMMIGRATION PROCEDURES, PLEASE CONTACT EITHER YOUR FOREIGN STUDENT ADVISOR ON CAMPUS OR A NEARBY IMMIGRATION AND NATURALIZATION SERVICE OFFICE.

SEVIS

FAMILY NAME: Jones _____   FIRST NAME: Mike _____

Student's Copy

N0004095710

Student Employment Authorization:

Employment Status: Type:

Duration of Employment - From (Date):   To (Date):
Employer Name:
Employer Location:

Comments:

Event History
Event Name: Event Date:
Registration   03/13/2007

Current Authorizations: Start Date: End Date:

This page when properly endorsed, may be used for reentry of the student to attend the same school after a temporary absence from the United States. Each certification signature is valid for one year.

Name of School:

AMY BULLOCK		DSO	06/19/2007	Any City, MD
Name of School Official	Signature of Designated School Official	Title	Date Issued	Place Issued (city and state)
Name of School Official	Signature of Designated School Official	Title	Date Issued	Place Issued (city and state)
Name of School Official	Signature of Designated School Official	Title	Date Issued	Place Issued (city and state)
Name of School Official	Signature of Designated School Official	Title	Date Issued	Place Issued (city and state)

Form I-20 A-B (Rev. 04-27-88)N

DS-2019 Accompanied by a Form I-94

Nonimmigrant exchange visitors (J-1) must have an I-94 accompanied by an unexpired DS-2019, specifying the sponsor and issued by the U.S. Department of State. J-1 students working outside the program indicated on the DS-2019 also need a letter from their responsible school officer. (See page 37 for Form I-94/I-94A)

REMEMBER:

a. Hiring employees without complying with the employment eligibility verification requirements is a violation of the employer sanctions laws.

b. This law requires employees hired after November 6, 1986, to present documentation that establishes identity and employment eligibility, and employers to record this information on Form I-9.

c. Employers may not discriminate against employees on the basis of national origin or citizenship status.

OMB No. 1615-0047; Expires 06/30/08

Department of Homeland Security
U.S. Citizenship and Immigration Services

Form I-9, Employment Eligibility Verification

Instructions
Please read all instructions carefully before completing this form.

Anti-Discrimination Notice. It is illegal to discriminate against any individual (other than an alien not authorized to work in the U.S.) in hiring, discharging, or recruiting or referring for a fee because of that individual's national origin or citizenship status. It is illegal to discriminate against work eligible individuals. Employers **CANNOT** specify which document(s) they will accept from an employee. The refusal to hire an individual because the documents presented have a future expiration date may also constitute illegal discrimination.

What Is the Purpose of This Form?

The purpose of this form is to document that each new employee (both citizen and non-citizen) hired after November 6, 1986 is authorized to work in the United States.

When Should the Form I-9 Be Used?

All employees, citizens and noncitizens, hired after November 6, 1986 and working in the United States must complete a Form I-9.

Filling Out the Form I-9

Section 1, Employee: This part of the form must be completed at the time of hire, which is the actual beginning of employment. Providing the Social Security number is voluntary, except for employees hired by employers participating in the USCIS Electronic Employment Eligibility Verification Program (E-Verify). **The employer is responsible for ensuring that Section 1 is timely and properly completed.**

Preparer/Translator Certification. The Preparer/Translator Certification must be completed if **Section 1** is prepared by a person other than the employee. A preparer/translator may be used only when the employee is unable to complete **Section 1** on his/her own. However, the employee must still sign **Section 1** personally.

Section 2, Employer: For the purpose of completing this form, the term "employer" means all employers including those recruiters and referrers for a fee who are agricultural associations, agricultural employers or farm labor contractors.

Employers must complete **Section 2** by examining evidence of identity and employment eligibility within three (3) business days of the date employment begins. If employees are authorized to work, but are unable to present the required document(s) within three business days, they must present a receipt for the application of the document(s) within three business days and the actual document(s) within ninety (90) days. However, if employers hire individuals for a duration of less than three business days, **Section 2** must be completed at the time employment begins. **Employers must record:**

1. Document title;
2. Issuing authority;
3. Document number;
4. Expiration date, if any; and
5. The date employment begins.

Employers must sign and date the certification. Employees must present original documents. Employers may, but are not required to, photocopy the document(s) presented. These photocopies may only be used for the verification process and must be retained with the Form I-9. **However, employers are still responsible for completing and retaining the Form I-9.**

Section 3, Updating and Reverification: Employers must complete **Section 3** when updating and/or reverifying the Form I-9. Employers must reverify employment eligibility of their employees on or before the expiration date recorded in **Section 1**. Employers **CANNOT** specify which document(s) they will accept from an employee.

A. If an employee's name has changed at the time this form is being updated/reverified, complete Block A.

B. If an employee is rehired within three (3) years of the date this form was originally completed and the employee is still eligible to be employed on the same basis as previously indicated on this form (updating), complete Block B and the signature block.

C. If an employee is rehired within three (3) years of the date this form was originally completed and the employee's work authorization has expired **or** if a current employee's work authorization is about to expire (reverification), complete Block B and:

1. Examine any document that reflects that the employee is authorized to work in the U.S. (see List A **or** C);
2. Record the document title, document number and expiration date (if any) in Block C, and
3. Complete the signature block.

What Is the Filing Fee?

There is no associated filing fee for completing the Form I-9. This form is not filed with USCIS or any government agency. The Form I-9 must be retained by the employer and made available for inspection by U.S. Government officials as specified in the Privacy Act Notice below.

USCIS Forms and Information

To order USCIS forms, call our toll-free number at **1-800-870-3676**. Individuals can also get USCIS forms and information on immigration laws, regulations and procedures by telephoning our National Customer Service Center at **1-800-375-5283** or visiting our internet website at **www.uscis.gov**.

Photocopying and Retaining the Form I-9

A blank Form I-9 may be reproduced, provided both sides are copied. The Instructions must be available to all employees completing this form. Employers must retain completed Forms I-9 for three (3) years after the date of hire or one (1) year after the date employment ends, whichever is later.

The Form I-9 may be signed and retained electronically, as authorized in Department of Homeland Security regulations at 8 CFR § 274a.2.

Privacy Act Notice

The authority for collecting this information is the Immigration Reform and Control Act of 1986, Pub. L. 99-603 (8 USC 1324a).

This information is for employers to verify the eligibility of individuals for employment to preclude the unlawful hiring, or recruiting or referring for a fee, of aliens who are not authorized to work in the United States.

This information will be used by employers as a record of their basis for determining eligibility of an employee to work in the United States. The form will be kept by the employer and made available for inspection by officials of U.S. Immigration and Customs Enforcement, Department of Labor and Office of Special Counsel for Immigration Related Unfair Employment Practices.

Submission of the information required in this form is voluntary. However, an individual may not begin employment unless this form is completed, since employers are subject to civil or criminal penalties if they do not comply with the Immigration Reform and Control Act of 1986.

Paperwork Reduction Act

We try to create forms and instructions that are accurate, can be easily understood and which impose the least possible burden on you to provide us with information. Often this is difficult because some immigration laws are very complex. Accordingly, the reporting burden for this collection of information is computed as follows: **1)** learning about this form, and completing the form, 9 minutes; **2)** assembling and filing (recordkeeping) the form, 3 minutes, for an average of 12 minutes per response. If you have comments regarding the accuracy of this burden estimate, or suggestions for making this form simpler, you can write to: U.S. Citizenship and Immigration Services, Regulatory Management Division, 111 Massachusetts Avenue, N.W., 3rd Floor, Suite 3008, Washington, DC 20529. OMB No. 1615-0047.

OMB No. 1615-0047; Expires 06/30/08

Department of Homeland Security
U.S. Citizenship and Immigration Services

Form I-9, Employment Eligibility Verification

Please read instructions carefully before completing this form. The instructions must be available during completion of this form.

ANTI-DISCRIMINATION NOTICE: It is illegal to discriminate against work eligible individuals. Employers CANNOT specify which document(s) they will accept from an employee. The refusal to hire an individual because the documents have a future expiration date may also constitute illegal discrimination.

Section 1. Employee Information and Verification. To be completed and signed by employee at the time employment begins.

Print Name: Last	First	Middle Initial	Maiden Name

Address (Street Name and Number)	Apt. #	Date of Birth (month/day/year)

City	State	Zip Code	Social Security #

I am aware that federal law provides for imprisonment and/or fines for false statements or use of false documents in connection with the completion of this form.

I attest, under penalty of perjury, that I am (check one of the following):
- [ ] A citizen or national of the United States
- [ ] A lawful permanent resident (Alien #) A _____
- [ ] An alien authorized to work until _____
  (Alien # or Admission #) _____

Employee's Signature	Date (month/day/year)

Preparer and/or Translator Certification. *(To be completed and signed if Section 1 is prepared by a person other than the employee.) I attest, under penalty of perjury, that I have assisted in the completion of this form and that to the best of my knowledge the information is true and correct.*

Preparer's/Translator's Signature	Print Name

Address (Street Name and Number, City, State, Zip Code)	Date (month/day/year)

Section 2. Employer Review and Verification. To be completed and signed by employer. Examine one document from List A OR examine one document from List B and one from List C, as listed on the reverse of this form, and record the title, number and expiration date, if any, of the document(s).

List A	OR	List B	AND	List C
Document title: _____		_____		_____
Issuing authority: _____		_____		_____
Document #: _____		_____		_____
Expiration Date (if any): _____		_____		_____
Document #: _____		_____		
Expiration Date (if any): _____				

CERTIFICATION - I attest, under penalty of perjury, that I have examined the document(s) presented by the above-named employee, that the above-listed document(s) appear to be genuine and to relate to the employee named, that the employee began employment on *(month/day/year)* _____ and that to the best of my knowledge the employee is eligible to work in the United States. (State employment agencies may omit the date the employee began employment.)

Signature of Employer or Authorized Representative	Print Name	Title

Business or Organization Name and Address (Street Name and Number, City, State, Zip Code)	Date (month/day/year)

Section 3. Updating and Reverification. To be completed and signed by employer.

A. New Name (if applicable)	B. Date of Rehire (month/day/year) (if applicable)

C. If employee's previous grant of work authorization has expired, provide the information below for the document that establishes current employment eligibility.

Document Title: _____	Document #: _____	Expiration Date (if any): _____

I attest, under penalty of perjury, that to the best of my knowledge, this employee is eligible to work in the United States, and if the employee presented document(s), the document(s) I have examined appear to be genuine and to relate to the individual.

Signature of Employer or Authorized Representative	Date (month/day/year)

LISTS OF ACCEPTABLE DOCUMENTS

LIST A **Documents that Establish Both Identity and Employment Eligibility**		LIST B **Documents that Establish Identity**		LIST C **Documents that Establish Employment Eligibility**
	OR		**AND**	
1. U.S. Passport (unexpired or expired)		1. Driver's license or ID card issued by a state or outlying possession of the United States provided it contains a photograph or information such as name, date of birth, gender, height, eye color and address		1. U.S. Social Security card issued by the Social Security Administration *(other than a card stating it is not valid for employment)*
2. Permanent Resident Card or Alien Registration Receipt Card (Form I-551)		2. ID card issued by federal, state or local government agencies or entities, provided it contains a photograph or information such as name, date of birth, gender, height, eye color and address		2. Certification of Birth Abroad issued by the Department of State *(Form FS-545 or Form DS-1350)*
3. An unexpired foreign passport with a temporary I-551 stamp		3. School ID card with a photograph		3. Original or certified copy of a birth certificate issued by a state, county, municipal authority or outlying possession of the United States bearing an official seal
4. An unexpired Employment Authorization Document that contains a photograph (Form I-766, I-688, I-688A, I-688B)		4. Voter's registration card		4. Native American tribal document
		5. U.S. Military card or draft record		5. U.S. Citizen ID Card *(Form I-197)*
5. An unexpired foreign passport with an unexpired Arrival-Departure Record, Form I-94, bearing the same name as the passport and containing an endorsement of the alien's nonimmigrant status, if that status authorizes the alien to work for the employer		6. Military dependent's ID card		6. ID Card for use of Resident Citizen in the United States *(Form I-179)*
		7. U.S. Coast Guard Merchant Mariner Card		
		8. Native American tribal document		7. Unexpired employment authorization document issued by DHS *(other than those listed under List A)*
		9. Driver's license issued by a Canadian government authority		
		For persons under age 18 who are unable to present a document listed above:		
		10. School record or report card		
		11. Clinic, doctor or hospital record		
		12. Day-care or nursery school record		

Illustrations of many of these documents appear in Part 8 of the Handbook for Employers (M-274)

Part Two
When You Must Complete the Form I-9

You must complete the Form I-9 every time you hire any person to perform labor or services in return for wages or other remuneration. This requirement applies to everyone hired after November 6, 1986.

Ensure that the employee fully completes Section 1 of the Form I-9 at the time of the hire - when the employee begins work. Review the employee's document(s) and fully complete Section 2 of the Form I-9 within 3 business days of the hire.

If you hire a person for less than 3 business days, Sections 1 and 2 of the Form I-9 must be fully completed at the time of the hire – when the employee begins work.

You DO NOT need to complete a Form I-9 for persons who are:

1. Hired before November 7, 1986, who are continuing in their employment and have a reasonable expectation of employment at all times;

2. Employed for casual domestic work in a private home on a sporadic, irregular, or intermittent basis;

3. Independent contractors; or

4. Providing labor to you who are employed by a contractor providing contract services (e.g., employee leasing or temporary agencies).

NOTE: You cannot contract for the labor of an alien if you know the alien is not authorized to work in the United States.

Completing the Form I-9

Section 1

Have the employee complete Section 1 at the time of the hire (when he or she begins to work) by filling in the correct information and signing and dating the form. Ensure that the employee prints the information clearly.

If the employee cannot complete Section 1 without assistance or if he or she needs the Form I-9 translated, someone may assist him or her. The preparer or translator must read the form to the employee, assist him or her in completing Section 1, and have the employee sign or mark the form in the appropriate place. The preparer or translator must then complete the Preparer/ Translator Certification block on the Form I-9.

You are responsible for reviewing and ensuring that your employee fully and properly completes Section 1.

NOTE: Providing a Social Security number on the Form I-9 is voluntary for all employees unless you are an employer participating in the USCIS E-Verify Program, which requires an employee's Social Security number for employment eligibility verification. You may not, however, ask an employee to provide you a specific document with his or her Social Security number on it, to avoid unlawful discrimination. For more information on the E-Verify Program, see Part Six. For more information on unlawful discrimination, see Part Four.

Figure 1: *Instructions for Completing Section 1: Employee Identification and Verification*

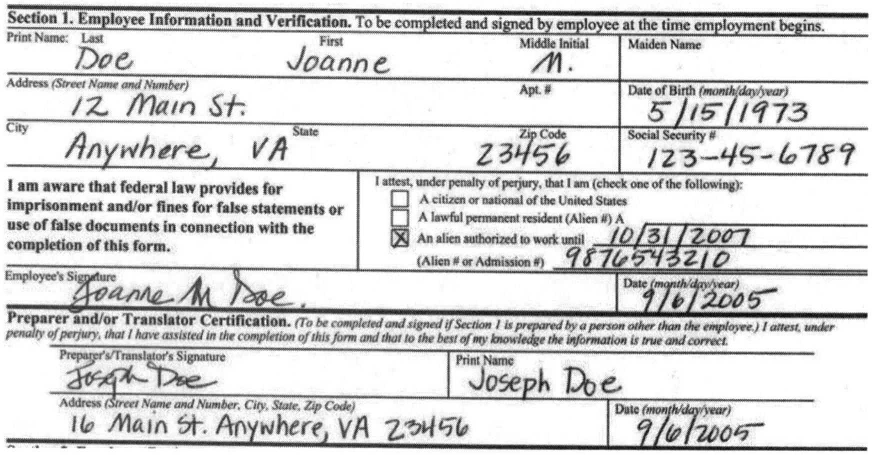

1. Employee enters full name and maiden name, if applicable.
2. Employee enters current address and date of birth.
3. Employee enters his or her city, state and Social Security number. Entering the Social Security number is optional unless the employer verifies employment eligibility through the USCIS E-Verify Program.
4. Employee reads warning and attests to immigration status.
5. Employee signs and dates the form.
6. If the employee uses a preparer or translator to fill out the form, that person must certify that he or she assisted the employee by completing this signature block.

Section 2

The employee must present to you an original document or documents that establish identity and employment eligibility within 3 business days of the date employment begins. Some documents establish both identity and employment eligibility (List A). Other documents establish identity only (List B) or employment authorization only (List C). The employee can choose which document(s) he or she wants to present from the Lists of Acceptable Documents. This list appears in Part Eight and on the last page of the revised Form I-9, dated June 5, 2007.

Examine the original document or documents the employee presents and then fully complete Section 2 of the Form I-9. You must examine one document from List A, or one from List B and one from List C. Record the title, issuing authority, number, and expiration date (if any) of the document(s); fill in the date of hire and correct information in the certification block; and sign and date the Form I-9. You must accept any document(s) from the Lists of Acceptable Document presented by the individual which reasonably appear on their face to be genuine and to relate to the person presenting them. You may not specify which document(s) an employee must present.

NOTE: If you participate in the E-Verify Program, you may only accept List B documents that bear a photograph.

In certain circumstances, employers, recruiters and referrers for a fee must accept a receipt in lieu of a List A, List B, or a List C document if one is presented by an employee. A receipt indicating that an individual has applied for initial work authorization or for an extension of expiring work authorization is NOT acceptable proof of employment eligibility on the Form I-9. Receipts are never acceptable if employment lasts less than 3 business days.

Receipts and other documents that serve as proof of temporary employment eligibility that employers can accept are:

1. Receipts for the application of a replacement document where the document was lost, stolen, or destroyed, which can be a List A, List B, or List C document. The employee must present the replacement document within 90 days from the date of hire.

2. The arrival portion of a Form I-94 with an attached photo and a temporary I-551 stamp, which is a receipt for a List A document. When the stamp expires, or if the stamp has no expiration, one year from date of issue, the employee must present the Form I-551 Permanent Resident Card.

3. The departure portion of the Form I-94 with a refugee admission stamp, which is a receipt for a List A document. The employee must present, within 90

days from date of hire, Form I-766, or a List B document and an unrestricted Social Security card.

When the employee provides an acceptable receipt, the employer should record the document title in Section 2 of the Form I-9 and write the word "receipt" and any document number in the "Document #" space. When the employee presents the actual document, the employer should cross out the word "receipt" and any accompanying document number, insert the number from the actual document presented, and initial and date the change.

Figure 2: *Section 2: Employer Review and Verification*

1.
Section 2. Employer Review and Verification. To be completed and signed by employer. Examine one document from List A OR examine one document from List B and one from List C, as listed on the reverse of this form, and record the title, number and expiration date, if any, of the document(s).

List A (and OR)	List B AND	List C
Document title: *Employment Authorization*		
Issuing authority: *USCIS*		
Document #: *9876543210*		
Expiration Date (if any): *10/31/07*		
Document #:		
Expiration Date (if any):		

CERTIFICATION - I attest, under penalty of perjury, that I have examined the document(s) presented by the above-named employee, that the above-listed document(s) appear to be genuine and to relate to the employee named, that the employee began employment on

2. *(month/day/year)* *9/6/2005* and that to the best of my knowledge the employee is eligible to work in the United States. (State employment agencies may omit the date the employee began employment.)

Signature of Employer or Authorized Representative *Jolene Doe*	Print Name *Jolene Doe*	Title *Owner*

3. Business or Organization Name and Address *(Street Name and Number, City, State, Zip Code)*
Jolene's Jellybean Factory, 123 Broadstreet Way, Anywhere, VA 2745   Date *(month/day/year)* *9/6/2005*

1. Employer records document title(s), issuing authority, document number, expiration date from original documents supplied by employee. See Part Eight for the Lists of Acceptable Documents.
2. Employer enters date of hire (i.e. first day of work).
3. Employer attests to examining the documents provided by filling out the signature block.

Minors (Individuals under Age 18)

If a minor – a person under the age of 18 – cannot present a List A document or an identity document from List B, the Form I-9 should be completed in the following way:

1. A parent or legal guardian must complete Section 1 and write "Individual under age 18" in the space for the employee's signature;

2. The parent or legal guardian must complete the "Preparer/Translator Certification" block;

3. You should write "Individual under age 18" in Section 2, under List B; and

4. The minor must present a List C document showing his or her employment eligibility. You should record the required information in the appropriate space in Section 2.

Figure 3: *Completing the Form I-9 for Minors*

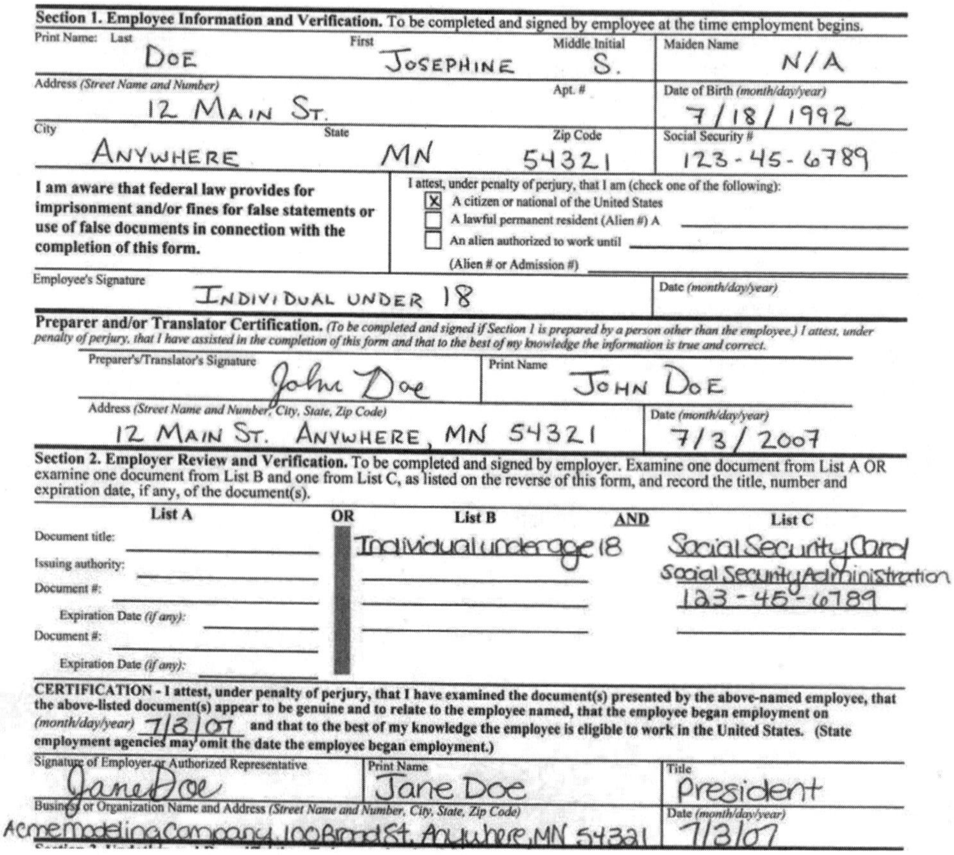

1. A parent or legal guardian of a minor employee completes Section 1 and writes, "Individual under age 18" in signature space.
2. A parent or legal guardian completes the Preparer and/or Translator block.
3. Employer enters "Individual under age 18" under List B and records the List C document the minor presents.

Employees with Disabilities (Special Placement)

If a person with a disability, who is placed in a job by a nonprofit organization or as part of a rehabilitation program, cannot present a List A document or an identity document from List B, the Form I-9 should be completed in the following way:

1. A representative of the nonprofit organization, a parent or a legal guardian must complete Section 1 and write "Special Placement" in the space for the employee's signature;

2. The representative, parent or legal guardian must complete the "Preparer/Translator Certification" block;

3. You should write "Special Placement" in Section 2, under List B; and

4. The employee with a disability must present a List C document showing his or her employment eligibility. You should record the required information in the appropriate space in Section 2.

Figure 4: *Completing the Form I-9 for Employees with Disabilities (Special Placement)*

1. A representative of a nonprofit organization, parent or legal guardian of an individual with a disability completes Section 1 and writes, "Special Placement" in signature space.
2. The representative, parent or legal guardian completes the Preparer and/or Translator block.
3. Employer enters "Special Placement" under List B and records the List C document the employee with a disability presents.

Electronic I-9 and E-Verify Vendors

Company	E-Verify Integration?	Vendor Self-Description
Form I-9 Compliance, LLC 24 Corporate Plaza, Suite 100 Newport Beach, CA 92660 Phone: 866-359-4949 Email: From web site Web Site: www.formi9.com	Yes (alliance With Verifications, Inc.)	As the first Designated Agent of the DHS/SSA to beta test the web services version of the Basic Pilot Program (E-Verify), Form I-9 Compliance, LLC (Fi9) enables employers to mitigate risk attendant to I-9 Form administration. Fi9's "Smart" error-detecting web based electronic I-9 Form seamlessly integrates with E-Verify. "Click-to-Sign" electronic signature functionality provides employers a paperless I-9 Form program. Fifty customized reports help to comprehensively manage the I-9 process. Fi9 provides professional auditing, training, and consulting services, scanning and indexing of paper I-9 Forms and verifies SSN through the SSNVS.
HireRight 5151 California Avenue Irvine, CA 92617 Phone: 800-400-2761 Email: info@HireRight.com Web Site: www.hireright.com/employment-eligibilityverification.html	Yes	The HireRight I-9 Solution™ is delivered on-demand and is designed to help employers streamline, automate and administer their employment eligibility program and meet state and federal regulations. It offers electronic management of I-9 forms and includes integrated employment eligibility verification through DHS E-Verify. The HireRight I-9 Solution simplifies the management of an employment eligibility program by providing flexible settings, smart features and the process automation required to efficiently facilitate employer and employee procedures in one central location on the Web. HireRight is a designated agent for the DHS E-Verify Program. For more information on the HireRight I-9 Solution, visit: www.HireRight.com/I9.
I-9 Compliance P.O. Box 491570 Redding, CA 96049 Phone: 800-300-1821 Email: ContactUs@I9compliance.com Web Site: www.i-9compliance.com	Yes	I9compliance.com (a designated E-verify agent) is a recognized leader in "end to end" I-9 form compliance solutions. Features include: Electronic Form i-9 submission, SSN duplication alerts, and step-by-step instructions for each phase of form completion, automated expiration notices, retroactive Form i-9 electronic storage and audit wizards. Ensure that you and your locations are in complete compliance with DHS, ICE, and state and federal guidelines. Easy to use reporting capabilities and multiple permission levels give you nationwide insight to your employment eligibility process – simplifying management. Part of the Preemploy.com complete screening services offering. Contact us today for a free demonstration.

continued on next page

Company	E-Verify Integration?	Vendor Self-Description
I9Advantage 5747 Perimeter Drive Suite 110 Dublin, OH 43017 Phone: 866-432-4056 Email: sales@i9advantage.Com Web Site: www.i9advantage.com	Yes	i9 Advantage provides simple employment eligibility verification solutions that enable organizations to minimize Form I-9 risk. Our team consists of full time software engineers, training and usability experts along with an AV rated immigration attorney. Our drive to build a high quality and intuitive system has helped us become the number one solution for total workforce compliance in the United States.
i9Check 1501 Cameron Avenue #110-22 West Covina, CA 91790 Phone: 866-210-1634 Email: sales@i9check.com Web Site: www.i9check.com	Yes	Cost-effective I-9 software designed by legal counsel experienced in I-9 law. Users may electronically complete the I-9 in its entirety or section by section via the General Questionnaire. The GQ also allows for additional orientation documents for expanded paperless new hire processing. Remote I-9 processing is also available. Software modifies List A, B, C options depending on new hire's status and tracks different visa types. System accepts receipts and reverifies, transfers, terminates, and rehires with ease. i9Check also provides training, auditing, and consulting services.
I9eXpress 11432 Lackland St. Louis, MO 63146 Phone: 314-214-7000 Email: From web site Web Site: www.talx.com/Services/I9eXpress		
I-9Zoom INSZoom.com Inc. 6111 Bollinger Canyon Road Suite 440 San Ramon, CA 94583 Phone: 925-244-0600 Email: sales@inszoom.com Web Site: http://www1.inszoom.com/solutions/i9ims/i9ims_overview.html		

continued on next page

Company	E-Verify Integration?	Vendor Self-Description
LawLogix's Guardian 2828 N. Central Avenue Suite 1125 Phoenix, AZ 85004 Phone: 877-725-4355 ext. 1 Email: I9sales@lawlogix.com Web Site: www.lawlogix.com/I-9_Compliance_LLX.html	Yes	Guardian is a web-based, paperless I-9 compliance system that produces error free electronic I-9s with digital signatures. Guardian includes both HR and Employee interfaces with powerful error checking and reporting tools to help you complete, store and track your I-9s. Our seamless E-Verify integration assists federal and state law compliance needs and provides instant response from DHS. Guardian is SOX/SAS70 compliant with a detailed audit trail to assist with your "Good Faith Defense." Guardian is backed by the best customer support and training in the industry. We offer comprehensive migration of preexisting I-9s including scanned images of I-9s.
Lookout Services 5909 West Loop South Suite 300 Bellaire, TX 77401 Phone: 888-522-6704 Email: From web site Web Site: www.lookoutservices.net	Yes	Lookout Services® is the nation's leading provider of web-based error-detecting I-9 Form compliance and seamless E-Verify services. We are the only company of our kind which installs software behind a company firewall. Proven scalable to any environment, Lookout is integrated into the hiring process of the nation's largest employers. Lookout was founded by immigration lawyers in 1998 and pioneered technology driven by legal logic designed to virtually eliminate errors and omissions on the I-9 Form. Lookout's technology is certified by DHS Web Services and approved as a Designated Agent for E-Verify. Lookout Services is a certified Woman Owned Business.
Tracker I-9 ImmigrationTracker 315 Montgomery Street Suite 750 San Francisco, CA 94104 Phone: 415-808-8800 Email: sales@trackeri9.com Web Site: www.trackeri9.com	Yes	Tracker I-9 is the advanced electronic system for processing and managing I-9 forms, and synching with E-Verify – from the immigration software company most trusted by corporate America since 1998, ImmigrationTracker. Distinguishing features: 1. Installs on-site for unmatched data security and guaranteed continued operation; 2. Intuitive web interface gives controlled web access to employer representatives; 3. Comes integrated with ImmigrationTracker, for full compliance with Section 3 and DHS records; 4. Includes configurable reminders, reports and other tools for tracking and auditing; 5. Has built-in error alerts and compliance guides by our award winning staff attorneys. An E-Verify Designated Agent and a Microsoft® Gold Partner. www.TrackerI9.com

continued on next page

Company	E-Verify Integration?	Vendor Self-Description
Verifications Inc. 6900 Wedgwood Road N Suite 120 Maple Grove, MN 55311 Phone: 866-455-0779 Email: sales@verificationsinc.com Web Site: www.verificationsinc.com/applicantemploymenteligibility.html	Yes	Verifications' Electronic I-9 Forms and Legal Right to Work checks allow employers to electronically prepare I-9 Forms and verify work eligibility through the E-Verify program. Electronic I-9 Forms Processing simplifies collection, storage, and management of I-9s. Error detection and help functions ensure accuracy while management alerts 90, 60, 30-days prior to work authorization expiration ensure you retain valued employees. The result is an accurate, paperless way to collect, store and manage I-9s. E-Verify/Legal Right to Work queries the SSA and DHS databases to confirm work eligibility. Email alerts and step-by-step user guidance are provided to manage through the tentative non-confirmation process.

Index